JUL 2 0 2005

3 —10—14

12/28/2017

ST ANTONY'S/MACMILLAN SERIES

General editors: Archie Brown (1978–85) and Rosemary Thorp (1985–), both Fellows of St Antony's College, Oxford

Roy Allison FINLAND'S RELATIONS WITH THE SOVIET UNION, 1944–84
Said Amir Arjomand (*editor*) FROM NATIONALISM TO REVOLUTIONARY ISLAM
Anders Åslund PRIVATE ENTERPRISE IN EASTERN EUROPE
Omer Bartov THE EASTERN FRONT, 1941–45, GERMAN TROOPS AND THE BARBARISATION OF WARFARE
Gail Lee Bernstein and Haruhiro Fukui (*editors*) JAPAN AND THE WORLD
Archie Brown (*editor*) POLITICAL CULTURE AND COMMUNIST STUDIES
Archie Brown (*editor*) POLITICAL LEADERSHIP IN THE SOVIET UNION
Archie Brown and Michael Kaser (*editors*) SOVIET POLICY FOR THE 1980s
Victor Bulmer-Thomas STUDIES IN THE ECONOMICS OF CENTRAL AMERICA
S. B. Burman CHIEFDOM POLITICS AND ALIEN LAW
Helen Callaway GENDER, CULTURE AND EMPIRE
Renfrew Christie ELECTRICITY, INDUSTRY AND CLASS IN SOUTH AFRICA
Robert O. Collins and Francis M. Deng (*editors*) THE BRITISH IN THE SUDAN, 1898–1956
Roger Cooter (*editor*) STUDIES IN THE HISTORY OF ALTERNATIVE MEDICINE
Wilhelm Deist THE *WEHRMACHT* AND GERMAN REARMAMENT
Robert Desjardins THE SOVIET UNION THROUGH FRENCH EYES, 1945–85
Guido di Tella ARGENTINA UNDER PERÓN, 1973–76
Guido di Tella and Rudiger Dornbusch (*editors*) THE POLITICAL ECONOMY OF ARGENTINA, 1946–83
Guido di Tella and D. C. M. Platt (*editors*) THE POLITICAL ECONOMY OF ARGENTINA, 1880–1946
Guido di Tella and D. Cameron Watt (*editors*) ARGENTINA BETWEEN THE GREAT POWERS, 1939–46
Saul Dubow RACIAL SEGREGATION AND THE ORIGINS OF APARTHEID IN SOUTH AFRICA, 1919–36
Simon Duke US DEFENCE BASES IN THE UNITED KINGDOM
Julius A. Elias PLATO'S DEFENCE OF POETRY
Ricardo Ffrench-Davis and Ernesto Tironi (*editors*) LATIN AMERICA AND THE NEW INTERNATIONAL ECONOMIC ORDER
David Footman ANTONIN BESSE OF ADEN
Heather D. Gibson THE EUROCURRENCY MARKETS, DOMESTIC FINANCIAL POLICY AND INTERNATIONAL INSTABILITY
Bohdan Harasymiw POLITICAL ELITE RECRUITMENT IN THE SOVIET UNION
Neil Harding (*editor*) THE STATE IN SOCIALIST SOCIETY
John B. Hattendorf and Robert S. Jordan (*editors*) MARITIME STRATEGY AND THE BALANCE OF POWER
Richard Holt SPORT AND SOCIETY IN MODERN FRANCE
Albert Hourani EUROPE AND THE MIDDLE EAST
Albert Hourani THE EMERGENCE OF THE MODERN MIDDLE EAST
J. R. Jennings GEORGES SOREL
A. Kemp-Welsh (*translator*) THE BIRTH OF SOLIDARITY
Paul Kennedy and Anthony Nicholls (*editors*) NATIONALIST AND RACIALIST MOVEMENTS IN BRITAIN AND GERMANY BEFORE 1914
Richard Kindersley (*editor*) IN SEARCH OF EUROCOMMUNISM

Maria D'Alva G. Kinzo LEGAL OPPOSITION POLITICS UNDER
AUTHORITARIAN RULE IN BRAZIL
Bohdan Krawchenko SOCIAL CHANGE AND NATIONAL CONSCIOUSNESS
IN TWENTIETH-CENTURY UKRAINE
Gisela C. Lebzelter POLITICAL ANTI-SEMITISM IN ENGLAND, 1918–1939
Nancy Lubin LABOUR AND NATIONALITY IN SOVIET CENTRAL ASIA
C. A. MacDonald THE UNITED STATES, BRITAIN AND APPEASEMENT,
1936–39
Robert H. McNeal TSAR AND COSSAK, 1855–1914
David Nicholls HAITI IN CARIBBEAN CONTEXT
Patrick O'Brien (editor) RAILWAYS AND THE ECONOMIC DEVELOPMENT
OF WESTERN EUROPE, 1830–1914
Amii Omara-Otunni POLITICS AND THE MILITARY IN UGANDA, 1890–1985
Roger Owen (editor) STUDIES IN THE ECONOMIC AND SOCIAL HISTORY
OF PALESTINE IN THE NINETEENTH AND TWENTIETH CENTURIES
Ilan Pappé BRITAIN AND THE ARAB–ISRAELI CONFLICT, 1948–51
D. C. M. Platt and Guido di Tella (editors) ARGENTINA, AUSTRALIA AND
CANADA: STUDIES IN COMPARATIVE DEVELOPMENT, 1870–1965
J. L. Porket WORK, EMPLOYMENT AND UNEMPLOYMENT IN THE
SOVIET UNION
Irena Powell WRITERS AND SOCIETY IN MODERN JAPAN
Alex Pravda (editor) HOW RULING COMMUNIST PARTIES ARE GOVERNED
T. H. Rigby and Ferenc Fehér (editors) POLITICAL LEGITIMATION IN
COMMUNIST STATES
Hans Rogger JEWISH POLICIES AND RIGHT-WING POLITICS IN IMPERIAL
RUSSIA
Marilyn Rueschemeyer PROFESSIONAL WORK AND MARRIAGE
A. J. R. Russell-Wood THE BLACK MAN IN SLAVERY AND FREEDOM IN
COLONIAL BRAZIL
Nurit Schleifman UNDERCOVER AGENTS IN THE RUSSIAN
REVOLUTIONARY MOVEMENT
Amnon Sella and Yael Yishai ISRAEL THE PEACEFUL BELLIGERENT, 1967–69
Aron Shai BRITAIN AND CHINA, 1941–47
Lewis H. Siegelbaum THE POLITICS OF INDUSTRIAL MOBILIZATION IN
RUSSIA, 1914–17
H. Gordon Skilling SAMIZDAT AND AN INDEPENDENT SOCIETY IN
CENTRAL AND EASTERN EUROPE
David Stafford BRITAIN AND EUROPEAN RESISTANCE, 1940–45
Nancy Stepan THE IDEA OF RACE IN SCIENCE
Verena Stolcke COFFEE PLANTERS, WORKERS AND WIVES
Jane E. Stromseth THE ORIGINS OF FLEXIBLE RESPONSE
Marvin Swartz THE POLITICS OF BRITISH FOREIGN POLICY IN THE ERA
OF DISRAELI AND GLADSTONE
Rosemary Thorp (editor) LATIN AMERICA IN THE 1930s
Rosemary Thorp and Laurence Whitehead (editors) INFLATION AND
STABILISATION IN LATIN AMERICA
Rosemary Thorp and Laurence Whitehead (editors) LATIN AMERICAN DEBT
AND THE ADJUSTMENT CRISIS
Rudolf L. Tōkès (editor) OPPOSITION IN EASTERN EUROPE
Jane Watts BLACK WRITERS FROM SOUTH AFRICA
Robert Wihtol THE ASIAN DEVELOPMENT BANK AND RURAL
DEVELOPMENT
Toshio Yokoyama JAPAN IN THE VICTORIAN MIND

Racial Segregation and the Origins of Apartheid in South Africa, 1919–36

Saul Dubow

 in association with
ST ANTONY'S COLLEGE
OXFORD

First published 1989

Published by
THE MACMILLAN PRESS LTD
Houndmills, Basingstoke, Hampshire RG21 2XS
and London
Companies and representatives
throughout the world

Printed in Hong Kong

British Library Cataloguing in Publication Data
Dubow, Saul, 1959–
Racial segregation and the origins of
apartheid in South Africa, 1919–36. —
(St Antony's/Macmillan Series).
1. South Africa. Apartheid, 1919–36
I. Title   II. St Antony's College
III. Series
323.1′68
ISBN 0–333–46461–3

Series Standing Order

If you would like to receive future titles in this series as they are
published, you can make use of our standing order facility. To place a
standing order please contact your bookseller or, in case of difficulty,
write to us at the address below with your name and address and the
name of the series. Please state with which title you wish to begin your
standing order. (If you live outside the United Kingdom we may not
have the rights for your area, in which case we will forward your order
to the publisher concerned.)

Customer Services Department, Macmillan Distribution Ltd
Houndmills, Basingstoke, Hampshire, RG21 2XS, England.

190334

Contents

Preface

South Africa has undergone enormous political upheaval since 1982, when I began to research the history of segregation. At that time the economy was still relatively buoyant and the Nationalist government, together with large business corporations, were confidently undertaking a significant range of reformist initiatives. In view of these developments the response of the forces of opposition was uncertain, and those who, in 1983, claimed that the state was in deep crisis, seemed to be engaged in a measure of wishful thinking.

There have been dramatic changes since then. Towards the end of 1984 it became evident that the new constitution (which at one point seemed set to enlarge the state's mandate by incorporating significant elements of the coloured and Indian middle class) was rebounding on the government. In the months that followed a wave of popular militancy led to mass insurrection in black townships throughout the country. The state responded in the way it knew best; with an unprecedented level of brutality and repression unleashed both within the country and beyond its borders. The imposition of a national state of emergency in June 1986 was followed by a massive crackdown on political organisations and a sustained attempt by the state to crush all forms of dissent. Those who, at the height of the 1984–6 insurrection, predicted that the state was about to yield to the forces of popular opposition, have since been forced to reassess their position in more sober terms. The speed of events and the volatility of the current situation make nonsense of any prognosis about the future of apartheid.

For the historian, one of the key questions which requires answering is not just how long the present regime will survive, but also how apartheid has been able to endure for so long. In addressing this problem a thorough understanding of apartheid's historical predecessor – segregation – is vital. This study therefore considers how segregation became the organising ideology of white supremacy during the interwar years, how it gained the effective consent of those it excluded from power, and how it sought to legitimise a system of government based on domination and exploitation.

Many writers have addressed the question of segregation, though few have done so in any systematic fashion. Marian Lacey's important book, *Working for Boroko*, comes closest to satisfying the need for a comprehensive treatment of the topic, though I am critical of her approach and conclusions. Martin Legassick's provisionally titled work, *Capitalism and Segregation*, might have been a brilliant contribution to the debate, but it was never completed. Nevertheless, my own work has been greatly stimulated by his lead. The insights of other writers have also had an important impact on the direction of my research. In particular, I think of Shula Marks's suggestive work on Natal, William Beinart's writings on the Transkei, John Cell's comparative study of segregation in South Africa and the American South, and Paul Rich's treatment of liberalism between the wars.

In the course of researching and writing this book, which began life as an Oxford doctoral thesis, I have been helped by many people. The librarians and staff of Rhodes House, Oxford, Jagger Library at the University of Cape Town, the Witwatersrand University Department of Historical Papers, and the Institute of Commonwealth Studies, London, all saw a great deal of me. They were generous with their time, patience and interest.

Throughout my research I have been supported by bursaries and scholarships administered by the University of Cape Town. In my final year as a student I was awarded the Beit Senior Research Scholarship by Oxford University. I am indebted to both universities for this support, without which it would have been impossible either to begin or complete this study. It was as a British Academy post-doctoral research fellow at the Institute of Commonwealth Studies, London, that the task of transforming an unwieldy thesis into book form was accomplished. The support of both these institutions has likewise been invaluable.

There are many friends both in England and South Africa who helped me a great deal; some by sharing their houses and meals, others by simply reminding me of the world outside my work. I learned much from extended talks with William Beinart, who read various drafts of the thesis and helped me to sharpen up some of my inchoate ideas. Shula Marks read both the thesis and the final manuscript. Her penetrating criticisms led me to make important revisions at a late stage and I am grateful for her encouragement over the past year. I have always been able to trust the careful judgement of my supervisor, Stanley Trapido, who allowed me freedom to explore and never sought to impose his views. His mastery and intuitive understanding of South African history is special. Stanley and Barbara have also shown me exceptional hospitality and friendship: their door has always been (literally) open.

In Oxford and in London John Lazar traded ideas, commented on draft chapters and advised on the finer points of apartheid ideology. Susan Rosenberg conceived the cover of this book and executed it with imagination and enthusiasm. I have benefited from the informed (and critical) interest of my parents, their sustained encouragement and support. It is difficult to record my thanks to them adequately. Bryony's rigorous editorial skills were indispensable during the final stages of the thesis. In encouraging me to reconsider passages which I would have preferred to forget about, she helped me to overcome my inertia and to improve the coherence of the manuscript as a whole. To her, I am more than grateful.

Finally, a note on language. For the purposes of contextual accuracy I have repeatedly used words which, in today's parlance, would offend many. I have therefore employed single inverted commas to indicate where words (like 'native') are used in their historical context. If I have not stuck rigidly to this rule, it is only in order to avoid pedantry.

SAUL DUBOW

List of Abbreviations

AAC	All-African Convention
ANC	African National Congress
CNC	Chief Native Commissioner
CPSA	Church of the Province Archives, University of the Witwatersrand
DRC	Dutch Reformed Church
GG	Archives of the Governor General, Pretoria
ICU	Industrial and Commercial Workers' Union
JAH	*Journal of African History*
JSAS	*Journal of Southern African Studies*
JSC	Joint Select Committee
JUS	Archives of the Justice Department, Pretoria
KCM	Killie Campbell Library Manuscript
MP	Member of Parliament
NA	Archives of the Native Affairs Department (pre-Union) Pretoria
NAC	Native Affairs Commission
NAD	Native Affairs Department
NEC	Native Economic Commission
NEC	*Report of the Native Economic Commission (1930–32)*
NRFA	Non-Racial Franchise Association
NTS	Archives of the Native Affairs Department (post-Union), Pretoria
OFS	Orange Free State
OUP	Oxford University Press
PM	Archives of the Prime Minister's Office, Pretoria
PSC	Public Service Commission
SACP	South African Communist Party
SAIRR	South African Institute of Race Relations
SAJE	*South African Journal of Economics*
SAJS	*South African Journal of Science*
SANAC	South African Native Affairs Commission
SAP	South African Party
SC	Select Committee
SDK	Archives of the Public Service Commission, Pretoria
SNA	Secretary of Native Affairs
SNC	Sub-Native Commissioner

TES	Archives of the Treasury, Pretoria
UCT	University of Cape Town
UG	Union Government
UNISA	University of South Africa
Wits	University of the Witwatersrand

Introduction

Most people are familiar with the meaning of 'apartheid'. Whether
through television images, newspaper reports or general reading,
they have at least some understanding of the unique system of racial
discrimination and economic exploitation which it embodies. Apartheid is conventionally regarded as having been introduced following
the electoral victory of the Nationalist Party under Dr Malan in 1948.
But fewer people are aware that it has a precursor in 'segregation',
a policy dating back to the beginning of the twentieth century, and
which in many repects established the ideological and political framework out of which apartheid was constructed and refined.

The adoption of segregation as a national political programme
represented an attempt to systematise relations of authority and
domination in a heterogeneous society which had only recently been
conquered and unified into a single state. Segregation denotes a
complex amalgam of political, ideological and administrative
strategies designed to maintain and entrench white supremacy at
every level. It was elaborated in the context of South Africa's experience of rapid industrialisation and was intended to defend the
prevailing social order from the threat posed by the growth of a
potentially militant African proletariat. As an ideological justification
of political inequality, segregation was founded on the dual principle
that (i) the recognition of Africans' right to land ownership was
conditional on the sacrifice of their claims to common citizenship,
and (ii) that Africans were the wards of their white 'trustees', under
whose benevolent guidance they would be encouraged to develop
autonomously. *Paternalism*

During the inter-war years, which constitute the focus of this study,
segregation was conventionally portrayed in terms of the imposition
of a 'frontier mentality' on the attitudes of the twentieth century.
Thus segregation was understood in terms of a battle between two
competing ideologies: on the one hand, the tradition of the Boer
Republics that there should be no equality between blacks and whites
either in church or state; on the other hand, the commitment of the
'liberal' Cape to the slogan 'equal rights for all civilized men south
of the Zambezi'. This interpretation was given impetus and authority

by liberal historians such as Eric Walker and C.W. de Kiewiet and it persisted until at least the 1960s. More recently, however, segregation has been treated as essentially a product of the industrial era. It was not, Martin Legassick argues, 'a policy produced by the imposition of earlier social attitudes on the new conditions of South African industrialization'. Rather, it was integrally linked to the process of industrialisation itself.[1] Legassick's important insight has now won widespread academic acceptance, but there remains considerable disagreement about the precise nature of the relationship between segregation and industrialisation.

One interpretation seeks to emphasise the notion that segregationist policies were instrumental agents in the development of capitalism in South Africa. Thus Wolpe argues that segregation functioned to subsidise industry's labour costs by ensuring that the burden of the social reproduction of the labour force was partly met by the precapitalist economies of the reserves.[2] Marian Lacey adopts a related version of this thesis, insisting that segregation was the process whereby competing capitalist interests combined to reduce Africans to the status of a 'super-exploited' labour force.[3]

The root problem with the positions of both Wolpe and Lacey is that they conceive of segregation far too narrowly in terms of the alleged interests or 'needs' of capital. A more subtle interpretation conceives of segregation more broadly as 'a set of policies specifically designed to cope with the strains of a society undergoing rapid industrialization'.[4] This argument, which emphasises segregation as a policy of social containment, was first outlined by Legassick. But Legassick's understanding of segregation was not always consistent, for at other times he appears to commit himself to the idea that segregation was consciously adopted as part of the active promotion of capitalist development. The following passage indicates this tension in his work:

> . . . the elaboration of the policy of 'segregation' was a specific and self-conscious attempt to formulate a 'native policy' appropriate to conditions of capitalist economic growth. And this not even in the 'weak' sense of preserving an existing social structure under new conditions, but rather in the 'strong' sense of elaborating a policy which would actually promote such growth in the specific conditions which existed in South Africa.[5]

My own understanding of segregation tends to the first interpretation set out above, namely, that the relationship between segregation and capitalist development should be interpreted in the 'weak' sense of preserving the existing social structure under conditions of rapid industrial growth. Further, it may be argued that segregation worked in the long-term interests of capitalism by helping to secure the social conditions for the reproduction of capitalism as a system.[6] However, this is not to say that segregation was the best, most efficient or indeed the only way to secure capitalist development. Rather, it is to suggest that segregation had at least as much to do with the ideological legitimation of white domination as with the requirements of capital accumulation.

In an influential article published in 1978 Shula Marks captures some of the essential structural and ideological ambiguities embedded in segregation. It was

> a many-faceted policy made up of varying components which could be and were subtly shifted in response to circumstance and to the needs of different interests of the dominant white group in South Africa. Indeed its great strength as an ideology was its very elasticity, its ability to serve the needs of very many different interests and to absorb 'elements stemming from the way of life of classes and fractions other than the dominant class or fraction'.[7]

John Cell's comparative study of segregation in South Africa and the American South (which is in many repects an elaboration of the work of Marks and Legassick) highlights the deliberate ambiguity inherent in segregationist ideology. 'Confusion', he points out, 'has been one of segregation's greatest strengths and achievements.'[8] The ideas in this book owe a great deal to the insights of Legassick and Marks and they build on the important work of Cell and Rich.[9] Yet whereas Legassick and Cell are primarily concerned to establish the origins of segregation in the two decades following the Anglo–Boer War, this work concentrates on the establishment of 'high' or 'mature' segregation during the inter-war years.

Before the First World War segregationist ideology was relatively undeveloped as a systematic political doctrine – despite its existence on the statute books in the forms of measures such as the 1911 Mines and Works Act or the 1913 Natives Land Act. It was the unprecedented rise of urban black protest immediately after the war's conclusion that brought the 'native question' to the fore. George Heaton Nicholls has commented, with some justification, that aside from the 'highly controversial' 1913 Land Act, which in any case was inoperative in the Cape and unevenly administered elsewhere, 'the Union had no recognized Native policy' before 1920.[10] The passage of Smuts's Native Affairs Act in that year represented an important watershed. It was, as Nicholas Cope points out, 'the first step in the implementation of political segregation in the Union', for it established the principle that African political activity should be divorced from 'white' South Africa and 'ushered in a period of intense debate on "native policy" during which state ideology was refined and clarified'.[11]

An important index of this changing political environment may be measured by the new meaning accorded to the term 'race'. Up until the mid–1920s, observes Sir Keith Hancock, the argument within the white political world about the proper relationship to be established between English and Afrikaans-speaking South Africans had, by 'common consent', exercised priority over the argument as to the proper relationship between blacks and whites. 'In the political vocabulary of that time, the word racialism seldom if ever referred to the colour question.'[12]

The definite association of race with colour is reflected in the intensified concentration on the 'native question'. The 1920s and 1930s saw a vast outpouring of 'expert' writings on the subject, as well as the establishment of university departments teaching Bantu studies and social anthropology. This new interest was also given expression in artistic form: works of fiction such as Sarah Gertrude Millin's *God's Step-Children* (1924), William Plomer's *Turbott Wolfe* (1926), Heaton Nicholls's *Bayete!* (1923) and Ethelreda Lewis's *Wild Deer* (1933), all reflect a heightened awareness amongst contemporary observers of the centrality of black-white relations in South Africa. Adriaan J. Barnouw, who toured South Africa in 1932 at the expense of the Carnegie Corporation in order to undertake an 'on the spot' study of Afrikaans language and literature, referred to Jochem van Bruggen's *Booia* as 'a new departure in Afrikaans literature', since it was the first such novel to be exclusively concerned with 'native life' and to have a 'native' as its hero. This represented a recognition of the important fact that the 'African landscape is not complete without the Bantu'.[13]

In 1926 Sarah Gertrude Millin noted, with reference to the visual arts, that 'lately, the Kaffir is being tentatively introduced'.[14] Perhaps she was familiar with the work of Irma Stern, whose fascination with 'tribal life' led her to Zululand and Swaziland in the 1920s, where she sought to reveal the 'inner character' of Africans in their 'natural environment'.[15] Margery Perham remarked in her 1929 journal on the new 'artistic interpretation' of the native, and mentioned the work of Alfred Palmer, an artist whose 'drawings and bronzes of Zulu chiefs reveal all the wisdom of the tribal patriarch, their dignity and courage . . .'[16] Writing in 1930, Leonard Barnes described the innocent vitality and nobility of 'tribal' Africans in the most enthusiastic terms:

> In the limbs and features of the Bantu lurk treasures of exotic beauty, the richness and variety of whose possibilities western artists are only now beginning to explore. It is an unforgettable experience to stand at evening on the verandah of a veld homestead watching the 'boys' come in from their work in the fields. They gather in a group at a shed near by, some laughing their loud musical laughter, some dancing a comic, shuffling dance, others standing a little aloof, silent, meditative, statuesque.[17]

The artistic idealisation of the 'primitive races' may be interpreted as a reaction to the experience of rapid industrialisation which, by the late 1920s, appeared set to engulf and destroy Africans' 'traditional' social structures. Notably, the reconstitution of a 'primitive' idyll has a counterpart in the emerging discipline of anthropology, many of whose practitioners sought to uncover the essence of 'primitive mentality' and to proclaim the integrity and inherent worth of different 'cultures'.[18]

II

The first part of this book begins by analysing the transformation of segregation from an abstract social theory at the turn of the century into a hegemonic or consensus ideology amongst white South Africans during the inter-war years. The first official exposition of segregation is to be found in the 1903–5 South African Native Affairs Commission (SANAC). It outlined a theory of territorial separation whereby Africans were to be accorded land in specially demarcated reserves – a policy which was subsequently given expression in the 1913 Land Act. Adam Ashforth describes SANAC as a scheme of ideological 'legitimation' associated with the construction of the South African state in the post Boer War era:

In the SANAC Report, the fundamental elements of a scheme of legitimation for a racially-divided and labour-repressive state can be clearly traced. That scheme embodies a set of theoretical relations between land occupation and political rights and obligations; between territory and citizenship. The SANAC Report was the first official South African document to elaborate an account of the political relationship between division of territory and citizenship. In so doing, it composed what might be termed a structure of legitimacy; one that was to become characteristic of the South African state in the twentieth century.[19]

SANAC's articulation of a theory of 'differential sovereignty' was given formal expression in the concept of 'segregation'.[20] The essential terms of this ideological package carried through to inform the core of General Hertzog's 1926 Native Bills, which proposed to extend Africans' land rights as a *quid pro quo* for their surrender of the common franchise.

The fact that segregation set out a well defined theory of rights and obligations and that its proponents sought to invest it with at least a semblance of moral and intellectual authority, means that it cannot be easily dismissed as a thinly disguised rationalisation of white domination. As John Cell puts it:

Segregation was not the crude and rigid system that much of the historical literature has presumed. Those who believed in it were by no means abnormal or mentally ill. Segregation triumphed for the very reason that it *was* flexible and sophisticated. Mystifying, rationalizing and legitimizing a particular configuration of caste and class, it enabled white supremacy to survive in an increasingly threatening world . . . Far from being the crude, irrational prejudice of ignorant 'rednecks', segregation must be recognized as one of the most successful political ideologies of the past century. It was, indeed, the highest stage of white supremacy.[21]

English-speaking intellectuals like Howard Pim, Maurice Evans, Charles Templeman Loram and Edgar Brookes were amongst the most important exponents of segregationist ideas in the first two decades of the twentieth century. These men figure prominently throughout this work. With the partial exception of Evans, who died in 1920, all of them played important roles in the liberal establishment after the First World War. Until the mid-1920s at least they viewed segregation as a just and pragmatic policy, which would preserve white supremacy while facilitating the development of Africans along 'separate lines'.

The early theorists of segregation drew their ideas from a variety of sources. They were initially concerned to distance themselves from the species of *laissez faire* universalist liberalism which they associated with mid-Victorian missionaries and politicians of the Cape Colony. They were conscious of the social problems associated with the rise of an industrial working class in Britain and the painful process by which it gradually gained a voice in the political establishment. Their understanding was informed too by the British colonial experience and early experiments in indirect rule and trusteeship. The history of Jim Crow legislation in the American South and the ideas of Booker T. Washington convinced them that 'social differentiation' was a natural human state.[22] Africans, they concluded, were ideally suited to a rural existence where they could aim at achieving agricultural self-sufficiency while being shielded from the harsh alien world of 'industrialism'. This is not to suggest that segregation was seen in terms of a return to a pre-industrial past. On the contrary, it was above all a modernising ideology which sought to defuse the intensity of social conflict that industrialisation would inevitably bring.

Pseudo-scientific doctrines of social Darwinism and eugenics exerted a further important influence on South African social commentators of the 1920s and 1930s. It was these theories which lay behind the concern to preserve 'racial purity', the common speculation about the innate intelligence of different races, an unquestioning acceptance of the 'evils' of miscegenation, and a highly charged fear about the 'degeneration' of both black and white races in the industrial context. Explicit theories of racial science were relatively muted in South Africa, but they were nonetheless widely evident in implicit forms.

Liberal segregationists presented the ideology of differentiation as an intrinsically moderate, common-sense policy worthy of widespread acceptance. They frequently depicted segregation as a compromise between 'identity' or 'assimilation', on the one hand, and 'repression' or 'subordination', on the other hand. The apparently naive policies of the nineteenth-century Cape became the stereotypical representation of the former option, while the latter was characterised as being typical of the 'northern' or 'Boer' tradition. Frequent references were made to the emerging discipline of social anthropology. Here the pluralist and relativist notion of 'culture' seemed to offer a useful escape from the constraints of various evolutionist theories. 'Culture' promised to transcend the manifest limits of both the Victorian 'civilising thesis' (which envisaged a universal upward progression of 'primitive' peoples from a state of 'barbarousness') as well as social Darwinist theories (which assumed the existence of an innate and immutable racial hierarchy). Segregation was therefore regarded by some as an acceptable and humane means by which to encourage the development of different 'cultures' along the lines of their 'natural advance'.

The small but influential group of missionaries, social workers, intellectuals and administrators who may be termed 'liberal segregationists' were vitally concerned to limit the socially divisive effects of rapid industrialisation. The convergence of a white and black proletariat in the cities convinced them that the existing structure of South African society was at risk. They therefore looked to the development of the rural areas in order to contain conflict in the urban areas and advocated segregation as a means of protecting African society from the harshness of 'industrialism'. By seeking to ameliorate social conflict liberal segregationists may be said to have helped guarantee the conditions necessary for the growth and reproduction of capitalism, though it would be mistaken to suppose that they engaged in special pleading on behalf of capitalist interests.

A number of liberal segregationists, most notably Edgar Brookes, were closely associated with the elaboration of Hertzog's Native Bills in the early and mid–1920s. In return for their intellectual and political support they hoped to influence the direction of state policy and to ensure that segregation would be implemented in a benevolent fashion. However, by about 1927–8 liberal segregationists, especially those grouped around the Joint Council movement, began to distance themselves from Hertzog. Brookes went so far as to recant publicly his former advocacy of segregation.

An important reason for the change of heart was the gradual realisation that Hertzog's policies were becoming increasingly repressive. The passage of the 1926 Colour Bar Act and the 1927 Native Administration Act contributed much to this growing perception. Liberal segregationists were also responding to the general intensification of African resistance to white authority and, in particular, to the more radical demands made by their African compatriots within the inter-racial Joint Councils movement. A further source of doubt derived from within liberal thinking itself.

Research conducted by the historian W.M. Macmillan and the economist S.H. Frankel demonstrated convincingly that segregation was
no longer viable in view of the thorough integration of black and
white in a unitary economic system. The clear implication was that
the 'native question' could not be dealt with in isolation from Union
policy as a whole. This perception also served to underline what
is perhaps segregation's dominant contradiction: that whereas its
ideology was given material life as a result of fears arising from South
Africa's rapid industrialisation process, the economic integration of
black and white which that very process entailed gave the lie to
schemes which envisaged the implementation of segregation in a fair
or equitable manner.

However brief the liberal flirtation with segregation was, its consequences were long-lasting, for liberal intellectuals played a major role
in defining the parameters of segregationist discourse. In portraying
segregation as a compromise between the polar opposites of 'identity'
and 'subordination', they laid the ground for its emergence as a
hegemonic ideology within white South Africa. The very flexibility
of segregationist discourse added to its attraction. It provided a ready
vocabulary which spoke to different interests within the dominant
classes: to farmers segregation meant a ready supply and even distribution of cheap labour, capitalists were reassured that the system of
migrant labour on which they had come to depend would remain
undisturbed, and white workers hoped that segregation would
protect them from competition in the job market. Many Africans
were also drawn into the language of segregation by the promise of
more land and the potential that trusteeship offered for the development of the rural areas and the restoration of traditional authority.
Thus segregation commanded the effective consent, if not always the
active support, of a very wide range of political constituencies.

Segregation was not designed in the first instance to quicken the
pace of capitalist accumulation, though it was certainly broadly
compatible with capitalist development and often advantageous to
particular capitalist sectors. It was primarily a defensive political
strategy intended to contain the vast social forces unleashed by the
industrial process. The widely perceived decline in the ability of the
reserves to feed their inhabitants, 'tribal dissolution', and the rapid
migration of African men and women into the cities, greatly alarmed
contemporary observers. Precise figures are hard to come by, but
the most reliable estimate of African urbanisation was probably made
by H.A. Shannon, who calculated that the urban African population

rose from 336 800 in 1904, to 587 200 in 1921, and 1 146 600 in 1936.[23] Thus when Colonel Stallard announced in 1930 that 'the problem before South Africa at the present time is whether or not the black population is going to be the proletariat of South Africa', he raised a question that was exercising the minds of politicians, 'native administrators' and social theorists alike.[24]

Those who feared the emergence of an African proletariat were not necessarily worried about an immediate threat to the stability of the state. But in a variety of ways white South Africans sensed that a qualitative change in the familiar relations between black and white was well under way. The possibility that a class or pan-Africanist sentiment might transform familiar forms of colonial domination and resistance was for many a truly frightening prospect. It was a feeling that was strongly reinforced by the eugenist-inspired notion that 'white civilisation' would inevitably decline as a result of its confrontation with 'hordes of black barbarians'. The less precisely whites understood the nature of the forces giving rise to the emergent African proletariat, the more threatening those forces appeared. For example, Helen Bradford remarks that the 'moral panic' which engulfed Eastern Transvaal landlords in the 1920s was

> far more closely related to what the I.C.U. represented than what it did. It both made latent conflicts visible, and also violated norms about the place of Africans in a racist society . . . the I.C.U. condensed images of the 'vrotsige kaffer' who had killed a farmer; of American Negroes promising black liberation; of 'educated, yet foul-smelling blacks' who were breaking down class and racial barriers; and of 'detribalisation', Communism and the end of white supremacy.[25]

III

The second part of this book is concerned with the Native Affairs Department (NAD) and its relation to segregation. Since the 1970s there has been a great deal of a theoretical nature written about the South African state, but little in the way of empirically based studies. In his 1981 review of the historical literature John Lonsdale writes:

> . . . there emerges a narrowly purposive yet rather abstract picture of the South African state; it has a mind of its own and is

seen to do things virtually on its own, despite (or rather because of) the great press of conflicting capitalist interests upon it . . . the state has emerged as a sentient being organizing capital's hegemony.[26]

Though many writers have been prepared to concede the state's 'relative autonomy' from its 'material base', this willingness has not always been reflected in practice. In the existing historical literature we are often left with a capital/state-centric view of the South African political economy in which little is actually known about the nature of the state or the complexity of its workings.

One of my objectives is to 'deconstruct' or 'disaggregate' the NAD in the inter-war years so as to cast light on its relation to segregation. It is well established that in the post-1948 apartheid era the Native or Bantu Affairs Department was a key agent in the process of social engineering. The partnership of Hendrik Verwoerd as Minister of Native Affairs and Werner Eiselen, his Secretary of Native Affairs, is rightly considered to have been of crucial importance in the conception and implementation of apartheid. Conversely, the retreat from grand apartheid in recent years has, amongst other important changes, meant breaking up the Bantu Administration Department as a single entity, with almost unlimited powers over the lives of black South Africans.[27]

The position of the NAD was appreciably different during the inter-war years. It was then a politically weak and administratively fragmented arm of the state. Outside of the Transkei, which consti- tuted the Department's chief administrative and ideological reference point, the NAD lacked cohesive identity. Moreover, it remained subordinate in crucial respects to the far more powerful Department of Justice. By comparison with the latter department the NAD was regarded as a benign, almost liberal, institution, which was distinctly 'sympathetic' towards the needs of Africans.

There is much truth in the assertion that the state is a 'material condensation' of various class forces and that, as such, it is beset with internal contradictions.[28] In South Africa the state has always exhibited a confusing mixture of highly repressive and rather more conciliatory behaviour: its right hand often appears to be quite out of touch with its left. During the inter-war years the NAD often appeared reluctant to act in an overtly repressive manner towards Africans. It sought instead to soften the harsh conditions occasioned by the industrialisation process and to discourage extreme forms of exploitation. Though it was receptive to the needs of capital, the NAD was not the blunt instrument of the captains of industry. The Department's primary objective was to 'keep the balance' between black and white and to secure cohesion within the wider social fabric. Despite its considerable powers, the scope of social engineering which the NAD could undertake was in any case limited by the residual power and potential for resistance within African society. For this reason the implementation of segregation was shaped in important respects, as William Beinart suggests, by the manner in which rural people on the 'periphery' struggled to defend their material and cultural resources.[29]

The NAD was acutely conscious of the threat to social stability posed by the rapid disintegration of the reserve economies and the uncontrolled influx of an African proletariat into the cities. Images of rebellion and anxious references to a 'developing sense of race consciousness' among Africans were widely pervasive within the administration from the early 1920s. In this context the Native Affairs officials generated an internal ideology which was expressed in terms of a protective relationship towards its African 'wards'. The coherence and credibility of this ideology determined that the NAD be seen to function on behalf of Africans' interests. It was an imperative which ensured that, in a number of instances, the NAD constrained the use of its powers and attempted to mitigate some of segregation's harsher aspects.

The NAD constantly sought to reconcile its 'protective' role with its manifestly coercive functions. But this proved to be a balancing act which the Department found increasingly difficult to sustain as the realities of segregation became apparent. The ideology of benevolent paternalism had developed out of early forms of colonial domination and it flourished where relations of domination were mediated by personal contact between rulers and ruled. But these governmental forms were steadily undermined as capitalist relations eroded existing social boundaries and encouraged the formation of political constituencies with an explicit class content.

The state's adoption of segregation as a national policy during the 1920s and 1930s influenced the development of the NAD, just as the NAD conditioned the implementation of segregation. In the decade following Union the Transkei constituted the NAD's strongest administrative component. It was here that the bureaucratic ideology of 'sympathetic paternalism' can be seen to have developed most clearly. This administrative ethic laid particular stress on the individual magistrate's personal authority and the special relationship he was supposed to enjoy with the people under his control. It may be characterised as an essentially pragmatic form of patriarchal rule, informed by residual traces of the Victorian 'civilising mission'. Many considered that these qualities were inappropriate to the requirements of white South Africa in the era after the First World War. In 1923 the NAD was substantially reorganised, ostensibly on the grounds of 'efficiency and economy'. The result was a further weakening of its already fragile authority with respect to the Department of Justice. The NAD responded to this onslaught by restating its administrative and ideological objectives in closer accord with the prevailing segregationist discourse. The Department drafted a monumental bill which finally emerged as the Native Administration Act of 1927. It embraced a comprehensive strategy of 'retribalisation' while greatly enhancing the nature and scope of the Department's jurisdiction. Accompanied by the assertion of technocratic values and in the name of 'efficiency' and 'uniformity', the NAD's administrative structure was consolidated and centralised. Indeed the groundwork was laid for its subsequent emergence during the apartheid era as a powerful 'state within a state'. Ironically, although many of these changes were made in the name of the mythologised 'Transkeian tradition', the 1927 Act was strongly resisted by Transkeian officials themselves, who rightly regarded it as a major threat to their region's administrative autonomy.

As segregation became more and more part of the state's legislative fabric, the ideology of the NAD underwent change. By degrees its lingering idiom of benevolent paternalism was submerged by a more robust and purposeful bureaucratic apparatus which, over time, became increasingly repressive. This process was observed by (among others) Margery Perham, who commented in 1929 that 'the whole spirit informing the native administration is changing' as 'Hertzog's Afrikaner Government fastens its grip'.[30]

Viewed from within, this transformation was not always smooth. There was conflict both within the NAD and between the NAD and other state departments over the allocation of resources, the exercise of political authority, and the direction that state policies should take. These conflicts were often registered in ideologically encoded terms whose internal logic has to be understood in order to comprehend fully the material context in which they occurred. It is therefore assumed in this work that state ideology should be treated as more than just a gloss on departmental activities or a crude rationalisation of hidden political agendas. Bureaucratic ideology is not confined to official pronouncements or the content of government commissions. One has also to consider the ethic and style of government, the living assumptions of administrative officials, and the vocabulary according to which competing interests and policies come to be formulated and contested.

IV

The final part of this work is concerned with the passage of General Hertzog's Native Bills. As enacted in 1936 they completed the nation-wide division of land envisaged by the 1913 Land Act, abolished the non-racial Cape franchise, and established the Natives' Representative Council in its stead. My analysis of the land and franchise bills considers their passage from the point of view of the major parliamentary parties as well as the various black and white opposition groupings. Here again I explore the way in which segregation developed into a consensus ideology through the 1920s and 1930s, the equivocal attitude to segregation displayed by key opposition figures, and the way in which pressure for the abolition of the non-racial Cape franchise was linked to the anxieties of whites about the emergence of a politically conscious African proletariat.

Before 1934, the year in which the Nationalists and the South African Party (SAP) combined to form the United Party, the two major white parliamentary parties appeared to differ substantially on the issue of segregation. The most important area of disagreement regarded the continued existence of the Cape African franchise. In reality, however, these differences were relatively superficial; they turned on matters of style and approach rather than on fundamental policy. It was short-term political interest that invariably kept the parties apart rather than matters of essential principle. The SAP was internally divided. A number of its Cape parliamentarians (who were dependent on the support of African voters for their electoral majorities) vigorously opposed the abolition of the Cape franchise. By contrast, other SAP parliamentarians, especially those in Natal, were determined to end the non-racial franchise. These contradic-tions were embodied in the person of General Smuts, leader of the

SAP, who vacillated and prevaricated on the Native Bills in a desperate attempt to avert an open split developing within his party. Like Hertzog, Smuts was a convinced segregationist. Smuts, however, tended towards a more accommodationist form of segregation, which traced its origins from the 1894 Glen Grey Act through to the 1920 Native Affairs Act. This tradition was founded on the establishment of political and territorial segregation, but it did not entirely rule out the possibility of gradually incorporating an emergent African peasantry or urban elite into the structures of white power. Its tone was characterised by a form of benevolent paternalism which stressed continuously the need for 'consultation' between blacks and whites. By contrast, Hertzogite segregation was defined more sharply. Its character was narrowly exclusionist, emphasising colour rather than class as the key point of social and political distinction. Outright domination rather than collaboration was the central motif. Thus it was the Nationalists who insisted, in spite of strong SAP opposition, on the 1926 industrial Colour Bar Act, and it was they who exploited the 'black peril' most crudely at election time.

Within these parameters there was basic agreement between the SAP and the Nationalists on the need to preserve white supremacy. Racial segregation can indeed be seen as the counterpart to the creation of a unified white South African nation. Earlier, reference was made to the transformation in meaning during the 1920s of the word 'race'. Whereas it had previously applied to relations between English and Afrikaners, it now became applicable to whites and blacks. This change in application is indicative of the process by which a unified sense of white identity was engendered through the exclusion of blacks from civil society. There is indeed an integral link between Hertzog's native policy, on the one hand, and his championing of a (white) South African nationalism, on the other hand. This idea was well understood by, among others, J. Albert Coetzee, then a student and subsequently a leading Afrikaner nationalist intellectual, who sent Hertzog a pamphlet in 1933 entitled 'Nation Building in South Africa'. Its basic premise was that in order to 'build up a White nation in South Africa', it was 'essential that the principle of differentiation shall be the principle of Native policy'.[31]

William Ballinger arrived at a similar conclusion in 1930, though from a rather different perspective. In his view it was the common interest in maintaining an adequate supply of cheap African labour which united the white political parties. Conversely, the division within white politics was conditioned by rivalry for the control of that supply of African labour:

> Native policy is the driving force of the greater part of politics. Flag controversy, compulsory bilingualism in Government services, government control of the academic personnel of the Universities – all are involved in the struggle for strategic advantage, for securing the occupation of vital points by the forces of one or the other political groups. It is a 'fight for position'. Beneath the 'armed peace' is the basic economic antagonism – on native policy. All Union politics are Native Affairs.[32]

Ballinger's assertion that all Union politics were 'native affairs' was a provocative insight which would have surprised many contemporary observers. Nevertheless, it was vindicated by the paradox that just as the 'native question' began to achieve national prominence during the 1920s, the major political parties undertook to prevent native affairs becoming a 'political football'. The attempt to prevent the 'native question' from becoming a divisive issue within white politics is itself suggestive of the process by which white political solidarity was achieved at the expense of black participation in the common society. In the event the possibility of immediate political advantage ensured that neither white party kept its promise to keep native affairs out of politics. This was made especially apparent during the 'black peril' election of 1929. Indeed the very attempt to exclude the 'native question' from white party politics underlines its centrality; by the 1920s 'native policy' had become a pivotal concern of what has been referred to as South Africa's 'racially exclusive bourgeois democracy'.[33]

George Heaton Nicholls, the radical segregationist ideologue and SAP politician, was keenly aware of the importance of settling the issue of political representation once and for all. Nicholls regarded the non-racial franchise as a democratic institution symbolising the potential political equality of white and black. For that reason alone it would have to go. In its place Nicholls advocated the ideology of trusteeship and the recreation of 'tribalism'; by redirecting Africans' political energies towards 'communalism', he hoped to avert the threat of 'communism'. Many others shared Nicholls's fears even if they did not express them with quite such clarity. General Hertzog was particularly adept at transforming the idea of black political advancement into a generalised sense of panic. He did so by conflating – in defiance of rational argumentation – the urbanisation of Africans, their education, miscegenation and the 'swamping' of whites at the polls.

One of the outstanding features of the Native Bills was the failure of opposition groupings, whether within parliament or outside it, to mount an effective campaign against them. Liberals grouped around the Joint Council movement or the Institute of Race Relations orchestrated much of the opposition to the Bills. Many of them, however, like Rheinallt Jones, Howard Pim, Alfred Hoernlé or Edgar Brookes, had either supported segregation in the past or else retained a lingering sympathy with its basic philosophy. After 1928 their commitment to the non-racial franchise was generally expressed with more conviction. Nevertheless, they remained essentially pragmatic, seeking constantly to arrive at a compromise settlement with the government.

This rather timid strategy of persuasion and negotiation was sharply criticised by liberals of a more traditional mould associated with the Non-Racial Franchise Association (NRFA). Individuals like Sir James Rose Innes or Henry Burton clung tenaciously to the universalist ideals embodied in the non-racial franchise. This does not mean, however, that they were 'democrats' in the modern sense of the word, i.e. defined at least partly by a belief in a universal suffrage. On the contrary, the ageing patrician survivors of the nineteenth-century Cape liberal tradition were convinced that white supremacy, which was associated with 'civilisation' rather than colour, would be preserved most effectively by the political incorporation of an educated African elite into its ranks. They were quite prepared to support raised franchise qualifications should the African electorate be seen to be expanding too rapidly.

White liberals exerted an important moderating influence on African organisations. But it would be wrong to lay the blame for the failure of Africans to mount an effective campaign against the Native Bills on white political intervention. Aside from the ICU (which was deeply fractured from within) and the Communist Party (which imploded in the late 1920s) there was little attempt to build a mass-based national organisation with the capacity to articulate popular demands. A significant element of the African political establishment was strongly committed to the liberal Christian values associated with the Cape franchise. As exemplified by Prof. D.D.T. Jabavu, this tendency predominantly voiced the aspirations of an 'improving' African elite who sought inclusion in civil society in recognition of their having satisfied the criteria of 'civilisation'.

A range of African political figures, from the representatives to the annual Pretoria Native Conference to the African National Congress or the All-African Convention, remained susceptible to the elusive promises of segregation. Hertzog's insistence on the interdependence of the land and franchise bills rendered it extremely difficult for African leaders to reject segregation outright. By proposing to extend the size of the reserves in return for the loss of the Cape franchise, Hertzog cynically exploited the manifest landhunger of many Africans. Moreover, the emergence of various strands of Africanist sentiment in the 1920s – though often expressed in terms of a militant rejection of white authority and a desire to restore traditional institutions and values – was not necessarily incompatible with segregationist thinking. The cry of 'Africa for the Africans' signalled in part a retreat from the aspirations to equal political rights as well as a tacit acceptance of differentiation along racial lines.

Although most African organisations expressed varying degrees of opposition to the Native Bills, they did not reject them outright. There were frequent instances in which individual African spokesmen contradicted themselves (just like their white liberal counterparts) by condemning segregation publicly, while maintaining rather more flexible positions privately. In a situation where political power was overwhelmingly concentrated in white hands it would, however, be inappropriate to suggest that African leaders collaborated with their oppressors. The ambivalence of the dominated classes with respect to segregation was founded in political and economic weakness rather than in an acquiescent acceptance of their subject status. Nevertheless, it is instructive to contrast the situation in the 1920s and 1930s with the present: whereas the opponents of segregation in the inter-war years by and large sought inclusion in the existing structures of society, the opponents of apartheid in contemporary South Africa reject the legitimacy of the state and therefore seek to transform its very nature.

Part I

Part I

1 The Elaboration of Segregationist Ideology, c. 1900–36

1 EARLY EXPONENTS OF SEGREGATION

Historians hold a multiplicity of views as regards the historical origins of segregation. Some writers, like Marian Lacey and Richard Parry, trace segregation back to the nineteenth-century Cape and the provisions of Cecil Rhodes's 1894 Glen Grey Act.[1] It has been suggested too that the experience of British rule in Basutoland provided a model for some of the early theorists of segregation.[2] During the inter-war years and beyond there was a widespread assumption (especially amongst liberal scholars) that the origins of segregation were to be found in the racial attitudes characteristic of the 'frontier tradition' and in the institutions of the nineteenth-century Boer republics. Against this view, David Welsh has claimed that the antecedents of segregation and apartheid are to be found in the Shepstonian policies of colonial Natal. It is in Natal, Welsh argues, that the demarcation of native reserves, the state's use of chiefs for administrative purposes and the recognition of customary law, were pioneered.[3]

The salience of Natal is also highlighted by Shula Marks, who gives the argument a fresh analytical twist. In her study of that region Marks shows that segregation was a means whereby capital and the colonial state came to terms with the 'still pulsating remains of powerful African kingdoms'. Segregationist policies were therefore not simply imposed by an all-powerful state; they emerged out of a complex process of struggle which was 'profoundly shaped' by the 'structures and social relationships of African precapitalist society'.[4] The importance of Natal – which, of all South Africa's regions most closely resembles a colonial/settler frontier – is further underlined by the fact that many of the principal advocates of twentieth-century segregation, e.g. Maurice Evans, C.T. Loram, Edgar Brookes and G.H. Nicholls, were closely associated with that province.

There are sound reasons to support all the above claims for the paternity of segregation, and it would therefore be misleading to cite one region to the exclusion of all others. Indeed it was ideologically advantageous to South Africa's early twentieth-century social engineers that segregationist precedents could readily be demonstrated in all the provinces of the Union of South Africa; for, in the context of the centralisation of the state after 1910, segregation could be shown to be a consistent feature of the Union's diverse political and constitutional traditions.

At this point it is worth noting that of all the competing explanations for the origins of segregation-apartheid, the theory of Afrikaner nationalist responsibility is perhaps the least convincing. That view is exemplified by such historians as C.W. de Kiewiet and Eric Walker, who portray segregation in terms of the imposition of a retrogressive 'frontier mentality' on the attitudes of the twentieth century, and C.M. Tatz, for whom segregation represents the victory of the racially exclusive North over the liberal traditions of the Cape.[5]

Although now a somewhat discredited view amongst academic historians, the misleading notion of apartheid as the eccentric creation of racist Afrikaners continues to enjoy wide provenance. In a recent book the BBC radio journalist Graham Leach, for instance, tells us that apartheid 'was a policy steeped in the Afrikaner's 300 years of history' and, even more inaccurately, that 'it was South Africa's first attempt at solving its racial problem'.[6]

This sort of account ignores the fact that the first group of theorists to outline a systematic ideology of segregation were English- rather than Afrikaans-speaking, and that many of them were associated with the inter-war tradition of South African liberal thought. Prime Minister Hertzog, who was directly responsible for the passage of the 1936 Native Bills, promoted segregation as a white supremacist rather than an Afrikaner, and he derived most of his ideas from English-speaking thinkers. It is notable that the Afrikaner Broederbond, that powerhouse of twentieth-century Afrikaner nationalist ideological thought, only began to shift its concerns from Anglo-Afrikaner relations to the 'native question' in the mid to late 1930s, by which time segregationist ideology was already deeply entrenched.[7] The earliest examples of Afrikaner proto-apartheid theory date from the early 1930s, but although they bear the distinctive imprint of Christian-Nationalist thinking and embrace a purist view of total separation, in substance they are largely derivative of already extant segregation and trusteeship ideology.

The first use of the word 'segregation' remains a matter of historical conjecture. Martin Legassick tentatively traced its first occurrence back to around 1908.[8] John Cell considers it 'truly remarkable' that the report of the 1903–5 South African Native Affairs Commission (SANAC) did not actually employ the term, even though it advocated a policy of 'territorial separation'.[9] (In fact, the word 'segregation' *does* occur in paragraph 190 of the report.[10]) Paul Rich recently claimed that 'segregation' was first used in 1903 by the Cape Liberal lawyer Richard Rose Innes 'to rationalise a policy of establishing "native reserves" in order to induce a ready supply of black labour for the mines and farms'.[11] But the word also crops up during the opening of the 1902 Cape Parliament, when the governor general declared that it was 'necessary for the Government to be endowed with larger powers than they now possess to effectually carry out the policy of segregation . . .'[12] It may well turn out that 'segregation' was used even earlier than that.

The search for the first use of 'segregation' in South Africa should not obscure the more significant point that segregation became an established political keyword only in the first two decades of the twentieth century. One of the first theorists to outline a reserve-based segregation strategy was J. Howard Pim, who did so in a paper which he delivered at the invitation of Sir Godfrey Lagden to the 1905 meeting of the British Association.[13]

The essence of Pim's argument was that it was preferable for Africans to remain in reserves, rather than their being established in 'locations' surrounding the industrial areas. He explained:

> For a time the location consists of able-bodied people, but they grow older, they become ill, they become disabled – who is to support them? They commit offences – who is to control them? The reserve is a sanatorium where they can recruit; if they are disabled they remain there. Their own tribal system keeps them under discipline, and if they become criminals there is not the slightest difficulty in bringing them to justice. All this absolutely without cost to the white community.[14]

It has been suggested that this quotation furnishes evidence for the validity of the reserve-subsidy theory of segregation as advanced by Harold Wolpe.[15] But when viewed in the context of Pim's paper and his other writings, the emphasis of such an interpretation appears to be misplaced. Pim's advocacy of the reserves occurs as an attempt to refute two prevailing arguments: the first claimed that Africans were occupying land which could be better utilised by whites; while the second contended that the reserves would deprive whites of labour by offering Africans an alternative form of subsistence. Both views therefore implied that Africans should be moved to locations close to large industrial centres where they would be compelled to enter into wage labour.[16]

Pim rejected this analysis (partly on moral grounds) but chiefly because he felt that 'location' Africans would in time constitute an intolerable economic and administrative burden upon white society. The Basutoland precedent apparently demonstrated that, even under 'tribal' conditions, Africans would be compelled – on economic grounds – to enter the labour market.[17] Moreover, experience of the American South in the post-emancipation era supposedly proved that 'the tendency of race feeling is towards segregation' and that 'the greatest benefit each race can confer upon the other is to cease to form part of the other's system'.[18]

On this reading Pim's advocacy of reserve segregation was not in the first instance a manifesto for cheap labour. His primary concern was with the maintenance of social discipline and control, which, he considered, would be most effectively sustained, under conditions of rapid industrialisation, through the existing 'tribal' system of the reserves. Thus it was Pim's intention to demonstrate that territorial segregation was *compatible* with (rather than *necessary* to) the development of industry, and that such a strategy would help to ensure the preservation of social order.

This interpretation of Pim's reserve policy is consistent with other writings in his private papers. In 1904, the year before his address to the British Association, Pim drafted 'A Note on Native Policy'. In this document he argued that, notwithstanding the mutual economic dependence of blacks and whites, it was to the advantage of both communities to be separate. The 'most ordinary reasons of [white] self-preservation' he explained,

> prevent our simply turning him [the African] loose in the country and allowing him to find his own level, for whatever veneer of civilization he may have acquired will rapidly under these circumstances disappear, and unless he is controlled, he will rapidly relapse into barbarism, in which condition he will be a source of endless trouble and difficulty to his white neighbours.[19]

It was 'obviously far easier' to keep Africans 'under some form of discipline' when they lived as 'a native community' than if they were scattered throughout the white population.[20] Yet Pim firmly rejected the notion that 'native policy' should be founded solely in the material interests of whites. It was fallacious to assume that by

> making him of the greatest use to the white man, he will also develop naturally to his own best advantage . . . I absolutely deny our right to base a native policy on the idea of our making the greatest possible use of the native races.[21]

Notably, references to social Darwinist and environmental theories are a dominant feature of Pim's early writings on the native question. Thus he took it for granted that physical differences were merely 'outward signs of mental and moral differences', and he cited Africans' alleged 'lack of a sense of responsibility, want of foresight, arrest of mental development and distinctive modes of thought . . .'[22] Pim also adhered to the common eugenic doctrine that Africans would 'degenerate' morally in the urban environment, thereby constituting a danger to white society. These beliefs reinforced his conviction that Africans should, so far as possible, be excluded from 'white civilisation'. Indeed, in evidence to the SANAC Commission, Pim argued that native policy should be predicated on the undeniable fact of racial difference, from which it followed as 'a necessary conclusion that you cannot give the Native his full rights as a citizen of a white State'.[23]

As he grew older, Pim's Quaker-influenced moral outlook emerged more clearly. From 1905 he insisted that it was wrong, as well as unnecessary, to tax Africans so heavily as to enforce their proletarianisation. Writing after the 1913 Land Act, which he welcomed, Pim rejected the industrial colour bar, arguing that it was tantamount to slavery and would lead to the 'deterioration of the white race . . .'[24] In later years Pim emerged as one of the most prominent liberal critics of segregation and gained a wide reputation as a philanthropist and 'friend of the natives'. His earlier eugenic beliefs were either abandoned or discreetly allowed to lapse.

In sum, during the period when Pim was an advocate of segregation, he conceived of it as a creative and prudent solution within the art of the politically possible. Given the reality of capitalism's labour requirements, he regarded segregation as a compromise between total separation on the one hand and the danger of unrestrained urbanisation on the other hand. This prudence was also informed by a moral position which led Pim to criticise segregation if it was intended for the sole benefit of whites. It is only if we understand Pim in these terms that his later critique of segregation becomes explicable.

Although Pim was one of the original exponents of segregation, his views remained largely outside the public domain, for they were presented in the form of lectures to specialised discussion groups, such as the Fortnightly Club, and diffused silently amongst Milner's mandarins.[25] The first thorough-going and broadly disseminated theory of segregation was Maurice Evans's *Black and White in South East Africa*, first published in 1911.[26] Evans's book enjoyed a wide circulation and was frequently cited in political debate.[27] Subtitled 'a study in sociology', it is noteworthy as one of the first in a tradition of 'expert' writings on the 'native question'. *Black and White* was strongly influenced by Evans's understanding of social conditions in the American South, to which he later devoted an entire study.

According to Evans, segregation was wrongly dismissed by the 'average person' as 'a Utopian chimerical idea' on account of its misassociation with the concept of total segregation. Yet, in a modified form, he believed that it embodied 'a great truth'.[28] Just as the Native Affairs Department was later to argue, Evans portrayed segregation as a natural synthesis of different regional approaches to native administration, each of which contained 'something of value'. By so doing he wished to demonstrate both its practicality and its pedigree.[29] Evans went on to establish three cardinal principles for the government of the native races:

(1) The white man must govern.
(2) The Parliament elected by the white man must realise that while it is their duty to decide upon the line of policy to be adopted, they must delegate a large measure of power to those especially qualified, and must refrain from undue interference.
(3) The main line of policy must be the separation of the races as far as possible, our aim being to prevent race deterioration, to preserve race integrity, and to give both opportunity to build up and develop their race life.[30]

These three principles resonate strongly with the colonial paternalism of trusteeship ideology, of which segregation was a variant. It will be observed that Evans's positive assertion of white supremacy is mitigated by an acknowledgement that native policy would have to be executed justly, and that considerable devolution of power with adequate mechanisms of consultation would have to be introduced. Like other writers of his time, Evans was strongly informed in his work by the language of eugenics, leading him, for example, to warn against miscegenation and the effects of inter-racial contact in the industrial sphere. Though not an advocate of total segregation, he believed that it was imperative to '. . . let the roots of the Abantu people remain in the soil of their country', where they would be subject to the wholesome restraints of tribal life and shielded from 'degeneration and despair'.[31]

Just as Afrikaner theorists of apartheid were later to argue, Evans stressed that segregation demanded an important material sacrifice from whites in the form of a generous land settlement. 'We cannot have our cake and also eat it', he warned.[32] In Evans's view segregation was incompatible with rapacious economic greed, and it was therefore not in the long-term interests of whites to submit to immediate calls for cheap African labour:

> For our own ultimate good . . . the points of contact of the races are already too many and too close, and to multiply them and intensify them for what is at bottom, our economic gain, is a policy likely to be fraught with evil for both races. The easy way is the perilous way.[33]

After Evans, the next landmark work on the 'native question' was the publication in 1917 of Charles Templeman Loram's *The Education of the South African Native*.[34] The significance of Loram's work lies in its attempt to articulate a detailed and differential educational policy appropriate to segregation. A number of sub-themes already present in Evans's writings are amplified in this work. For instance, Loram is strongly concerned to solve the native question in 'a scientific fashion' by employing the specialist insights of anthropologists, ethnologists and psychologists. In seeking technical solutions to social problems, Loram exhibits a firm belief in the supposedly objective methods of positivist science.

Like Evans, Loram's segregationist proposals bear the strong imprint of the American South, where he had spent 15 months studying Negro educational institutions. Another important feature of Loram's work is its concentration on the findings of racial science. Although his conclusions about the alleged inferiority of Africans remain ambiguous, Loram devoted considerable sections of the *Education* to an assessment of Africans' actual and potential mental capacities. He conducted a series of intelligence tests in Natal based on similar experiments on American negroes by W.H. Pyle, M.J. Mayo and Louise F. Perring.[35]

Like Evans, Loram is critical of the general indifference towards the 'native problem'. He claimed that only when faced by rebellion, labour scarcity, or competition in the cities, did the white man sit up and take notice; and even then such interest was momentary. Loram identified three schools of thought, which he termed the 'Repressionists', the 'Equalists' and the 'Segregationists'. Repressionists, he argued, regarded Africans as being inferior to whites and therefore fit for manual labour alone. Diametrically opposed were the Equalists (Exeter Hall philanthropists and certain European missionaries) who, 'basing their arguments on a common humanity, plead for equality of treatment for White and Black.'

In rejecting both these 'extremes', Loram embraced the Segregationists as a worthy 'midway' party. This school 'would attack the problem in a scientific fashion' and (with reference to Evans's three cardinal principles) 'would endeavour to give the Bantu race every circumstance to develop on the lines of its racial genius'. Strict segregation was, however, impractical in a country 'whose very existence is said to depend on a supply of cheap black labour', and in a situation where the tribal system had suffered irreparable decay.[36]

Finally, we should turn our attention to Edgar Brookes's well known *History of Native Policy*.[37] This work was originally submitted as a doctoral thesis to the University of South Africa and may be considered to be the first full-length archivally based treatise on the subject of segregation. Brookes's *History* is also significant on account of the controversy it evoked and the wide circulation it achieved among policy-makers. Segregation, he ceaselessly argued, was the

> way out between the Scylla of identity and the Charybdis of subordination. We have seen it in the administrative, in the legal, in the political, in the economic, in the religious and in the social sphere as not merely a plausible or advisable, but as the inevitable, solution. In trying to arrive at a general formula, we are in no doubt that differentiation is the formula to be accepted – differentiation, without any implication of inferiority.[38]

Brookes counterposed complete segregation with what he termed 'Partial' or 'Possessory' segregation. He dismissed complete segregation on the grounds that 'a certain amount of Native labour will always be necessary in South African economic life'.[39] Nevertheless, his sympathies at this stage were with those advocating a white labour policy, and he echoed the idea that Africans were fundamentally unsuited to industrialism.

Brookes's notion of possessory segregation amounts to a thorough statement of liberal-minded practical paternalism. Central to his thinking was the need to preserve the independent existence of the white and black races. He assumed that the natural place of Africans was on the land and affirmed the 'horror' of racial intermarriage. But Brookes felt that it was wrong to institute needless discrimination, such as the horizontal job colour bar. The duty of the white man was 'to civilise as well as control, to develop as well as protect'.[40]

Brookes's *History* is distinctive, both because it was published under the patronage of Hertzog himself, and also because it was the first extensive analysis of segregation. In a sense it was the last, for, with the publication of Hertzog's Native Bills in 1926, segregation came to the fore as declared government policy. Before this date the exponents of segregation were essentially self-appointed experts attempting to influence the content of what was still a vague, undefined theory within white ruling circles. Henceforth most of the literature dealing with segregation was written as commentary or critique, rather than as an explication of its policies.

2 'CULTURAL ADAPTATION'[41]

The foregoing section has indicated how, in the presentation of segregation as part of an historic compromise, the language of scientific racism, and of eugenics in particular, constituted an important component of its ideological discourse. During the second half of the nineteenth century there was a spectacular explosion of biologically based racial science in the English-speaking world. Evolutionist thought, exemplified by the Darwinian theory of natural selection, came to be applied to the human situation, and to groups rather than individuals. Scientists across a range of disciplines set themselves the task of classifying the world's races according to a 'natural' hierarchy. Biology, notes Greta Jones, helped to 'create the kind of moral universe in which nature reflected society and vice versa'.[42]

By the turn of the century the doctrine of eugenics, founded by Francis Galton, was strongly pervasive in Britain and the United

States. This theory was predicated on the idea that social and political objectives could be efficiently achieved through the deliberate manipulation of genetic pools. Eugenics drew strongly on the late-nineteenth-century fear of working class discontent and was infused with an 'air of catastrophism'.[43] According to Galton, Western civilisation was on the decline; it could only be saved through the adoption of radical measures involving social and biological engineering. Within Britain, eugenics was primarily addressed to the questions of social class. It was viewed (often as not by political progressives) as a means of coping with poverty as well as the physical degeneration and moral 'degradation' of the urban proletariat. Moreover, its language and applications were readily transferred to the colonial domain, where it came to be addressed to questions of race.[44]

The rise of the eugenics movement in the second half of the nineteenth century is indicative of a general decline in confidence about the inevitability of human progress, the Whiggish assumption which so strongly informed the British imperial mission. A similar tendency is discernible in South Africa, where a number of writers have remarked on a distinct ideological shift in the late-nineteenth-century Cape. Parry, for example, has demonstrated the manner by which the 'amalgamationist' policies ascribed to Sir George Grey were gradually undermined by the turn of the century: although the rhetoric of 'civilising the backward races' persisted, the combination of administrative difficulties and the new conditions occasioned by the mineral revolution combined to rob the liberal vision of its practical force.[45]

Similarly, Russell Martin's analysis of the Transkeian administration shows how, particularly after the wars of 1877 and uprisings of 1880–1, officials became ever more sceptical of the potential for success of the Victorian 'civilising mission'. By slow degrees 'the orthodoxy of Grey who had sought to promote "civilisation by mingling" became the heterodoxy of the Transkeian magistrates who set their face against what they called "amalgamation" '.[46] This reassessment of social evolutionary theory appears to have been true of the British Colonial Office as a whole. Thus Hyam, writing of the Liberal government of 1905–8, claims that by this time 'the mid-Victorian objective of turning Africans into black Europeans had long been given up . . . the tendency was towards segregation rather than assimilation'.[47] Notably, Hyam ascribes this change to the historical experience of colonialism, as well as to the teachings of 'pseudo Darwinian science'.[48]

In South Africa the lived relations of paternalism which bound black and white together presented white supremacy as part of the natural order of things. To an extent this assumption obviated the need for an elaboration of explicit theories of racial superiority as evidenced in Britain or the United States. Aside from relatively marginal individuals like Fred Bell, there appears to be a relative absence of virulent scientific racism in early-twentieth-century South Africa. This point has recently been made by Paul Rich.[49] In making it, however, Rich has underrated the extent to which scientific racism was an *implicit* component of the political discourse of the time. Indeed it is perhaps by virtue of the fact that racist assumptions were so prevalent in the common-sense thinking of early-twentieth-century South Africa that the relative absence of eugenist or social Darwinist theories is to be explained.[50]

The imagery of social Darwinism is clearly discernible in three important areas of political debate: speculation about the relative intelligence of blacks and whites, the almost universally expressed horror of 'miscegenation', and fear of racial 'degeneration' following upon the uncontrolled development of a black and white proletariat in the cities.

In the view of many, Africans were 'naturally' part of the land. Cities were portrayed as an 'alien environment' for which they were supposedly not yet ready. The urban environment was commonly described as the site of vice and immorality, 'influences far too potent for his [the African's] powers of resistance'.[51] The phenomenon of 'poor whiteism' was frequently held up as a perfect illustration of the tendency of civilisation to decline. Concern was especially expressed for the physical and moral well-being of Africans in the cities. Notably, urban social welfare became an important area of liberal activity in the 1920s, as attempts were made to prevent 'demoralisation' and to defuse the potential for social and industrial conflict.

The language of eugenics is strongly evident in the contemporary obsession with 'miscegenation' and the creation of 'hybrid races' – a preoccupation which was by no means confined to South Africa alone.[52] Miscegenation among the working classes was held to sap the fibre of white civilisation and its most vulnerable point. Similarly, 'race fusion' was portrayed in the most apocalyptic terms by such eugenist-inspired catastrophists as Ernest Stubbs and George Heaton Nicholls.[53] Maurice Evans associated himself (as did many white liberal thinkers) with the opinion of the 'average white South African' that the 'admixture in blood of the races is the worst that can happen, at least for the white race, and perhaps for both'.[54] So strong was feeling on this point that African notables took care to distinguish their political claims from the implication that they desired 'social equality' – often as not, a euphemism for miscegenation.

The dangers of miscegenation were powerfully exploited at the hustings. In his speeches on segregation Hertzog warned of the vulnerability of white civilisation in the face of the numerical preponderance of Africans, and he frequently equated political rights for Africans with 'swamping'.[55] The full force of these warnings escape us today, as they have eluded those liberal historians who naively attempt to show by means of figures that Hertzog's fears of the rapid expansion in the African franchise were unfounded.[56] But the impact of 'swamping' or of the 'rising tide of colour' is rendered more comprehensible when set in the prevailing mood of the time, with its paranoia about civilisation's retrogressive tendencies and its vulnerability in the face of the 'virile' mass of 'barbarians' who were 'flooding' into the cities.

The impact of nineteenth-century racial science also served to confirm the popular justification of white supremacy, which looked to the Bible for its authority. According to this interpretation, which became especially prominent within Afrikaner nationalist thought from the 1930s onwards, Africans were forever destined to be 'hewers of wood and drawers of water' on account of their being descendants of the children of Ham. As de Kiewiet succinctly observes, 'Religion and science each seemed to lend the weight of its peculiar authority to the elevation of one race over another'.[57]

The problem of genetic inheritance provoked three major questions with respect to Africans: their innate as opposed to their potential mental capacities, whether their intellect was 'originative' as well as 'imitative', and whether their mental development was 'arrested' after adolescence.[58] Results of intelligence tests, frequently derived from American models then in vogue, were often invoked in support of arguments for or against segregation.[59]

Speculation about the relative mental capactiy of the different races was by no means confined to those who may obviously be considered to be racists. Prominent liberal thinkers, such as J.D. Rheinallt Jones, C.T. Loram, and Alfred Hoernlé, all addressed themselves to the question of innate intelligence at one time or another.[60] A.R. Radcliffe-Brown, then professor of social anthropology at the University of Cape Town, was equivocal on the matter.

He thought it likely that there were some physiological differences between whites and blacks, but supposed these would not make a vast amount of difference.[61] The general consensus as expressed by the black author S.M. Molema was that 'neither capacity nor incapacity have been shown conclusively to be characteristic of the backward races, or more plainly, of the African race'.[62] A similar conclusion on the indeterminacy of intelligence testing was reached by Werner Eiselen in 1929.[63] Eiselen was then a lecturer in ethnography and Bantu languages at Stellenbosch University, but later served as Secretary of Native Afairs under Hendrik Verwoerd, in which capacity he played a central role in the implementation of apartheid.[64]

If most writers agreed that the matter of biological differences between the races was in doubt, this did not prevent them from making inferences based on their own prejudices and suspicions. For some, innate racial differences were manifestly obvious; the only question which remained was the extent to which Africans could be expected to bridge the intelligence gap. In the case of others, the inconclusive results of scientific research offered hope for the ultimate achievement of liberal ideals. In general, however, to pose the question of biological differentiation in itself presupposed some acceptance of segregation: a policy of 'differentiation', it seemed clear, was the best social laboratory in which the true capacity of Africans could be tested.

South Africa's transition from a mercantile to an industrial economy in the late nineteenth century forms the historical context in which the assumptions of classic liberalism were called into question.[65] But it was only during the first two decades of the twentieth century that the full social implications of capitalist industrialisation became apparent. Among its more important manifestations were the growth of urban slums and the emergence of working class radicalism, as well as a growing awareness of the rapid dissolution of the 'tribal system' and the inadequate agricultural capacity of the reserves. It was with these processes in mind that social theorists began to draw on the brand of liberal reformism and collectivist thought which had been gathering strength overseas.

In this regard it should be observed that the liberalism which developed after the Anglo–Boer War and coalesced on the Witwatersrand during the early 1920s was born in explicit opposition to its Cape forebears. Although in some respects the inheritors of the Cape tradition, the new establishment-liberalism eschewed fundamental tenets of the mid-Victorian project. The writings of Loram and Brookes rejected the policies of identity and assimilation. In their hands 'civilisation' was replaced by 'culture', 'progress' became synonymous with 'differentiation', while individualism was subsumed into the collective interests of 'racial groups'. Whereas the racist policies of the nineteenth-century Boer republics were associated with 'repression' and Victorian liberalism with 'identity', segregation came to be portrayed as transcending these opposites. An intellectual organising principle was required to validate this compromise or synthesis; and the anthropological notion of culture came to serve the purpose admirably.

The study of anthropology in South Africa was institutionalised during the decade after the First World War.[66] In 1921 A.R. Radcliffe-Brown, one of the acknowledged founders of modern social anthropology, was appointed to the newly established chair of social anthropology at the University of Cape Town. Within a few years all four teaching universities in the country had departments offering courses in 'Bantu studies' and anthropology, or their equivalents. From the outset anthropology was looked to as a source of applied knowledge. Influential individuals, such as C.T. Loram, J.D. Rheinallt Jones, James Duerden and Jan Smuts, all stressed the role that anthropology could play in providing a solution to the so-called 'native question'.[67] In the words of Radcliffe-Brown, social anthropology was 'not merely of scientific or academic interest, but of immense practical importance . . .' Given a situation where the economic, social and cultural of the 'native tribes' was being 'altered daily', Radcliffe-Brown extolled the value of anthropological knowledge in 'finding some social and political system in which the natives and the whites may live together without conflict . . .'[68]

For a variety of reasons the instrumental effects of anthropology on state policy were limited.[69] But its contribution to the formulation of segregationist ideology was pronounced as a result of claims which made reference to its intellectual authority. For key members of the liberal establishment, a number of whom were strongly influenced by early social anthropology, the nascent theory of 'culture contact' offered new and valuable insights into the 'changing native'. Its recognition of the complexity of African society, and of the distinctive nature of African 'culture', informed their efforts to provide for the differential development of Africans. As an empirical science of a distinctive 'native mentality', anthropology was eagerly seized upon by experts seeking positivist 'solutions' to the 'native question'.[70]

George Stocking, the American historian of anthropology, has convincingly demonstrated how the work of Franz Boas and his students in the period 1900–30 served to 'free the concept of culture from its heritage of evolutionary and racial assumptions, so that it could subsequently become the cornerstone of social scientific disciplines completely independent of biological determinism'.[71] The influence of the Boasian school, explains Stocking, generated a specifically anthropological concept of culture which was distinctly *relativistic*. This was contrasted with the humanist sense of culture, 'which was absolutistic and knew perfection'. Thus, whereas 'Traditional humanist usage distinguishes between degrees of "culture"; for the anthopologist, all men are equally "cultured".'[72]

As disseminated through Bronislaw Malinowski (and possibly through Franz Boas), a popular notion of 'culture' came to serve as a credible linguistic peg upon which the segregationist compromise was hung. Both the liberal 'civilising mission' and scientific racism shared the linear asumptions characteristic of evolutionist thought, yet both these theories jarred with those who favoured a form of separate development without repression. The notion of 'culture' offered a way out of these constraints. It did so by incorporating – and transcending – the evolutionist assumptions of liberal assimila-tionists (who believed in the capacity of the black man 'to rise'), as well as of racist 'repressionists' (who based their policies on the assumption that the position of Africans on the evolutionary scale or the 'Great Chain of Being' was fixed at a lower point than whites).

Consideration of the ways in which the term 'culture' was popularly used in the 1920s and 1930s, reveals an intriguing diversity in its connotations. 'Culture' was sometimes employed as a synonym for 'civilisation', whereby it was seen as a universally transmissible quality on an ascending evolutionary scale. At other times, however, it was employed as a synonym for 'race', in which case it took on an immutable character. Used in the first sense, culture was perfectible, whereas in the latter case it was static in virtue of its being biologically determined. It was out of these contradictory meanings that a distinc-tive, anthropologically derived notion of culture developed. Though implicitly racist and openly hostile to traditional theories of assimi-lation, this sense of 'culture' allowed room for a gradual process of racial 'upliftment'.

A paradigmatic example of this mode of thought is evident in General Smuts's celebrated 1929 Oxford lectures in which he outlined his personal view of segregation.[73] Smuts rejected the opinion which saw the 'African as essentially inferior or sub-human, as having no soul, and as being only fit to be a slave'. But he also rejected the converse, whereby the 'African now became a man and a brother'.[74] Although this view had given Africans a semblance of equality with whites, it had destroyed 'the basis of his African system which was his highest good'.[75] Both these policies, according to Smuts, had been harmful: the solution was to be found in a policy of differential development or segregation. 'The new policy', he explained, 'is to foster an indigenous native culture or system of cultures, and to cease to force the African into alien European moulds.'[76]

G.P. Lestrade, the government ethnologist, argued similarly that the culturally assimilated and missionary-educated native was somehow fraudulent ('about as original as a glass of skimmed milk') and that it was necessary instead to 'build up a good Bantu future' on the basis of their own culture.[77] In 1931 he informed the Native Economic Commission:

> . . . there is a middle way between tying him [the native] down or trying to make of him a black European, between *repressionist* and *assimilationist* schools . . . it is possible to adopt an *adaptationist* attitude which would take out of the Bantu past what was good, and even what was merely neutral, and together with what is good of European culture for the Bantu, build up a Bantu future.[78]

Lestrade's formulation of cultural adaptationism was to become a crucial organising theme for the Native Economic Commission's advocacy of segregation. Thus in 1932 the Commission 'unhesitatingly affirm[ed]' its adherence to Lestrade's concept of adaptationism, which it considered to be 'not only the most reasonable but also the most economical approach to the native question'.[79]

The concept of 'adaptation', which in biology refers to the manner in which an organism becomes fitted to its environment, was especially suited to the vocabulary of segregation. If differentiation between species was a feature of the natural world, it was (by a process of inference) true of society as well. Thus J.E. Holloway, the Chairman of the NEC, defined adaptation in such a way that it functioned as a biological metaphor for separate development:

> The adaptationist aims at transforming, at giving shape and direc-

tion to what is growing, or, to vary the metaphor, at grafting on the existing stock. His view of human beings is essentially evolutionary. They are a part of the conditions which have created them. Their reactions are largely conditioned by their racial past, and are therefore difficult to destroy.[80]

At this point it is necessary to insert a note of caution: although it derived from and was shaped by the emerging discipline of anthropology, the popular notion of 'culture' and of 'cultural adaptation' should not be too closely associated with the modern discipline of social anthropology. Isaac Schapera, for example, was strongly critical of Lestrade's theory of cultural adaptation as adopted by the NEC, since he laid stress on the dynamic qualities of 'culture'. In Schapera's view the penetration of Western civilisation in the form of 'the missionary, the teacher, the trader, the labour recruiter, and the farmer' was irreversible. Changes in one aspect of culture inevitably reacted upon other aspects, and it was therefore impossible to 'bolster up the Chieftainship and Native legal institutions . . .'[81]

It is clear that Schapera had absorbed W.M. Macmillan's historical insights into his own understanding of anthropology. Macmillan had been bitterly contemptuous of the 'rather doubtful doctrines' of anthropology from as early as 1923, attacking the liberal establishment for its concern with anthropological studies and complaining angrily of the 'paralysing conservatism' of its approach.[82] In Macmillan's view rural poverty and tribal disintegration had 'already gone too far'. It was therefore 'more urgent that we see he [the African] is provided with bread, even without butter, than to embark on the long quest to "understand the Native mind".'[83]

The concept of 'cultural adaptation' was widely appropriated for use in the political domain. In the hands of George Heaton Nicholls, the Natal politician and prominent segregationist ideologue, it was imperative to recreate a tribally based culture or 'ethos'. The alternative to adaptation was assimilation, which 'substitutes class for race' and would inevitably 'lead to the evolution of a native proletariat inspired by the usual antagonisms of a class war'.[84] Werner Eiselen also emphasised the need to recognise and encourage 'Bantu culture' in order to promote a policy of differentiation. 'The duty of the native', he explained, was 'not to become a black European, but to become a better native, with ideals and a culture of his own.'[85]

The language of cultural adaptation was of distinct advantage in the attempt to associate South African segregation with the wider

imperial policies of indirect rule and trusteeship. This linkage consti-
tutes a major theme of Smuts's 1929 Oxford lectures, wherein he
sought to demonstrate that the South African policy of differentiation
was enshrined in the trusteeship clauses of the League of Nations
Covenant.[86] In his keynote statement on the draft Native Bills in
1935 George Heaton Nicholls reinforced this connection, suggesting
that the essence of the Bills differs 'in no way in principle from the
new conception of native government which is embraced in the word
"trusteeship" and translated into administrative action through a
policy of "adaptation" in all British States'.[87] The policy of adaptation, he added, was not new to South Africa 'where the people
have learnt their anthropology at first hand from actual contact with
native life'.[88]

In Britain Lord Lugard's doctrine of indirect rule had likewise
been lent theoretical coherence through its association with social
anthropology and, in particular, the Malinowskian concept of
'culture contact'. Rich has recently emphasised the intellectual
contribution during the 1890s of the writer and traveller Mary
Kingsley, who challenged the jingoistic certainties of high-Victorian
British imperialism and championed the instrinsic worth of African
societies. Kingsley's legacy of 'cultural relativism' may therefore be
regarded as having anticipated the theory of indirect rule, as well as
providing ammunition for later segregationists.[89]

The South African advocates of segregation sought to accommodate themselves to ideas forwarded by the proponents of indirect
rule – a task made considerably easier by the fact that both groups
shared the vocabulary of 'culture', 'adaptation', and 'parallelism'.
This similarity in discourse was a source of considerable embarrassment during the inter-war years to British social anthropologists and
commentators, for whom South Africa was increasingly seen as a
retrogressive or aberrant member of the Empire.

It is indeed revealing that the attempt to distinguish indirect rule
from segregation was somewhat awkwardly accomplished. Margery
Perham, in her elaboration and defence of indirect rule, claimed that
it was 'strange that segregation and indirect rule should have been
confused'.[90] She argued that whereas segregation was characteristic
of the 'mixed territories', indirect rule had only been applied in
the 'purely native territories'; and she contrasted the doctrinaire
artificiality inherent in the strategy of preserving indigenous cultures
in South Africa with the essential flexibility characteristic of indirect
rule. Perham's arguments were elaborated at greater length by Lucy

Mair, for whom indirect rule was not a magic formula whose essence could be deduced theoretically. In the final analysis, Mair contended, the distinction between Nigeria and Tanganyika (where the finest attributes of indirect rule were apparently exemplified) and South Africa (which was based on the selfish preservation of white 'supremacy') could only be judged empirically.[91]

Perham and Mair were undoubtedly correct in their concern to distance indirect rule from segregation – no doubt Kingsley would have wished to do the same. But their manifest difficulty in doing so is testament to the power of the language of cultural adaptation in lending credibility to the ideology of segregation.

3 SEGREGATION AFTER THE FIRST WORLD WAR

Thus far we have considered some of the core elements which went into the creation of segregationist ideology. Yet from the vantage point of someone writing in the early 1920s it was not at all clear that segregation was approved government policy. It is true that significant segregationist legislation was firmly planted (in embryonic form at least) on the statute books by 1920: the 1911 Mines and Works Act, the Native Labour Regulation Act of the same year, the 1913 Native Land Act and the 1920 Native Affairs Act, are amongst the most important examples. Together with the pass laws, this legislation laid down job discrimination and territorial separation, as well as mechanisms by which labour could be controlled and coerced. Nevertheless, these measures were seldom interpreted as integral elements of a unified ideological package.

For example, whereas the 1913 Land Act promised segregation, plans for its implementation had in fact been deferred to an unspecified date in the future. The 1916 Beaumont Commission and the 1918 Local Committees, which were intended to finalise the land question, encountered constitutional and political difficulties and were consequently dropped. The 1917 Native Administration Bill, with its key proposals for administrative segregation, was likewise abandoned. Prime Minister Botha's native policy had, in the words of Hancock, 'come to a dead stop'.[92] Or at least it was perceived to have done so. Thus, in 1918 the Native Affairs Department concluded that an Urban Areas Bill would have to 'bide its time' because the policy (of segregation) as expressed by the 1913 Land

Act and the 1917 Administration Bill had 'not yet been fully accepted by the country'.[93]

It may therefore be concluded that the legislative and ideological continuity of segregationist policies was severely disrupted during the First World War and its immediate aftermath. Yet, with the introduction and passage of Smuts's Native Affairs Act in 1920, the 'native question' was forced back on the agenda as a matter of urgency. Many observers of a liberal disposition welcomed the 1920 Act, which focused attention on the question of separate political representation for black and white, as an enlightened measure, commending it as 'a great and hopeful step forward'.[94]

The decade of the 1920s witnessed an unprecedented upsurge in black political radicalism: a volatile, if contradictory, amalgam of working class militancy, rural populism and Africanist millenarianism. This ferment was intimately related to the declining productivity of the reserves, the development of capitalist agriculture and the quickening pace of proletarianisation. And it was largely as a reaction to these social processes that segregationist ideology gathered political momentum, until it became a sort of hegemonic ideology within white South Africa.

The marked change in the political environment after the First World War, a matter which was especially apparent to officials of the Native Affairs Department, was often expressed in terms of an 'awakening of racial consciousness'. On his return home to South Africa in 1919 after war service C.L.R. Harries, the Sub-Native Commissioner of Sibasa in the northern Transvaal, exclaimed that Africans had been 'awakened by the roar and noise of a universal war'. He laid great stress on political and economic changes, adding that Johannesburg had become the centre 'from which native political movements will, and in fact do already, radiate'.[95]

Similar points were made by many other officials and observers in the early 1920s.[96] In his introduction to the *Report of the Native Affairs Department for the Years 1919–1921*, Secretary of Native Affairs Edward Barrett noted astutely that events in the 3 years since the ending of the Great War had

> exercised a remarkable and unprecedented influence on Native thought. The growth of education and the increasing contact of the races had, during the last decade, rendered the mind of the Native much more accessible to the reports of current history and to European ideas . . . In the large industrial centres, too, the

position has been emphasised by the increased cost of living and the far from corresponding adjustment of Native wages . . . There has been a growing inclination among Native workers to adopt European methods for the redress of grievances, actual and assumed, and there has been a noticeable, if yet but little successful, attempt of the communist or Bolshevik section to capture and exploit the Native races for the purpose of the subversion of the present form of government . . . The inevitable development of race-consciousness has begun and is showing itself in the formation of associations for all kinds of purposes – religious, political, industrial and social. These may be at present shortlived and unstable – the product of immature thought – but they indicate how the wind blows and what importance is attached to European example.[97]

Barrett supported these claims with a detailed account of recent events, mentioning, *inter alia*, agitation in Bloemfontein in 1919 for higher wages and the arrest of H. Selby Msimang; the sanitary workers' strike in Johannesburg; strikes during 1919 at the Natal Collieries, the Messina Mine, and the Cape Town Docks; the 1919 deputation of the SANNC to England; the 1920 mineworkers' strike on the Rand; a riot in 1920 at the Lovedale institution; agitation for increased wages and an ensuing riot in 1920 at Port Elizabeth; and the 1921 Bulhoek incident at Queenstown.[98]

Scholars have frequently remarked upon the distinct sharpening in black political awareness during the immediate post-war decade.[99] In recent years these observations have been scrutinized with greater precision. In his perceptive study of the class dynamics of the black population on the Rand between 1917 and 1922, Philip Bonner, for example, draws attention to the intense radicalisation of black political leadership during the period 1918–20 as the Transvaal Native Congress confronted a powerful upsurge in working class agitation.[100]

Other recent work has broadened the focus of research to reveal a remarkable degree of militancy in the countryside during the 1920s. Most notably, Helen Bradford's sensitive analysis of the Industrial and Commercial Workers' Union (ICU) provides us with a vivid account of mass-based populist resistance in the rural areas. The introduction to her doctoral thesis begins dramatically:

Immediately after World War I, black protest almost unprecedented in scope and intensity swept through South Africa.

Sparked by soaring inflation, it assumed forms ranging from riots and boycotts to strikes and anti-pass campaigns. Erupting in almost every major town as well as in numerous rural areas, this resistance incorporated tens of thousands of unskilled African workers. It also fuelled the emergence of trade unions, and contributed to a realignment of forces on the black political scene.[101]

It must be said that the organisational coherence of the ICU differed markedly from region to region and its successes were often short-lived. But its phenomenal growth in the 1920s through large parts of Southern Africa is testimony to a high degree of mass mobilisation and popular discontent during this period. The Union's reputation as a communist-inspired organisation is reflected by the degree to which its activities were monitored by the Native Affairs Department. Thus, for many contemporary observers, the ICU – and particularly its leader, Clements Kadalie – constituted a profoundly dangerous threat to the existing social order. Indeed, there is strong evidence to suggest that the sedition clause of the 1927 Native Administration Act was specifically intended to curb the activities of the ICU and the influence of white communist 'agitators'.[102]

Pirio and Hill's research on the impact of Marcus Garvey's ideas in South Africa adds a further dimension to our understanding of popular radicalism during the inter-war years. They argue that Garveyite notions of 'Africa for the Africans' penetrated far more deeply into rural as well as urban black political consciousness than has been appreciated by earlier scholarship, and they emphasise the potency of its radical nationalist appeal.[103] This claim is reinforced by Bradford's observation that, by the mid-1920s, the belief that black Americans were about to liberate South Africa had 'permeated to the remotest rural districts'.[104]

The groundswell of black resistance in the 1920s initially caught the South African Communist Party (SACP) off-balance and led to a (painful) re-evaluation of the path that revolutionary change should take. Formed in 1921, the SACP addressed itself almost exclusively in its early years to the white working class. Yet in 1928 it adopted the policy of the 'Native Republic', a policy which – though largely dictated externally by the Comintern – represented a new-found awareness of the fact that South Africa's revolutionary potential lay predominantly with the black working class and peasantry. Henceforth the SACP became increasingly concerned to consolidate its alliance with the forces of African nationalism, as represented by the ANC and the ICU.[105]

The political turbulence of the early 1920s ensured that segregation-talk came to impinge more and more directly on the political agenda. In 1920 the governor-general remarked (in light of the Native Affairs Act of that year) that the principle of segregation was now generally accepted. But he was forced to add that there was 'some divergence of opinion as to what precisely the term "segregation" should be held to imply'.[106] The ambiguous character of segregation thrived in an environment where there was 'strong demand by the public for a "policy", just as when people are sick they want a pill or mixture that will "cure" the trouble'.[107]

Though General Smuts appeared to endorse segregation in 1920, it was increasingly (if confusedly) associated with J.B.M. Hertzog, who skilfully exploited the desire for a panacea solution to the native question by deliberately leaving the details of segregation obscure. Through the election year of 1924 the pro-SAP *Cape Times* exhibited marked frustration at its inability to pin Hertzog down on the meaning of segregation. It accused him of having 'always been clever enough to leave his meaning entangled in a mass of loosely-spun words, as vague and intangible as a collection of moonbeams'. This expedient, the newspaper noted, afforded Hertzog considerable room for manoeuvre, for he simply claimed to have been deliberately misrepresented or misquoted whenever political opponents chose to put a definite interpretation on his utterances.[108]

In the mid-1920s Hertzog was successfully indulging in a strategy of political kite-flying. The elusive quality with which he invested segregation was its very strength, for it drew differing groups into its discourse, always promising, never quite revealing. In Hancock's words, segregation was 'not a precisely defined programme but a slogan with as many meanings as anyone could want'. Even as the opposition tried to force Hertzog to define what he meant by the term, they might be left 'protesting that they too were segregationists'.[109]

The ideology of segregation was ambiguous but it was not vacuous. At the risk of oversimplification, there were two distinct segregationist traditions, whose distinctive strands coalesced in rough accordance with the fault lines of the major parliamentary parties. They may therefore be loosely associated with Smuts and Hertzog respectively.

On the one hand, Hertzogite segregation maintained strong

positions on the abolition of the Cape franchise, the white 'civilized labour' policy, the industrial colour bar, and the distribution of farm labour. Its tone was strident, it was racist in character and it emphasised the economic and political exclusion of Africans from a common society.

By contrast, Smutsian segregation drew on the incorporationist and 'protective' elements inherent in liberal segregation and made explicit reference to the paternalist idiom of trusteeship ideology. Unlike the Hertzogite variant, which was often understood as the logical extension of the 'Northern tradition', Smutsian segregation traced its antecedents back to the nineteenth-century Cape. The notion of 'parallel institutions' or 'differentiation' was said to derive from the pragmatic legacy of the 1894 Glen Grey Act. Smutsian segregation celebrated the reputed success of the Transkeian Councils and proclaimed the 1920 Native Affairs Act, which sponsored indirect statutory forms of black political representation, as the basis of a moderate segregationist solution.[110]

The question of the industrial colour bar was probably the issue on which the two segregationist traditions diverged most sharply. In combination with Hertzog's civilised labour policy, the job colour bar was designed to protect white labour against 'unfair' competition from reserve Africans. Liberal opinion was seemingly outraged at this explicit example of discrimination. In a sustained campaign against its introduction the *Cape Times* variously termed the colour bar 'pernicious' and both 'ethically and morally unsound'.[111] The Act was attacked by liberals as an infringement of individual human rights, an example of illegitimate state interference in the market, and a measure whose political and economic effects were bound to be counter-productive.

Much of the opposition mounted against the colour bar represented an alliance between proponents of *laissez faire* economic policies and those more inclined towards the expression of humanitarian sentiment. Yet, in spite of the opposition mounted against statutory job discrimination, it is notable that segregation itself was not under attack at this stage. Indeed some of the most outspoken opposition to the Bill emanated from such liberal paternalists as Brookes, Pim and Loram, who remained supporters of Hertzog. What distressed these individuals in particular was the *principle* of statutory discrimination, which it was feared would arouse unnecessary hostility amongst the African elite. The colour bar, it was pointed out, had long been a *de facto* feature of South African

life and it could effectively be maintained through indirect means –
for instance, through manipulation of the Wage Act.[112]

If the two segregationist traditions differed most strongly on the
question of the colour bar, on other issues there was a substantial
degree of convergence. The 1923 Urban Areas Act serves as a good
example. This measure managed to synthesise the findings of the
Stallard Commission (which argued that Africans' presence in the
urban areas should be restricted to their 'ministering' to the needs
of whites) with those of the Godley Commission (which, accepting
African urbanisation as inevitable, went on to propose measures
designed to improve the living conditions of permanently proletari-
anised Africans). In combining labour control with the 'protection'
of Africans the 1923 Act attracted significant support from liberal
segregationists, and the manner in which it was debated was
portrayed as a vindication of the 'consultative' spirit underlying the
1920 Native Affairs Act.[113]

Common to both strands of segregationist ideology was an
unashamed paternalism towards Africans and an unquestioning
commitment to the maintenance of white supremacy. There were
differences, however, as to what supremacy entailed, as well as the
means by which it was to be upheld. By the early 1920s the major
white political parties, together with significant elements of African
opinion, had come to accept segregation in its broadest terms. This
does not mean that there was unanimity about segregationist policies,
much less that it was universally welcomed. But arguments about its
content tended to revolve around matters of detail and differences
in interpretation rather than on the generally accepted principle of
consolidating a racially differentiated society.

4   THE LIBERAL BREAK WITH SEGREGATION

The formative role of key English-speaking advocates of segregation
was discussed at the beginning of this chapter. It was suggested that
such individuals as Howard Pim, Maurice Evans, Edgar Brookes
and C.T. Loram contributed significantly to the definition of the
'native problem', and that they helped to invest segregationist
discourse with a much needed vocabulary. Their views were internalised and repeated by liberal or benevolent segregationists, such
as J.H. Hofmeyr, who came to reject

policies which are based either on the repression of the native or
on his identification with the white man . . . The important thing
is not the native's inferiority, or his equality, or his superiority;
what is important is just the fact that he is different from the white
man. The recognition of this difference should be the starting-
point in South Africa's native policy.[114]

Hertzog's 1925 Smithfield speech, which is commonly accepted as
his first major statement of segregationist intent and the immediate
precursor of the 1926 Native Bills, is a case in point. According to
John Cell, C.T. Loram not only supported Hertzog's segregationist
programme, but helped him to draft speeches in its defence.[115] (In
private, Loram claimed to have written the Smithfield speech
himself.[116]) Paul Rich suggests that Maurice Evans's work played an
important role in the development of Hertzog's thinking during his
tenure as Minister of Native Affairs in 1912.[117] A.W. Roberts, a
liberal-minded colleague of Loram's on the Native Affairs
Commission and ex-teacher at Lovedale, also seems to have had
a hand in the process. At Hertzog's request he wrote a lengthy
memorandum with the cumbersome title 'Certain Reflections On
The Existence Of A Native People In South Africa, And Of The
Need For A Clear Policy In Dealing With Them'. It was submitted
just a few months before the Smithfield pronouncement. Roberts
covered a wide range of topics, maintaining that 'the ideal arrangement would be to have territorial segregation, with economic segregation only as far as possible'. He stressed the need for a 'definite
and if at all possible a final declaration on Native Policy'.[118]

Edgar Brookes's participation was more public, as was his renunciation of segregation a few years later. Hertzog himself arranged the
publication of Brookes's segregationist manifesto, *The History of
Native Policy*, which was published in 1924 by Nasionale Pers, the
Afrikaner publishing house, and paid for out of a trust fund given
over to 'national purposes'.[119] In 1924, moreover, Hertzog had
greeted Brookes's manuscript with 'immense pleasure' and wrote
him an enthusiastic letter expressing their 'perfect harmony of views
and sentiments . . . on this momentous question'.[120]

As a result of the alliance struck between the new Nationalist
Prime Minister and the young Pretoria academic, a relationship
which the latter was not slow to exploit, Brookes soon became
known as one of the key interpreters of segregation. The *Cape Times*
went so far as to speculate whether Brookes was 'a John the Baptist

who is making straight the way for the Prime Minister . . .'[121] In a series of articles published in 1926 Brookes fulfilled this role by defending the principles behind Hertzog's Smithfield proposals. Howard Pim was another liberal figure who devoted time to an explication of these proposals. In 1925–6, while still a declared supporter of segregation, he urged the need to secure additional areas for Africans under the 1913 Land Act and agreed the Cape franchise would have to be altered. At this stage the only point on which Pim departed from Hertzog's scheme in any significant respect was his opposition to the institution of a statutory colour bar.[122]

It can safely be concluded that as late as 1925–6, an important caucus of reformist liberals was favourably disposed towards the Smithfield proposals. It was seen as a courageous, forward-looking document, whose benign intentions were perhaps frustrated in certain respects by the political need to accommodate 'reactionary' interests. But if there were misgivings over the industrial colour bar and the abolition of the Cape franchise, these were suppressed for the moment. Instead of moving onto the attack, segregationist liberals hoped to strengthen the 'progressive' elements embodied in the Smithfield scheme through a process of rational discussion and discreet lobbying.

By the close of the decade, however, there was marked liberal disillusionment with the whole idea of segregation. The year 1927 seems to have been a key moment in the process of political reassessment. Indeed Legassick refers to this period as the first significant breach in thinking on native policy since Union, representing 'the birth of modern South African liberalism reconnecting with its antecedents in the Cape'.[123]

Brookes's recantation after 1927 is the most widely known and dramatic. Amidst profuse breast-beating he announced that his previous advocacy of segregation had been misguided. In 1926 Brookes was still advocating the Hertzog policy ('with certain necessary amendments') as an expression of 'wise and moderate liberalism'.[124] By October, however, his misgivings seemed to be getting the upper hand, and he asked for a private interview with Hertzog. Brookes submitted a memorandum proposing a number of detailed amendments to the Native Bills, though without attacking its principles as a whole. But it was evident that the lack of political representation for 'detribalised' and 'educated' Africans, 'like my friend Professor Jabavu', had begun to prey heavily on his conscience.[125]

Looking back, Brookes accounted for his support of segregation in terms of an emotional engagement with Afrikaner legend. He also cited his naive reliance on the positivism of J.H. Seeley, which led him to assume in the *History* that a careful study of the past would automatically disclose an infallible policy for the future. He came to realise too that he had been politically manipulated by Hertzog, who welcomed academic support from an unexpected source. Moreover, his support for segregation had been influenced by his political ambition, his youth and an 'exhilarating feeling of being a kind of power behind the throne . . .'[126] In rejecting segregation Brookes was significantly influenced by his visit in 1927 to the United States, where he imbibed the philosophy of Booker T. Washington and became convinced that 'the black man was capable of considerable achievement in a milieu of white civilisation'.[127]

Other liberal segregationists changed their views by incremental steps at about the same time. Howard Pim remained a qualified supporter of the Smithfield speeches until 1925–6. However, in his keynote address to the 1927 European-Bantu Conference, he argued that the reserve system 'had been shattered and it could not be rebuilt'. To astonished cries of 'no!' he was reported as saying that segregation was quite impossible 'except under conditions of slavery'.[128]

By 1929 Pim had become a supporter of common citizenship as the surest guarantee of South Africa's future stability, declaring himself a 'convinced believer in the principle enunciated by Mr. Rhodes of equal rights for all civilised men'.[129] This shift marked a conscious re-identification on his part with the (much idealised) brand of liberal universalism associated with the Cape; it also stood in direct contradiction to his earlier conviction that it was unwise 'to give the native full political rights in a white community'.[130]

The positions of Rheinallt Jones and Loram also appear to have shifted at about the same time, though their attitudes towards segregation remained somewhat more ambivalent. In 1925 Rheinallt Jones praised Hertzog for the boldness of his Smithfield declaration; yet in his 1927 address to the European-Bantu Conference Rhenallt Jones argued (following Macmillan) that 'natural economic and social law knew no colour bar' and that a 'national' rather than a specifically 'native' land policy was required. Territorial segregation should be seen 'not as a principle' but as a temporary 'expedient'.[131]

C.T. Loram's views appear to have changed least. As late as 1930 he was reported to have remained a supporter of Hertzog as 'the only man who can carry out a policy worth having, because he alone can sway the back-veld'.[132] By this time, however, whatever credentials he might have had as a liberal were under suspicion: Howard Pim, for example, regarded Loram as being untrustworthy, describing him as the 'Government servant every time with all the merits and defects of his class'.[133]

The liberal break with segregation was by no means neat or clean. A number of its prominent representatives continued a dialogue with segregation, thereby remaining within its consensual orbit. There were a variety of reasons for the growth of liberal discontent in the second half of the 1920s. Amongst these, the colour bar, the 1927 Native Administration Act and the failure to implement fully the provisions of Smuts's 1920 Native Affairs Act, were significant. The palpable hardening of debate following the publication of Hertzog's Native Bills in 1926 was another contributory factor. Also important was the response of African members of the Joint Council movement to the burgeoning social discontent in both the urban and rural areas, which was now more critical of the activities of their white liberal counterparts. Yet something more was required to weld these misgivings into a coherent critique of segregation's fundamental assumptions; it was from within the liberal intellectual paradigm itself that the economic basis of segregation and its relation to industrialisation came to be reformulated.

By the early 1920s the historian W.M. Macmillan was coming to realize that the plight of poor whites was essentially the same as that of poor blacks. His pathbreaking investigation into agrarian conditions led him to the important realisation that the South African political economy was a complex, interdependent whole. The economy of the reserves was integrally dependent on that of industry and it was therefore meaningless to talk about separate or differential development.[134]

Macmillan's insights were elaborated on and set within a more rigorous framework by his student, the economist S.H. Frankel, who wrote to Loram in 1926 announcing his intention to criticise the 'white labour viewpoint' of Edgar Brookes, and the assumption that 'welfare of the European can only be furthered by the separation of the economic activities of the white and native peoples'.[135] That same year Frankel addressed the Johannesburg branch of the Economic Society of South Africa. Now he attacked Brookes's position explicitly, claiming that there was no sense in speaking (as Brookes did) about 'economic aspects of the Native Problem', since that very problem was merely 'one aspect of South Africa's economic policy in general'.[136] The address was published in 1928. Here he reiterated Macmillan's argument that segregationist schemes were absurd 'in the face of an outworn and economically unsound tribalism, appalling overcrowding, ignorance and poverty'.[137] The essential interdependence of blacks and white rendered segregation impossible.

In Frankel's view the only means by which to end both black and white unemployment was to increase the 'national dividend'. African labour, he explained, was exploited – but it was not cheap. Robbed of incentive and the hope of self-advancement, Africans laboured 'in the spirit of slavery . . .' Their 'cheap' labour was therefore inefficient and thoroughly unproductive. It followed that only through the creation of a prosperous, economically assimilated African population could South Africa develop as a whole.[138]

In 1930 Brookes cooperated with Frankel in an article dealing with aspects of 'the poor white and the native'.[139] Acknowledging their debt to Macmillan, they credited him with having finally buried the 'conscience comforting "South African *idée fixe* that the native is a lucky being, able to live on very little, working only when it suits him – passing lightly between town house and country seat!".' The economic interdependence of whites and blacks determined that 'complete separation of two economies within one nation' was impossible: 'Segregation, if it could ever have been a success, would have had to be put into practice long ago when land was still easily available and when vested interests were few and recent'.[140] Macmillan's 'economic school' was never fully accepted by the liberal segregationists, but it effectively gave the lie to any sense in which segregation could practically be achieved within the framework of liberal principles.

2 Segregation and Cheap Labour

1 THE CHEAP-LABOUR THESIS

The early 1970s saw the emergence of a series of influential studies emphasising 'class' rather than 'race' as the appropriate analytical category by which to interpret South African history. Far from being an irrational and atavistic phenomenon, and therefore dysfunctional to South Africa's economic development, it was contended that racial discrimination had functioned to quicken the pace of capitalist accumulation. In a seminal article published in 1972 Harold Wolpe established a theoretical framework for the understanding of segregation. Drawing on the work of the Marxist anthropologist Claude Meillassoux, he declared that the policy of segregation was designed to maintain the productive capacity of the precapitalist economies in the reserves, so as to provide capitalist industry with a cheap supply of migrant labour.[1]

Wolpe's article was in some respects a development of an equally important paper circulated a year earlier by Martin Legassick in which he rejected the notion that segregation represented an imposition of earlier outdated racial attitudes on South Africa's process of industrialisation. Legassick argued instead (with reference to Stanley Trapido's formulation) that segregation was about the 'alliance of gold and maize'. In association with various coercive mechanisms it 'created and perpetuated the system of migrant labour which has characterized South Africa's road to industrialization'.[2]

The Legassick-Wolpe position, though by no means identical in all respects, served as a schematic overview of South Africa's history of industrialisation. Their argument was elegant, precise and forcefully put, but it lacked the nuances which more detailed empirical research would have revealed. F.A. Johnstone's contribution to the debate was a further important development in the early radical literature. In an article published in 1970 he debunked the view that economic growth was inconsistent with apartheid and white supremacy.[3] Johnstone's thesis focused on the system of racial discrimination in the gold mines around the period of the First World War. Its central contention was to deny that the industrial colour

51

bar was merely the consequence of race prejudice or chauvinism on the part of white workers. On the contrary, it was shown to be part of a wider structure of exploitation in which white and African workers were differentially oppressed for the greater good of capitalist interests.[4]

The first full-length study of the segregationist era to have emerged out of the radical milieu of the 1970s was Marian Lacey's *Working for Boroko*. This work, though incisive and original in parts, is flawed on account of its oversimplified conception of segregation. In Lacey's view segregation was 'not only compatible with economic growth, but was designed as a coercive labour system geared to ensure capitalist profitability'.[5] Thus she construes the period 1924–32 as the era in which intra-capitalist rivalry over access to supplies of cheap black labour was resolved. It saw the elaboration of a policy intended to solve 'one single overriding issue: how best to super-exploit all African workers in the interest of capitalist profitability and the national economy as a whole'.[6]

There is undoubtedly an essential element of truth in these claims, but without refinement and changes in emphasis they can only be proposed at the cost of considerable distortion. Segregationist policies were not simply a knee-jerk response to capitalist interests as a whole, much less to the particular needs of particular 'fractions' of capital. Segregation embodied a multitude of different policies grouped together under a common ideological umbrella; to capture its full meaning a somewhat broader analytical framework is therefore required.

The argument advanced in this chapter is that segregation should be seen as a *generalised* response on the part of the state to the problems wrought by industrialisation; specifically, it was intended to cope with the ecological and social collapse of the reserves, and the political threat posed by an uncontrolled and potentially uncontrollable African proletariat in the cities. As a strategy developed to defuse potential class, and social upheaval, it is plausible to argue that segregation operated in the long-term interests of capitalism by guaranteeing the social conditions for its continued reproduction. In this way the material basis of white domination was preserved. This proposition is subtly (but importantly) different from those formulations which imply that segregation was in the first instance concerned with the creation and reproduction of an ultra-cheap labour supply for agriculture and industry.

2 THE MINES

As applied to the development of mining capital, the cheap-labour or reserve-subsidy thesis has especial salience. Nevertheless, there are a number of serious problems associated with it, some of which may be mentioned in passing. An initial objection to the thesis is that it has never been satisfactorily proven. Theoretical issues pertaining to the nature of surplus value extraction and the 'reserve army' of the unemployed have been the subject of extensive theoretical debates, but the economics of migrant labour to the mines has never been subjected to detailed research. Nor has the migrant labour thesis been rigorously periodised, either with respect to the history of the mining industry or to the development of the reserves. The argument has been sustained by a small selection of richly illustrative contemporary quotations which, though suggestive, do not constitute hard empirical evidence.

A second objection to the cheap-labour thesis is that it relies heavily on functionalist and instrumentalist assumptions regarding the pattern of state intervention. According to Wolpe, the state was required to 'maintain production in the reserves at a level which, while not too low to contribute to the reproduction of migrant workers as a class, is yet not high enough to remove the economic imperatives of migration'.[7] The implication that the state possessed either the percipience or the capacity to intervene in the reserves so as to maintain the delicate equilibrium between subsistence production and dependence on migrant labour is open to considerable doubt. It is this implication which has contributed to the legacy in which the South African state is misleadingly seen as an omnipotent agent operating directly on behalf of capitalist interests.

A further objection to the cheap-labour thesis is its assumption that labour migrancy was the natural and most advantageous route to capitalist industrialisation in South Africa. Yet it is by no means certain that labour migrancy was always an option favoured by the mines. Indeed there is convincing evidence to suggest that, in the late nineteenth and early twentieth centuries, mine-owners might well have favoured the permanent settlement of African families on the mines on account of their inability to recruit sufficient labour. In the view of some mine managers permanent locations would materially alleviate chronic labour shortages as well as improve efficiency.[8] Moreover, Alan Jeeves's recent study of labour recruiting in the South African gold-mining economy dispenses with the notion that the migrant labour system was imposed at the simple behest of all-powerful capitalists and with the ready connivance of the state. Instead he shows that until the 1920s 'mine labour recruiting remained an unstable, expensive, conflict-ridden enterprise', and that it was established only through a process of intense struggle.[9]

The cheap-labour thesis has been attacked from the perspective of African societies themselves as well. Thus Beinart's study of Pondoland situates labour migrancy in the context of a complex struggle by Africans to protect their rural resources from the onslaught of capitalist penetration. He argues that 'migrancy, as a specific form of proletarianisation, arose initially out of the dynamics of power and authority within rural society as much as from the specific demands by capital'.[10] A similar point is made by Patrick Harries in demonstrating that migrant labour from the Delagoa Bay hinterland in the pre-colonial period was neither cheap nor a simple response to capital's labour requirements. Rather, it was conditioned by the structure of kinship relations and the manner in which chiefs and homestead heads utilized the system to defend their 'traditional' authority.[11]

In the literature on segregation between 1920 and 1936 the paucity of references to the mining industry is immediately striking. Published government reports, evidence submitted to select committees on the Hertzog Bills and the Native Affairs Department's archives as well, reveal very little material relevant to the relationship between the mining industry and segregationist policies. There is no direct mention of segregation, for example, either in the *1920 Low Grade Mines Commission* or the *1932 Low Grade Ore Commission*, both of which were centrally concerned with the supply of labour. A notable feature of the 1932 *Native Economic Commission*, which was a powerful advocate of the need for territorial segregation, is its relative lack of concern with the mining industry. Aside from the question of the industrial colour bar and general recruiting problems, the needs of the mining industry and its relationship to segregation received only peripheral attention.[12] Neither in the evidence nor in the Report itself is there any suggestion that the mining industry was particularly voluble in support of an extension (or, for that matter, a diminution) of reserves.

The explanation for this apparent lack of concern probably relates to the fact that, by the time of the First World War, the dominance of the mining industry in the political economy of South Africa was a *fait accompli*. The system of labour recruitment in the reserves had been regularised, as had cooperation with the state through the NAD's Director of Native Labour. Whether it was the most efficient system or not, labour migrancy had proved to be compatible with the profitability of the mines: it was the line of least resistance. The only aspect of segregation on which the mining industry expressed a strong opinion was on the still unsettled question of the legislative job colour bar, which it undoubtedly opposed. On the wider issue of territorial segregation, however, the interests of the mines and the state were in broad agreement.

The terms of this consensus (Yudelman refers to it as a 'symbiotic' relationship between state and capital) were hammered out of a shared historical experience, rather than as a result of covert arrangement agreed to by state and capital.[13] Despite serious differences over specific issues, such as levels of taxation of the mining industry, areas of recruitment etc., it was a tacit agreement that survived changes in government. With regard to segregation there was consensus that the integration of Africans into the general economic system was irreversible, and that migrant labour was indispensable to the gold-mining industry. Total segregation was therefore impossible. It was also recognised that a total collapse of the reserves and an uncontrolled congregation of an African proletariat in the cities had to be averted at all costs. The reserves would therefore have to be extended and the existing social structure bolstered.

During the early history of gold mining an exploitative combination of economic and extra-economic devices had been essential in order to procure labour in large numbers from the reserves. But, from around the First World War, and despite periodic labour shortages, the fragile ecology of large parts of the reserves was increasingly seen to be reaching the stage where the subsistence requirements of their inhabitants could not be satisfied. It therefore became a matter of considerable concern to prevent the reserves' collapse, and with it an unrestricted flow of labour to the cities. The fear of uncontrolled proletarianisation was exacerbated by the widespread belief that gold mining was a 'wasting asset', 'doomed to extinction' as ore reserves dried up.[14] The undeniable implication of this was that it would be imprudent to settle a permanent African labour force on the mines. For example, in 1922 the Joint Councils discouraged the movement of African women and children into the cities. While acknowledging that migrancy led to 'irregularities' in family life and that intermittent labour 'handicaps the mines', they nevertheless agreed that 'the social danger from this course is far less than if the mine surroundings become thronged with native women and children'.[15]

Major H.S. Cooke, the Director of Native Labour, adopted a similar position in 1931. He was entirely opposed to the 'Congo' system of establishing African families in the vicinity of the mines, fearing the breakdown of 'tribal control' and a proliferation of urban unemployment. Notwithstanding the problems associated with the system, Cooke regarded migrancy (as opposed to a settled labour policy) as 'the lesser of the two evils'.[16]

These fears became especially apparent in the wake of the 1929 world economic collapse: by 1931 according to H.M. Taberer, the mines were faced with a labour surplus, perhaps for the first time in their history.[17] The problem of surplus labour soon became a matter of serious concern and in 1932 Secretary of Native Affairs Herbst circularised all district native-affairs officials, advising them that there were 4000 unemployed Africans in Johannesburg and that the 'inflow of further labour should be restricted to the utmost'.[18] Although these circumstances were somewhat atypical, for many observers they were living proof of the social threat posed by the congregation of thousands of economically redundant Africans in the urban areas.

3   WHITE LABOUR

The anomalous position of the white worker has provided an important springboard in the debate over the relationship of capitalism to apartheid. In the post-war era a view prevailed among liberal economists and historians that industrial segregation had been brought about as a result of political pressure exerted by white workers who were intent on preserving their privileged economic position. Further, it was held that this state of affairs ran contrary to the rational interests of employers, for whom colour was supposedly immaterial.

This comfortable assumption came under sustained attack in the 1970s from a number of radical scholars. F.A. Johnstone disputed the view that racial discrimination was dysfunctional to capitalist development, arguing instead that the industrial colour bar was an integral part of the overall pattern of capitalist exploitation in South Africa.[19] Moreover, Rob Davies claimed that the racist division of labour and the economic benefits enjoyed by whites accorded with the interests of capitalist accumulation, since they precluded the possibility of a class alliance emerging between white and black workers.[20] The view that industrial colour discrimination has acted as an important agent in dividing the working class by restricting whites to supervisory roles is also expressed by Lacey, who states:

> The state's 'white labour' policy was . . . designed in the interests of capital and not the white worker . . . Even the few concessions that were made to the white worker – at the expense of his African counterpart – were a victory for capital.[21]

These interpretations have in turn been challenged by Merle Lipton and David Yudelman, for whom the argument that white workers adopted racist strategies in pursuance of their own narrow material interests does not pose any particular problem. Indeed Lipton argues that white workers actively promoted discriminatory practices, to the cost of both capital and black labour, and that their interests therefore reinforced their prejudices.[22] However, focusing on the issue of the industrial colour bar has caused the broad relationship between white labour and segregation policies to be bypassed.

This is somewhat surprising in view of the fact that white labour leaders were amongst the first politicians to embrace segregation. In the run-up to the formation of the South African Labour Party prominent protagonists of a white labour policy and territorial segregation, such as H.W. Sampson and Wilfred Wybergh, clashed with Archie Crawford and J.F. Trembath, who insisted that socialism did not recognise colour. It was the former argument that won out: the Labour party's 1910 manifesto called for separate representation for natives, a prohibition of native ownership of land in areas occupied by whites, and the provision of native reserves. Thus 'any pretence of non-racialism was abandoned and the party came forward unequivocally as a white labour organisation'.[23]

The champions of a white labour policy were in large measure responding to fears that cheap African migrant labour would 'undercut' the wages paid to whites. Thus W.M. Macmillan observed in 1924 that the relatively new phenomenon of white and black 'rustics' competing for unskilled jobs in the cities was 'almost sufficient explanation of the panic white demand for "segregation" of the blacks – segregation that is, as understood at the average political meeting'. A decade earlier Howard Pim had commented likewise that it was industrial competition which had 'given rise to the cry for segregation'.[24] It was therefore as a result of experience in the urban environment that segregation first became a popular slogan, and it was in the rural areas that solutions to these problems were sought.

The leaders of white labour, many of whom had encountered Marxist theory of some sort or another, were acutely aware of the reasons for the existence of ultra-cheap African labour. To varying degrees therefore they were opposed to the system of labour migrancy. Alan Jeeves notes that F.H.P. Creswell, the Labour politician and advocate of a white labour policy,

> anticipated almost completely the current radical view of migrant labour. Basic to his thinking was the view that migrant labour constituted unfair competition for whites, that it was a highly artificial system of mobilization and one which could not be sustained without the support of the state.[25]

In 1930 Walter Madeley (then leader of the splinter opposition Labour Party) declared in Parliament that all legislation contemplated by either of the two major parties had been 'framed and designed with one main objective; namely, using the native as a hewer of wood and a drawer of water, and in either event establishing him as a menace to our white civilization'.[26] Madeley's extended analysis bears a remarkable similarity to current versions of the cheap-labour thesis, except that he spoke against capital as a representative of white labour. Thus he contended that whereas there was sufficient territory dotted about the country into which to 'herd the natives' in anticipation of industrial and farming requirements, there was not enough land to allow for Africans' development along separate lines. Consequently he called for the provision of 'sufficient good and suitable land, not rubbish' for African use – failing which the 'degradation' of both whites and blacks would ensue.[27]

It was a sense of the threatening social consequences of competition between white and black labour which lent white workers' demands for segregation wider political significance. The unrestrained flood of cheap African labour into the cities, coupled with the growing 'poor white' problem, was commonly held to be to the detriment of both races. Large-scale white unemployment was seen to lead to crime and dangerous racial mixing, a situation which was perceived to pose a real threat to white supremacy itself.[28] These impressions were fortified by popular eugenist-derived theories stressing that industrialism and proletarianisation would lead inevitably to 'race degradation'. According to Ernest Stubbs, it was 'contact in the industrial field that has created and is creating still more white unemployment and that is sapping the supremacy and prestige of the white race'. This contact would lead to the 'utter and irretrievable ruin of the White races of South Africa'. The only solution would be the adoption of a policy of total segregation 'maintained on the basis of an all-black and an all-white economy'.[29] Stubbs was one of the few people who in the 1920s maintained the call for total segregation. But he was typical of a developing body of opinion which sought to cope with problems in the industrial sphere by adopting a policy of territorial segregation.

C.T. Loram, who was more representative than Stubbs of mainstream segregation thinking, argued that the political object in developing the reserves would be 'to offer a counter to the industrial antagonism growing between the Europeans and the natives, and that peaceful development of the native reserves would be the safest policy to pursue to pacify the growing industrialism of natives'.[30] The idea that the development of the reserves was a mechanism by which to retard the dangerous process of black proletarianisation was central to the conception of the *Native Economic Commission*. It was extremely concerned by the 'chronic state of chaos' of the labour market in the cities. The plentiful supply of casual African labour, which came to town 'only to earn enough cash to pay taxes and buy the few things which they require', exercised a depressing influence on the labour market. Wages for both unskilled white labour and permanently urbanised African labour, both of whom had no alternative income, were driven downwards, leading to great hardship. Moreover, the 'natural corollary' of low wages was poor standards of efficiency, and this was held to have exerted a negative effect on industry. 'The permanent cure for the urban wage problem must be looked for in the Reserves', concluded the Commission. Only the development of the reserves would 'have the effect of stemming the flow of labour to the towns, and of reducing the town labour problem to manageable proportions.'[31]

A similar line of argument had earlier been adopted by the influential *Economic and Wage Commission* of 1925, which recognised that 'the ultimate absorption of the native in European industry and agriculture' was an irreversible process. At the same time, however, it was necessary to avoid the 'unregulated drift' of Africans from the rural areas to the cities. The Commission therefore recommended an extension of the reserves as a means of affording protection to Africans 'in the difficult transition from primitive simplicity to the complexity of modern economic civilization'. Those Africans who were 'detribalised' and had 'no reserve to fall back on' therefore required the same legislative protection as 'weaker members of the European and coloured wage earning class'.[32] The Minority Report went so far as to compare the relatively fortunate position of Africans in the reserves to 'English workers before the enclosure of commons turned them into landless labourers dependent on any jobs they could obtain'.[33]

4   AGRICULTURE

The introduction of Hertzog's Native Bills in 1926 led white farmers and their agricultural unions into extensive debates about the implications of segregation. Perhaps more than any other natural constituency, however, farmers were by and large uninterested in segregation as an abstract idea. Aside from small pockets in the Eastern Cape, where the African franchise was a living political issue, agricultural unions were casually united in opposition to a common non-racial franchise. But on the issue of the Native Council Bill there was less unanimity, for although it was often acknowledged that some form of political representation had to be found for Africans, farmers were in the main hostile to any institution which might develop coherent political powers.[34]

By contrast, issues relating to the apportionment of land and labour concentrated the collective agricultural mind in a very real sense. The 1926 Land Amendment Bill, which was intended as the final word on the 1913 Land Act, proposed to demarcate further released areas for African occupation, and it embodied critical clause(s) governing the nature of squatting and labour tenancy relations. It was with these isues that white farmers were overwhelmingly concerned.

The 1926 Land Bill provided for land falling outside the scheduled areas (as defined in 1913) to be made available for African occupation. These so-called 'released areas' were based on the Beaumont and Local Committee Reports of 1916–18, and they were available for competitive purchase by both Africans and Whites. The total extent of the released areas proposed in 1926 was substantially smaller than had been envisaged in the decade before; moreover, they were no longer exclusively reserved for African occupation. From these facts Marion Lacey concludes that Hertzog effectively reneged on the earlier promise to create adequate native reserves. She argues that Hertzog, as the representative of farming capital, was primarily concerned with reducing the amount of land available to Africans – in order to boost the supply of labour to white farms.[35]

Though there is some truth in this view, it amounts to a considerable oversimplification. The reduction in land available to Africans since 1916–18 was primarily a consequence of the increasing capitalisation of white agriculture and rising land values. Securing labour for white agriculture was undoubtedly a major concern for Hertzog, but as Minister of Native Affairs he was also in charge of a department which was attempting to retain as much land for Africans as possible within the terms of segregation. Though receptive to farmers' demands, Hertzog was by no means their unwitting instrument.

White agricultural unions were generally agreed as a matter of principle that a strict policy of land segregation was advisable, for to reserve no land at all for exclusive African occupation would be to invite consequences of incalculable social danger. But there was no unanimity whatsoever on which, or how much, land should be released for African usage. The example of Natal is a case in point. In 1925 the Native Affairs Commission toured that province to ascertain farmers' attitudes to the proposals made by the 1918 Natal Land Committee. It reported a unanimous opinion that 'no more land should be set aside for exclusive Native occupation.'[36] White Natalians contended that their province had reserved a greater proportion of its total land area for Africans than any other, and that it was incumbent upon Africans to make more efficient usage of the land they already had.[37] Yet only 2 years later William Elliot, giving evidence on behalf of the Natal Agricultural Union to a Select Committee on the Native Bills, claimed that since 1925 there had been a considerable change in opinion in Natal on the land question. He declared that Natal was now prepared to make available for African use the extra land proposed by the 1918 Mackenzie Committee, and he asked the government to expropriate that land outright at fair market value.[38] When Elliot's evidence became known, it caused an uproar. Major J.R. Cooper, representing farmers in Natal's northern districts, insisted that Elliot had no authority to 'give away another million acres in Natal'. On the contrary, his constituency upheld the earlier position that 'not another inch of land should be given to the natives'.[39] This theme was reiterated by a number of other witnesses from Natal.[40]

As a result of this controversy the Natal Agricultural Union held a special conference in November 1927 to resolve the issue. The evidence of F.J. Carless, the Union's President, suggests that the meeting remained sharply divided amid fierce debate. Although strong resolutions on other aspects of the Native Bills were carried, the crucial issue of the released areas remained inconclusive. In the event, Carless maintained that Elliot's original evidence had been 'practically reaffirmed', adding that there would never be satisfactory agreement in Natal as regards the released areas.[41]

This episode suggests the difficulty in generalising about farmers' attitudes to the reserves. Certain farmers, whose land adjoined the potential released areas, were implacably opposed to the idea of granting any more land to Africans, for they feared that their own land would depreciate in value. There were those like Mr Colenbrander, who complained: 'A Zulu will not work, he is too wealthy. These natives are well off and they will not turn out of the location to work'. The amount of land available for Africans should therefore be restricted so as to 'tighten up' the whole question of labour.[42]

On the other hand, there were a substantial number of farmers, especially the wealthier ones, who took a longer view. Thus individuals like Sir Frederick Moore and W. Elliot supported C.A. Wheelwright, the Chief Native Commissioner of Natal, in his contention that more land would have to be made available to Africans. As Elliot explained, 'We employers think it is a very great safeguard and guarantee for the stability of the country if our locations are developed on modern lines'.[43] These men argued that it was a moral obligation to uphold the promises of the 1913 Land Act, and they were no doubt conscious of the need to preserve some semblance of the state's legitimacy among Africans. More especially, they took note of the congestion in African locations and warned that land would have to be found for the thousands of African squatter peasants and tenants who would be evicted from white farms with the passage of the proposed Land Act.[44]

There were sound political reasons for this prudence: C.A. Wheelwright estimated that there were 540 000 Africans in Natal living outside the scheduled areas as squatters and tenants. Many possessed considerable numbers of stock and there was insufficient land for them elsewhere should they suffer eviction. With regard to the northern areas of Natal, he warned, 'If that population is disturbed it is going to be a very serious difficulty. You are going to turn a body of people who have been perfectly affluent and contented into poor blacks'.[45] In expressing these fears Wheelwright was doubtless also considering the wave of ICU-inspired rural populism which was gathering force in Natal.[46]

A similar range of opinion is evident in the Eastern Cape. Jan Marais of the Cape Agricultural Union insisted that Africans had 'quite enough ground' and J.T. Brent, representing the Peddie Farmers' Association in the Ciskei, objected to 'absolutely any land being included in the released area'.[47] By contrast, T.W.C. Norton, the Chief Native Commissioner of the Cape, attested to the state of congestion in the Peddie district and suggested that it should be included in the released area.[48] At the 1926 Farmers' Conference in Pretoria Norton claimed that the Eastern Province was 'saturated with labour' and that were the Land Bill to be enacted, he did 'not know where these natives are going to be placed'. Other farmers from the Cape, like Mr Sinclair, also warned of the lack of sufficient land in the Eastern Cape for African use. 'We farmers', he explained, are 'living in danger of the overflow from these locations today . . . our areas are getting so congested that the farmers there are living in dread of what is going to happen in the near future.'[49]

If farmers differed on the amount of land that should be reserved for Africans, they differed too over the likely implications of defining the released areas. Many farmers insisted on a rigid demarcation of white and black areas, arguing that the land question should be settled once and for all. They objected to competitive purchasing in the released areas, claiming that where pockets of African farmers existed, the land values of surrounding white farms tended to depreciate. In these circumstances farmers either demanded that plans for the extension of African areas be dropped, or they demanded that their land be expropriated at its full market value.[50] But the concern over depreciation was not universally felt. Mr O.R. Nel from Natal gave evidence to the effect that farmers were purchasing land in the released areas 'on the off-chance that the Government will one day have to expropriate'.[51] General Hertzog himself was wise to this speculative aspect, observing that Africans had to pay more for land in the released areas than whites. In a number of instances, Hertzog explained, he had been approached by people 'with tears in their eyes' pestering him to include their land in the released areas.[52]

It is undeniably true that farmers' demands for a regular supply of cheap African labour for agriculture were ubiquitous. It is also the case that farmers constituted a powerful political lobby – an influence which no doubt increased with the election of the Pact government in 1924. Yet it would be a mistake to assume uncritically either the state's willingness or its ability to deliver the electoral goods.

Throughout the 1920s the Native Affairs Department came under sustained pressure both from farmers and the Agriculture Department to encourage a supply of labour to the white rural areas. Farmers complained of competition with the mines and of chronic labour shortages. But the NAD, though sympathetic to the farmers' predicament, was unwilling to become directly engaged in the recruitment of farm labour. The Department was convinced that the solution to the farm labour crisis was above all dependent on farmers' preparedness to offer higher wages and improve conditions of work. The NAD saw itself as the 'protector' of African interests and it was strongly concerned that engagement in actual recruiting would jeopardise its relatively benign reputation. It is highly unlikely, moreover, that the 1932 Native Service Contract Act 'could have bound roughly two million Africans in the white areas', as Lacey suggests.[53] For all its draconian intentions, and perhaps because of them, the Act was almost certainly a dead letter. Native Affairs officials were deeply suspicious of its practicability, and the NAD itself effectively refused to administer its provisions.[54]

The issues of labour tenant and squatting relationships were of vital concern to farmers, but again they were the cause of substantial disagreements.[55] With the intensification of capitalist agriculture and the increase of land values in the twentieth century, the issue of labour tenant and squatting relationships came to the fore. Labour tenancy and particularly rent squatting were considered to be inefficient, uneconomic, and severe obstacles to the even distribution of farm labour. But although there was unanimity that these systems of production would disintegrate with continued agricultural 'progress', they were nevertheless seen as a 'necessary evil', especially by those farmers who were not in a position to pay full cash wages.[56]

Chapter II of the 1926 Land Bill proposed to impose punitive licence fees on rent-squatters and to enforce the licensing of labour tenants – who, in addition, were required to render service for at least 180 days in the year. Its intention was therefore to eradicate rent-squatting and curb labour tenancy, so as to foster an even distribution of wage labour for white farmers and increase agricultural productivity.

These proposals aroused deep division. In the more 'backward' agricultural areas of the OFS, the northern and eastern Transvaal and parts of Natal, farmers defended existing squatting and tenancy relationships. Even where the desire to 'get rid of the labour tenant and squatter' was acknowledged, it was nonetheless asserted that 'the process [would] have to be gradual'.[57] In the Cape, where squatting and labour tenancy had by and large been eliminated, farming representatives were therefore able to state unequivocally that 'it is best to pay a man to work for you'.[58] However, the majority of the Transvaal Agricultural Union felt that Chapter II of the 1926 Land Bill should be omitted, fearing that potential African labour would simply take refuge in the released areas, where they would become unavailable for labour.[59] The Natal Agricultural Union likewise resolved in 1927 that Chapter II should be excised from the Bill, apparently reversing an earlier opinion that labour should be paid for in cash and that all systems in lieu of rent should be discouraged.[60]

The diversity of opinion as regards squatting and labour tenancy was made clear at the 1926 Farmers' Conference in Pretoria. A delegate from the northern Transvaal observed with justification that in areas like the Cape where farms were small, but valuable, and where labour was freely available for hire, labour tenancy was considered to be a nuisance. In the northern Transvaal, however, Africans had been subjugated relatively recently and it was only with the aid of labour tenants that the north was developed at all.[61] This view was further elaborated by Ernest Stubbs, who concluded on the basis of differences between the Cape, the Transvaal and Natal, that labour tenancy would have to be dealt with according to the differing conditions in the various provinces.[62] General Hertzog appears to have acknowledged this point, for he conceded that with more detail and information the law would have to take account of 'different Provinces according to their different circumstances'.[63]

In summary, it can be asserted that there was a range of opinion on the part of farmers as regards Hertzog's Native Bills, and that we should therefore be cautious of generalisations. It was almost invariably true that farmers demanded an adequate supply of labour and on conditions of contract which they considered to be in their own best interests. Furthermore, they wanted their land to retain or improve its value. However, there was no consensus on the most effective means to achieve these objectives.

Some farmers called for a rigid demarcation of land between Africans and whites whereby 'not an acre more' would be given over for African occupation. A minority – but an articulate and significant one at that – considered an extension of the released areas to be a necessity on political grounds, and there were even those who wished their lands to be included in the released areas for reasons of financial speculation. Similarly, relatively 'advanced' farming regions were keen to eradicate all squatting and to impose heavy restrictions on labour tenants. Others pleaded that the transition to wage labour should be gradual, fearing that they would otherwise lose their supply of labour altogether. Moreover, there was a multiplicity of views regarding the precise conditions under which labour should be hired. Segregation, as a political slogan, was therefore not an issue on which farmers were either 'for' or 'against' in any simple sense; it was a somewhat imprecise expression which provided the ideological and legislative framework within which competing sectors of agrarian capital sought to advance their material interests.

Extending this analysis, we may conclude that territorial segregation was, for different reasons, compatible with the general interests of mining capital, white labour and white agriculture. But it cannot be reduced to the direct sectoral requirements of any single constituency, much less to the triumph of one over another. Nor can it be seen as the inevitable or only possible route for capitalist development in South Africa. Segregation cannot therefore be fully comprehended by relating it only to the immediate needs of capital: it was a complex political package which was first and foremost concerned with ameliorating the threat to white supremacy posed by South Africa's process of rapid industrialisation.

5 THE RESERVES

The vast impact of industrialisation was strongly registered during the 1920s, as expert observers and politicians became increasingly alarmed at the declining agricultural capacity of the reserves, the dissolution of 'tribalism' and the 'drift' to the cities. William Miller Macmillan, the pioneer of South African agrarian and social history, was one of the first writers to give a coherent account of the parlous state of the reserves.[64] In his early career Macmillan had been concerned to analyse the poor white problem. He wrote an influential study of urban social conditions in Grahamstown in 1915, and followed this up in 1919 with a brilliant essay entitled *The South African Agrarian Problem*, in which he linked the growing problem of 'poor whiteism' to changing conditions in the countryside.[65]

Macmillan's analysis of the proletarianisation of whites, and of black/white competition in the job market, led him to an important discovery: that the forces leading to the impoverishment of poor whites were similar to those encountered by poor blacks. This was the basic theme of a series of newspaper articles which were published in 1924 as *The Land, The Native, and Unemployment*.[66] Here Macmillan stressed the novel thesis that 'the problem of white unemployment is fatally linked up with the poverty and unemployment of natives'. [67] He demolished the complacent myth of the reserves as rural idylls, insisting that they were often hopelessly congested and gripped by endemic poverty. 'The native', he asserted, was 'economically dependent on wage labour in industry, and not to any serious extent a lordly proprietor who may occasionally condescend to menial labour in the towns.'[68]

Macmillan's insights were confirmed by his 1925 survey of poverty in the Herschel district of the Ciskei, and refined in a seminal book published in 1930, *Complex South Africa*.[69] His distinctive theoretical contribution was to conceptualise the essential unity of the South African economy, and to explain the economic dependence of the reserves on capitalist industry. To this extent Macmillan's work may be regarded as having anticipated the emergence of underdevelopment theory some two generations later.

Macmillan was a radical in the South African context. His work led to the political conclusion that segregation was a bankrupt ideology because it failed to take account of the irreversible integration of Africans into the industrial economy. This argument had much to do with the qualified rejection of segregation by a number of key liberals in the late 1920s. But Macmillan's insights also had impact on (or perhaps coincided with) a growing body of official opinion which came to insist on some form of partial segregation as an urgent necessity. According to this view, the reserves would have to be bolstered up economically and socially in order to restrain the formation of an African proletariat. Macmillan seemed to suggest this himself when he wrote, 'We need labour. But our safety demands that labour come in as a steady stream, not in a flood that must overwhelm us'.[70] Dr James Henderson, the principal of Lovedale Institution in the Eastern Cape (with whom Macmillan had been in contact in 1923), was also witness to the deteriorating situation in the reserves. In 1927 Henderson submitted written evidence to the Parliamentary Select Committee on Hertzog's Native Bills. Speaking primarily from 20 years' experience in Victoria East, but with reference to the Ciskei as a whole, Henderson presented statistical evidence of the region's impoverishment. He calculated that whereas the population of Victoria East had doubled between 1875 and 1911, it had actually diminished since that date. Moreover, the proceeds of agricultural and pastoral produce had fallen by half in the 50 years from 1875 to 1925, while food purchases had increased.

Henderson concluded that the decline in agricultural production and the deterioration of commonages through overstocking had resulted in severe population congestion. A considerable proportion of the rural African population was dependent on wage labour, so that it was possible 'to describe some of the worse locations in the Ciskei, as slum suburbs of the Rand'.[71] These findings were published in the *South African Outlook* and they were also presented to 1927 Dutch Reform Church European-Bantu Conference.[72]

At the 1927 Conference Henderson's evidence was endorsed by Howard Pim. Clearly Pim's perspective had undergone change since 1905, when he described the reserves as a 'sanatorium' where Africans could subsist without expense to the white community. Referring to the Transkei, Pim argued that whereas the mines drew very little labour from the Transkei 25 years before, now in 1927 most adult males worked beyond its borders for a considerable part of the year. The impoverishment of the Transkei was principally due to the fact that migrants 'have never drawn a living wage', they were paid on the assumption that they required only 'the difference between their expenditure and the value of their lands.'[73]

The *Report of the 1932 Native Economic Commission* was the source of the most influential comment on the grave state of the reserves. The Commission drew attention to the problems of soil erosion, overstocking and the impending ecological collapse. In a now familiar phrase it warned against the '*creation of desert conditions*' throughout the Union's reserves.[74] Notably, the Commission's impressionistic survey of the reserves follows very closely the evidence submitted to it by R.W. Thornton, the Director of Native Agriculture. It was impressed too by the evidence of government ethnologist G.P. Lestrade, who argued that economic pressure on the reserves was largely responsible for the disintegration of 'tribal life'.

Implicit in the views of the Native Economic Commission was the sense that deteriorating conditions in the reserves would lead to the creation of a 'poor black' problem and that such a situation posed an untold political threat to the security of whites. This was certainly the belief of Director of Native Agriculture R.W. Thornton, who was convinced by 1932 that the labour market for Africans had contracted permanently – notwithstanding possible economic recovery. He warned that there was little time left in which to develop the reserves so as to prevent 'not another sudden labour crisis in the future but the arrival of a slower and more deadly "poor black" problem . . .'[75] According to Thornton, the emergence of a 'colossal permanent poor black problem' was a real possibility, and it threatened white South Africa with 'calamity'.[76]

By the early 1930s the impending collapse of the reserves was viewed primarily as a social and political threat, rather than in terms of the relationship between migrant labour and capitalist accumulation. This point appears to be underlined by Lord Hailey, who noted in 1938 that South African opinion 'now tends to lay emphasis on the existence of the reserves in the policy of social segregation, rather than on the influence it may exert on the supply of labour'.[77]

6   AN EMERGENT PROLETARIAT

In the decade following the First World War there was a pervasive fear of the emergence of a politicised African proletariat in the cities. Commonly expressed in terms of the growing 'native question', these fears were intensified by evidence of increasing social disorder in the post-war era. The word 'proletariat' occurs quite regularly in the political discourse of the time, but other words and phrases possessed even greater political currency. Notions of 'denationalisation', the 'dissolution of tribal bonds', 'industrialism', 'swamping' 'the rising tide of colour', etc., were frequently invoked. It was these evocative, if somewhat amorphous, ideas which coalesced in and reinforced segregationist ideology. When the image required association with something more definite, Clements Kadalie and the ICU were prominent symbols in the demonology. Anxiety, bordering at times on panic, was intensified by the assimilation into popular thought of widely prevalent eugenic theories which stressed the tendency of civilisation to 'decline'.

As seen in the last chapter, Maurice Evans's *Black and White in South East Africa* was an early segregationist manifesto emphasising the need to conserve 'tribal restraints' in the face of creeping 'industrialism'. According to Evans, some form of partial segregation was essential for the continued supremacy of the white race, even if this meant forgoing short-term economic advantage:

> Galling as it may be to the captain of industry to see thousands of more or less intelligent, exceptionally strong men and women all around and yet unavailable to him, the position would be made infinitely more difficult and embarrassing by any relief which could be given by breaking up their present life, and with it all standards of conduct and all the wholesome restraints to which they are accustomed. Torn from the present controls and sanctions and plunged into the whirlpool of city and industrial life, without even the occasional return to sweeter and healthier conditions, makes one who knows them shudder for their future. And if our own race life is to remain pure and our ideals uncontaminated, equally for us would such a course be disastrous. At whatever sacrifice of possible economic developments, the remedy for the present difficulty is not by rapid, and what may seem easy adjustment, but by more gradual means, at least as much of conservation as of transformation.[78]

It is a striking feature of Edgar Brookes's writings during the 1920s and 1930s that, despite his initial advocacy and subsequent rejection of segregation, the fear of an African proletariat remains a constantly echoed theme. In the *History of Native Policy* Brookes adopted a position similar to that taken by Evans, contending that 'industrialism' was foreign to Africans, whose 'natural state' was on the land. Though he accepted that a measure of economic integration was inevitable, Brookes warned against the

> massing of Natives in centres like the Witwatersrand . . . [which] leads gradually to the growth of an urban population, poor, squalid, propertyless, easily inflammable, whom the Bolshevik Third International has already designated the best material through which to spread communistic doctrine through Africa.[79]

In 1926, though still a segregationist, Brookes likened the South African economy to 'that of a slave-state'. He called for an amelioration in the working conditions of Africans, in order to defuse the threat of 'a Native Socialist Movement' – with which he associated Clements Kadalie of the ICU.[80] Two years later Brookes announced that segregation had failed 'because black South Africa does not want it, and because white South Africa is not prepared to make the sacrifices without which it cannot succeed'. He warned again that 'raiding ICU offices or putting Mr Clements Kadalie in gaol' would make no difference at all 'to an economic movement which, if history has any meaning, is as sure as tomorrow's sunrise'.[81] Thus although Brookes had distanced himself from segregation by the end of the decade, his appeals to guard against communism had, if anything, intensified. In his Phelps-Stokes lectures of 1933 Brookes contended that segregation would lead to Bolshevism by precluding the possibility of African advancement:

> Class becomes associated with something definite and tangible as colour. The stage is inevitably set for the 'class war'. As a member of the *bourgeoisie* myself, I hope it is not set for the 'dictatorship of the proletariat'. As a liberal I believe that only swift and far-reaching reforms and many more opportunities for self-realisation on the part of the Bantu can ensure the impossibility of such a dictatorship.[82]

The early Brookes viewed a measure of protective segregation as an essential means by which to prevent the emergence of a politicised African proletariat. From about 1928, however, he was increasingly aware that a policy of enforced segregation which precluded African advancement, would lead precisely to that result. Crucial to this change of heart was his realisation that economic integration rendered any equitable form of segregation an impossibility.

By contrast, the radical anti-liberal George Heaton Nicholls transformed the 'protectionist' strand of liberalism into a highly conservative brand of 'trusteeship'. As the SAP member for Zululand and member of the Parliamentary Joint Select Committee on the Native Bills, Nicholls played an important role in the framing of segregation. Nothing was more important to him than the need to prevent a politicised African proletariat from developing – a point on which he was ruthlessly clear. The essence of Nicholls's thinking was that parliamentary democracy or 'individualism' was 'completely unsuited to Bantu evolution', since it was opposed to 'chieftaindom'. He constantly reiterated the need to 'come back to the real essence of native life – communalism – a very different thing to communism. If we do not get back to communalism we will most certainly arrive very soon at communism.'[83]

In the cities a new generation of liberal Christian welfare workers, led by Fred Bridgman, Ray Phillips and Dexter Taylor (all of whom were affiliated to the American Board Mission) was intensely aware of the potentially explosive situation on the Rand. The suggestive title of Phillips's book, *The Bantu are Coming*, stressed the impact that industrial life was having on Africans. Phillips's brand of muscular Christianity emphasised the calling of the 'modern missionary', whose role was to engage in active social welfare programmes so as to protect Africans from corrupting political influences:

> South African is in flux. All is ferment. In a generation the native people of this land are being compelled to bridge a gap which the white races have taken hundreds of years to cross. A native heathen father is sitting in his grass hut in the country, living his life and fearing his fears as did his ancestors before him. You ask him where his son is. 'In Johannesburg'. To-day that son is in Johannesburg working as a motor-driver, piloting a high-powered motor-car through the thick of city traffic. To-night this son will put on his correct evening clothes and spend the evening at one of the fashionable nightclubs. Tomorrow (Sunday) he may go to church, or he may listen attentively while the white agitator and his native assistants seek to arouse in him a spirit of revolt against the capitalist, the missionary, and the white labour leader.[84]

Phillips's anxieties were shared by the Rev. Dexter Taylor, who was concerned about the 'rapid disintegration of Bantu social institutions' and the 'definite entrance of the native into the industrial life of the community'. Together with the influence of Christian education, these had 'produced an unstable condition in the political atmosphere'.[85] The threat of an emergent African proletariat was perceived (and exploited) too by all the main white political protagonists. Smuts, in his well known 1929 Oxford lectures stressed the need to preserve the integral nature of the 'native social system', and looked to anthropology as an intellectual source of support. He drew attention to the various agencies which had led to the 'weakening or disappearance of tribal discipline' and warned:

> If this system breaks down and tribal discipline disappears, human society will be resolved into its human atoms, with possibilities of universal Bolshevism and chaos which no friend of the natives, or

the orderly civilization of this continent, could contemplate with equanimity.[86]

General Hertzog was equally inclined to play the proletarian card. At the start of the 1926 Farmers' Conference in Pretoria he cautioned that unless Africans were given land, white farmers would be the first to suffer. The moment Africans' link with and love of the land was severed.

> your native drifts to the location and becomes useless and a menace . . . I do not want to speak about what will then be the result when we have driven those natives to take refuge in the cities and they have become the industrial class in the union.[87]

By the close of the conference Hertzog was even more explicit. He wrapped up the proceedings saying that Bolshevism 'was no idle fear' and claimed to have received 'fresh information' to the effect that strong attempts were being made to encourage Africans to combine with whites on the basis of class. The possibility of a class alliance, he concluded, was 'the greatest fear that is over-hanging South Africa . . .'[88]

Similar sentiments were aired during a private meeting in 1928 between Hertzog and Smuts, when Hertzog referred to the possibility that the Communist Party 'might join hands with the natives for political purposes, divide the whites very seriously and make a solution of the native question in future impossible'. Further postponement in dealing with the Segregation Bills was therefore impossible.[89] It appears that Smuts and Hertzog were in close agreement as regards the danger posed by 'agitators' and the threat of a politicised African proletariat.[90] But it was Hertzog who was particularly adept at turning these fears to his own political advantage. He did so with consummate skill a year later when he manipulated popular anxiety about 'swamping' into an election-winning formula during the 1929 'Black peril' election.

Spokesmen for white labour, such as Walter Madeley or Col. Stallard, also warned against the prospect of permitting a permanent black urban population to develop, lest it became politicised.[91] This spectre haunted all white political parties through the 1920s. It was sometimes raised with great clarity by individuals like Heaton Nicholls, though at other times it was merely alluded to in a suggestive fashion, perhaps in indirect support of some more immediate political objective. This combination of precision and vagueness only served to intensify popular anxiety over the 'native question' and led to increased political pressure for an early solution along segregationist lines.

In Part II, which considers the administrative implementation of segregation and the role of the Native Affairs Department in particular, these themes are developed further.

Part II

3 Structure and Conflict in the Native Affairs Department

1 THE NATIVE AFFAIRS DEPARTMENT (NAD)

In the years after Union the NAD was weak and poor, managing to attract only a tiny fraction of the state's total expenditure.[1] The Department was small, it was not well represented outside the Transkei and the Witwatersrand, and there were severe constraints on the promotional prospects open to its officers. Many observers regarded the NAD as the 'Cinderella of the ministerial family' and its prestige was correspondingly low.[2] Major Stubbs, for example, bemoaned the fact that the NAD administration in Pretoria was inadequately housed in a 'tumbledown bungalow' because 'being "Native" it is of small account'. As a Department 'without honour', it lacked 'both adequate organisation and, even, a real head'.[3]

As a result of Union, three separate Departments of Native Affairs, each with distinctive administrative characteristics, had been merged into one.[4] To a large degree the new Union Native Affairs Department was unified in name only. Not only were there differences in organisation between the NAD's constituent elements, but there were also variations in the statutes which each followed.

Expressed schematically, the structure of the NAD after 1910 can be summarised as follows: in the Transkei a chief magistrate administered native affairs with the aid of twenty-seven magistrates, all of whom were attached to the NAD. With the exception of Herschel and Glen Grey, the Ciskei was administered by magistrates of the Department of Justice. They were aided by 'Superintendents of Natives', who belonged to the NAD.[5] In the Transvaal all magistrates were controlled by the Department of Justice, and they were also native commissioners *ex officio*. The NAD appointed sub-native commissioners in predominantly African areas, and they were effectively responsible for the administration of native affairs. But they remained subject to the jurisdiction of the magistrates. In Natal magistrates were also attached to the Department of Justice; where necessary they were assisted in matters of native administration by a staff of 'Inspectors of Locations and Mission Reserves', who belonged to the NAD. Native administration in Natal and Zululand was coordinated by a Chief Native Commissioner (CNC), attached to the NAD and stationed at Pietermaritzburg. In the Orange Free State native administration, such as it existed, was likewise administered by Justice magistrates, though the NAD had representatives stationed at Thaba 'Nchu and Witzieshoek.[6]

Operating parallel with the district administration of the NAD was the Native Labour Sub-Department. A Government Native Labour Bureau was first established in 1907 by the Botha government in the Transvaal in order to regulate the supply of labour to the mines. The Native Labour Department was created in terms of the 1911 Native Labour Regulation Act and operated within the proclaimed labour districts of the Witwatersrand, the OFS and Natal. The Native Labour section was responsible for the supervision and control of African industrial workers. It comprised a Director of Native Labour (with headquarters in Johannesburg), and a staff of Inspectors and Protectors of Natives and Pass Officials. Their task was to administer the pass laws, deal judicially with minor offences, visit the mine compounds and 'generally watch over the welfare and interests' of Africans in the industrial areas.[7]

The complexity of these administrative arrangements meant that the NAD was fragmented by divergent, if not contradictory, sources of authority. Only in the Transkei was there a coherent and homogeneous NAD presence. The NAD of Union had grown out of the Transkei and the Transkei endured as its administrative and ideological reference point. Elsewhere NAD control was at best tenuous, and it was invariably subordinate to the far larger Department of Justice.

The dominance of the Department of Justice contributed in no small measure to the NAD's poor image. Magistrates of the Department of Justice who were charged with native administration considered their postings to far-flung rural districts as a preliminary, if necessary, hardship to be endured for the sake of their careers. When Third-grade Justice magistrate Frank White of Taungs was made a first-grade native commissioner in the NAD, he complained of having been converted from 'a third class poor white, to a first class Kaffir . . .'[8] This sort of contempt displayed by Justice officials towards the NAD, and the resentment it elicited in response, was to have important bearings on the NAD's development during the 1920s.

Until 1924, when Hertzog's plans for segregation began to gain momentum, the NAD languished in relative oblivion. Lacking a full-time ministerial head, it was nominally under the charge of Prime Minister Smuts or his deputy F.S. Malan, neither of whom, however, were able to devote sufficient time to running the Department. Those who believed that the interests of Africans would be most sympathetically served by an invigorated NAD, with strong political support in the cabinet, frequently called for the creation of a full-time Minister of Native Affairs.[9] The system whereby Malan deputised for Smuts as Minister of Native Affairs was frequently condemned on the grounds that the Department lacked adequate political representation in government. During a parliamentary debate on the 'Union's Native Policy', for example, F.S. Malan and Smuts were accused of having made contradictory statements, with the result that it was unclear where ultimate responsibility for the NAD lay. Hertzog taunted Malan by saying that he was nothing more than a clerk of the NAD; when Smuts protested, Hertzog responded 'Well, a head-clerk then'.[10]

The NAD's weakness was exacerbated by the fact that it lacked an effective departmental head. Between Union and 1923, when Major Herbst became Secretary of Native Affairs (SNA), there were four appointees to the post, no less than three of whom had been selected since 1918. Magistrate C.L.R. Harries provides us with a useful (if partial) description of these incumbents: Edward Dower, the first SNA, was a 'capable and charming man, but unfortunately his insatiable thirst detracted considerably from his virtues as an efficient officer'; J.B. Moffatt, his successor, died on the very day he telegraphed to accept the post; M.C. Vos, the next appointee, resigned his post after only 6 months; and Edward Barrett, who was compelled to resign in 1923 was dismissed by Harries with the words, 'a more unfortunate election could not have been made . . .'[11]

In common with most bureaucratic machines, the inner workings of the NAD were obscured from public view. Even where access to the NAD files is possible, it remains a difficult task to specify just where the locus of power was situated. Memoranda were often crudely initialled, left unsigned, or else stamped in the name of the SNA. Except on rare occasions, officials were unwilling to associate themselves with controversial points of view. Yet it is clear that the most important officials were the senior members of the Pretoria Head Office, the Director of Native Labour in Johannesburg, the Chief Native Commissioners of the Cape and Natal, and the Chief

Magistrate of the Transkei.[12] The opinions of this group of officers were regularly canvassed on matters of policy and administration.

The overwhelming preponderance of English-speaking officials throughout the NAD is immediately striking. Many administrators were the sons of missionaries and regarded 'native administration' as something of a secular mission. Others had pursued military careers before joining the civil service. There does not appear to have been a major infusion of Afrikaans-speaking officials into the NAD during the reign of the Pact government, or at least not into positions of authority.[13] Correspondence during the 1920s and early 1930s was conducted almost entirely in English.

Although there were no obvious ideologues in the upper reaches of the NAD hierarchy, many of the senior officers were steeped in the cautious gradualism associated with the liberal Cape tradition. The NAD was undoubtedly dominated by Cape officials: until the appointment of D.L. Smit in 1934, from the Department of Justice, every departmental head had served in the Transkeian or Cape administration. [14] With the partial exception of J.F. Herbst, they were strongly imbued with aspects of its well developed ethos of 'sympathetic paternalism'. Although this legacy was eroded during the 1920s and 1930s, as Hertzogite segregation came to define the limits of political discourse and as the Department became more closely centralised, traces of the Victorian 'civilising mission' and the ethic of liberal protectionism nevertheless survived. These residual forces acted to modify the implementation of segregation in important respects.

The intellectual mandarins of the NAD remain elusive. If any one officer has to be singled out in the period under review, it must be E.R. Garthorne, who replaced G.A. Godley as Under Secretary of the NAD in 1925. Garthorne was described by the Public Service Commission (PSC) as 'an officer of marked ability, though of an academical rather than an administrative type'.[15] C.L.R. Harries saw him as 'a sterling fellow, full of force and to my mind the only buttress to matters at Head Quarters'.[16] In pressing his claim to become the first secretary of the Native Affairs Commission Garthorne pointed out that he was 'to no little extent responsible' for the 1920 Native Affairs Act.[17] He was also the author of key departmental memoranda on matters of land policy and customary law, as well as being one of the draftsmen, if not the key architect, of the crucial 1927 Native Administration Act. Younger officials, e.g. Howard Rogers, P.A. Linington and J.S. Allison, also figured prominently in the formulation of policies and the framing of legislation during the 1920s and 1930s.

2 RESTRUCTURING THE NAD: THE PUBLIC SERVICE COMMISSION, 1922–3

The weak and fragmented state of the NAD was exacerbated after 1922 as a result of drastic cuts administered by the Public Service Commission (PSC). The PSC was created in 1912 as an independent body charged with reviewing all appointments and conditions of service in the civil service. But it soon came into acute conflict with the Treasury over the question of its effective sphere of jurisdiction. After 1914 the Commission's authority was further curtailed, leading to the resignation of key officers. By 1920 the PSC's members advised that 'unless its functions are extended there is no justification for its continued existence'.[18]

The PSC was reconstituted in 1921 under the chair of V.G.M. Robinson, and its powers were considerably enhanced. Thus began the period which Edgar Brookes has referred to as its 'brief golden age'.[19] Reinvigorated, the Commission zealously went about investigating the means for 'effecting economies and promoting efficiency in the Public Service . . .'[20] In 1922 it investigated a number of government departments and proposed various measures as part of the relentless quest for administrative 'economy' and 'efficiency'. The unpublished reports and correspondence of the PSC are rather more illuminating than its official publications. Even here, however, political machinations and hidden agendas are largely obscured by the dispassionate language employed by the Commission's technocrats.

In 1921–2 the NAD came under the scrutiny of the PSC, as a result of which a massive reorganisation of the Department was proposed. Fuelled by the economic depression then gripping South Africa, the PSC attempted to simplify the administration of native affairs and to make it more cost-effective. The Commission was initially attracted to the system operative in Zululand and the Transvaal, maintaining that the Transkei was over-administered and therefore needlessly expensive.[21] It criticised the tendency for different departments of state to appoint their own regional officials, since this led to a multiplication of government representatives in the same area. A cardinal principle of the Commission's reorganisation proposals was that the magistrate should function as the primary administrative authority in any district. The PSC therefore argued that in all districts apart from the Transkei and the Witwatersrand NAD staff should be incorporated within the Department of Justice and should be subject to the jurisdiction of its magistrates. In predominantly African areas, however, it was conceded that the NAD 'should have a voice' in the selection of the magisterial staff.[22]

The Public Service Commission went on to propose that the CNCs of Natal and the Cape be invested with 'definite status', so as to enable them to direct native affairs through the magistrate. It argued for a large reduction of the staff of the Native Labour Sub-Department in Johannesburg, which it considered to be 'needlessly large and expensive'.[23] The PSC also alleged that the administration of the NAD Head Office was 'ineffective and unsatisfactory'. It insisted that the entire reorganisation scheme hinged on the retirement of SNA Edward Barrett, who was regarded as 'lacking in the capacity and ability necessary to administer and control the large and important Department of Native Affairs'.[24] V.G.M. Robinson calculated that as a result of the intended changes a saving in salaries of approximately £4000 *per annum* would be achieved.[25]

With certain modifications, and in spite of strong resistance from the NAD, many of these proposals were carried into effect: Edward Barrett retired as SNA and was replaced by J.F. Herbst. Major H.S. Cooke succeeded Col. Pritchard, and became CNC of the Witwatersrand as well. Large cuts were effected in the NAD's regional establishment, principally as a result of the transfer of a number of native affairs staff to the Department of Justice. Others were simply made redundant. Thus, as a result of the PSC's intervention, the NAD's white staff was reduced from 528 to 419, and its African staff from 929 to 792.[26]

The Transkei's relative strength enabled it to withstand the worst ravages of the PSC. There are indications that the PSC initially considered administering substantial cuts to the Transkeian administration, perhaps even by transferring its entire magisterial staff to the Department of Justice. It certainly intended to reduce the number of independent Transkeian magistracies.[27] At a meeting with senior Native Affairs officials in November 1922, however, the Commission reported having encountered 'determined opposition at the present juncture to making any alterations' to the existing Transkeian system and concluded that 'a surrender to the first attack upon it can hardly be expected'.[28] A year later, the PSC had come to recognise that the system of NAD-administered magistrates 'works satisfactorily'.[29] But it appears that the Commission was successful in imposing a standardised system of 'grading according to station'. This measure was intended to avoid the anomalous situation whereby a senior magistrate might preside over a relatively unimportant district.[30] Transkeian magistrates preferred the existing system, since this allowed them to be promoted without being transferred.[31]

The Transkei's opposition to having any changes imposed on its administration was based on the notion that it was a unique system whose autonomy should be defended at all costs. Linked to this assertion was the frequent suggestion that any outside interference with the administrative philosophy or practice of the Department might lead to popular insurrection. In 1933, for instance, SNA Herbst, echoing complaints that the new grading system imposed by the PSC sacrificed local expertise, pointed out that a district 'quite insignificant as far as actual work is concerned may be a hot-bed of intrigue and dis-order requiring an experienced, fully trained, and trusted officer for its administration'.[32] Similarly, Chief Magistrate Welsh of the Transkei criticised the PSC for not having understood the 'essential differences' between a magistrate charged with administration in predominantly African as opposed to white areas. Native affairs officials had specifically political functions on top of their judicial responsibilities. He explained:

> They are the principal and almost sole reliable agencies for keeping the Government in touch with great areas and masses of people practically unknown to the ordinary European . . . Unless the greatest care is taken and unless the natives are kept in sympathy with the Government, which can only be done by trusted officers, the state of smouldering discontent which is already apparent in some quarters will spread and will lead to a state of affairs which can only be viewed with great anxiety.[33]

The enforced retirement of SNA Barrett as a result of the PSC's recommendations in 1922 was an embarrassing, even pathetic affair. Nevertheless, it serves to illuminate the growing challenge within the state to the NAD's established methods. After having learned that his position as SNA was in jeopardy on 30 December 1922, Barrett became desperate. He wrote a long and impassioned letter to Smuts in which he 'denounce[d] as cowardly subterfuge the charge of incapacity' levelled against him by the PSC.[34] Barrett complained that the PSC had produced 'no tittle of evidence' against him and that its report had come as a complete surprise. He contended that the very existence of an effective and specialist department was at issue and he claimed the support of CNC Norton and Chief Magistrate Welsh in his views. The PSC, Barrett said, was ill equipped to form a judgement on the 'higher aspects of native administration' which distinguished it from 'mere police administration and tax gathering'.[35]

But, in spite of these efforts to defend himself, Barrett made no progress. His case was considered by the Cabinet and in February 1923 he was coolly informed by Smuts that he would be retired immediately.[36] Stunned and hurt, Barrett continued to bemoan his misfortune and pathetically demanded reasons for his dismissal. Barrett's case was taken up publicly by Maurice Alexander, who suggested in Parliament that policy differences were the real reason for his dismissal. Smuts was typically evasive and attempted to deflect the issue on the spurious grounds of wishing to spare Barrett embarrassment. He asserted, untruthfully, that the Barrett affair and the PSC reorganisation scheme were unconnected. In a peroration calculated to defuse the matter Smuts referred to Barrett as a competent official and a 'good man', but added that the post of SNA required an 'exceptional man'.[37]

Despite the volume of correspondence surrounding Barrett's dismissal, it is difficult to prove the existence of any conspiracy between Smuts and the PSC. Smuts's role, in particular, is uncertain and the allegations against Barrett's competence must similarly remain open. But while there is no direct evidence to suggest the existence of a political conspiracy, it is apparent that, by the 1920s, the style of government epitomised by Barrett was falling into disfavour. In the light of the Bulhoek and Bondelswarts incidents and the increasing prominence of the 'native question' in general, it seems likely that Smuts and his associates felt that sterner and more directed native policies were required.

Barrett's dismissal and the reorganisation of the NAD were widely perceived as an attack on the Department's 'liberal' traditions. It occasioned a minor public outcry in which letters and telegrams of protest were sent to the Prime Minister's office by prominent individuals and clergymen.[38] The issue was also taken up in a crusading fashion by the English press. In the *Rand Daily Mail* Edgar Brookes wrote a series of articles on the 'Government of the Natives'. He identified Barrett as 'by natural inclination a friend of the natives . . .' – the very words which Barrett had used of his predecessor Edward Dower.[39]

Brookes's intention in these articles was to defend the need for a strong and independent NAD wholly devoted to the specialised task of native administration. He attacked the proposed transfer of the native affairs sub-native commissioners in the Transvaal to the Department of Justice, since this would mean 'placing them before the native no longer as fathers, but as correctors pure and simple'.[40] In his final article Brookes argued that the NAD's authority should be extended rather than curtailed. The tactful and 'liberal' traditions of the NAD were presented as essential to the maintenance of social and political stability.[41] Brookes's articles were backed by editorial comment in the *Mail*, the gist of which was conveyed in the headline, 'Wrecking the Native Affairs Department'.[42]

The retrenchment or transfer of native affairs officials in the Transvaal aroused especially strong condemnation. It generated a host of testimonies to the unique qualities of those individual officers whose posts were under threat. Typically, it was argued that 'this "economy" will be purchased at a very heavy price.'[43] As the *Cape Times* explained,

> it would be doing away with trained men who know native customs and who understand exactly how a native thinks. From such men the natives get more sympathetic treatment than it is possible to get from magistrates, all of whom are not linguists and as a body are not well versed in native affairs.[44]

Whether by design or not, the reorganisation of the NAD bureaucracy prefigured major changes in the administrative tone of the Department. In 1923 Barrett expressed his conception of the NAD as

> a body of carefully selected and trained officers, of high character, knowing the people, speaking the language, acquainted with their needs and shortcomings, in sympathy with their legitimate aspirations and thus best able to hold a just balance between white and black. With all its shortcomings, and floundering along through the mud, this is the ideal to which the Native Affairs Department aspires. This is our star.[45]

Far from helping his cause, this expression of Barrett's personal philosophy of native administration was, by the time he wrote it, virtually a self-indictment as far as his enemies were concerned. For Barrett's conception of the NAD as a well intentioned, if faltering, umpire of the races was archaic and out of tune with those who demanded clear and unyielding native policies.

Barrett's successor as SNA, Major John Frederick Herbst, was born in Swellendam, the son of a Prussian mercenary. He joined the Cape Civil Service in 1891 and worked in country districts. Later he went to the Transkei, where he served for some years as Magistrate of St Marks district. Herbst first came to public attention when, in 1908, as the Assistant Resident Magistrate of Rietfontein, he drafted a highly commended government report on the area.[46] Shortly after, Herbst consolidated his reputation, and came to the notice of John X. Merriman, by tracking down and arranging a settlement with the bandit leader Simon Kooper in Bechuanaland in 1908–9.[47] As Secretary for SWA (Namibia) during the military occupation, he was responsible for building up the territory's administration and he was awarded the CBE in 1919. Herbst came to attention again as a result of the Bondelswarts massacre in 1922. His appointment as SNA by Smuts in 1923 was based on his proven qualities as a trouble-shooter and administrator. This set him apart from previous SNAs, who had risen through the ranks of the Cape administration and had been promoted on account of their intimate knowledge of, and work in, native affairs.[48]

The view which sees Herbst as a 'martinet', and as an advocate of 'total control' along with the model of refurbished Natal traditionalism, is something of a caricature.[49] It is true that Herbst, unlike his predecessors, was not generally considered to be a 'Cape man' – despite his experience as a magistrate in the Transkei. As a technocrat Herbst was well suited to the task of rebuilding the NAD from within, but he was not a segregationist ideologue, nor was he insensitive to the distinctive ethos of 'sympathetic paternalism' traditionally associated with the NAD. Nevertheless, his appointment *did* mark a departure from the Cape policy of 'drift', so ridiculed by those who were impatient to 'solve the native question'. Moreover, it signalled the demise of the Transkei's dominance of the NAD, with its idealisation of gradualism, accommodation and consultation.

3   CONFLICT WITHIN THE STATE AND THE NATIVE ADMINISTRATION BILL

Weakened, fragmented and possessing only local influence, the NAD during the early 1920s was in no position to generate an ideology of segregation, much less to take the initiative in its implementation or administration. The Department lacked any dynamic sense of direction: its policies were essentially reactive; its strategy overwhelmingly dominated by the prerogative to contain, deflect and defuse conflict. The cuts administered to the Department by the PSC in 1923 had further reduced the NAD's already tenuous authority in regions outside the Transkei. By the mid-1920s, therefore, the Department was more concerned with re-establishing its effectiveness as an administrative entity than with planning a segregationist programme.

In view of the prescience sometimes ascribed to the South African state, it is paradoxical that the NAD's authority was reduced to its lowest point ever just before the inauguration of Hertzog's segregation proposals. It requires too much stretching of the imagination to suppose that the NAD's powers were deliberately proscribed at the PSC's behest in order to reconstruct it in a more powerful form. But in the event this is how things worked out: the cuts administered to the NAD in 1923 prompted the Department to reclaim its lost authority, so that by 1928 it was potentially more powerful than it had ever been. The revival of the NAD had much to do with the widespread realisation that, in order to implement segregation, the NAD required substantial strengthening. But although the existence of a political climate conducive to segregation was a necessary condition for the NAD's invigoration, it was not sufficient: much of the impetus for restructuring came from within the Department itself.

In consolidating its authority the NAD sought to redefine the legitimate scope of its jurisdiction so as to encompass virtually everything concerning 'native affairs'. This process brought the NAD into sharp conflict with other governmental departments, which resented the new challenge to their traditional administrative preserves. The struggle within the state over control of native affairs was largely obscured from public view, but it was an integral part of, and had significant implications for, the development of segregation.

The establishment of a Native Affairs Commission (NAC) in terms of the segregationist 1920 Native Affairs Act was perceived by the NAD as a potential encroachment on its administrative domain. The

NAD was piqued when Dr Loram of the NAC held discussions with Africans in New Brighton over the proposed Urban Areas Bill in 1921; its official report for 1919–21 referred to a confusion about the 'consultative and advisory functions of the Commission'.[50] In the same year SNA Barrett objected that the NAC's role in the Bulhoek Commission called for executive action 'alien to its province' and he expressed the fear that the Commission would come to be regarded as 'an instrument of Government action instead of a source of political wisdom'.[51] This charge was denied by A.W. Roberts, on behalf of the NAC, and he dismissed the 'retrograde proposal' that the NAC be restricted in its powers to consult with African opinion.[52] Bureaucratic squabbling such as this had little to do with serious ideological differences between the two bodies, but it was indicative of the NAD's sensitivity to any possible limitation of its powers.

As plans for territorial segregation took shape, more serious intra-departmental disputes came to the fore. The increasing strain in relations between the Lands Department and the NAD serves as a useful example. In accordance with the NAD's conception of itself as the 'protector' of African interests, the Department attempted to secure as much land as possible for lease or purchase by Africans. The 1913 Land Act deprived Africans of their unrestricted rights to purchase or lease land outside the scheduled areas, pending the demarcation of special areas for that purpose. But the recommendations of the Beaumont and 1918 Committees, which were set up to establish the boundaries for enlarged reserves, were not accepted by Parliament. Thus the status of what were to become the 'released' or 'dual' areas remained ambiguous, a problem which was exacerbated by the fact that both the NAD and the Lands Department claimed jurisdiction over them.

The NAD was anxious to keep the spirit of the 1913 Land Act by making available as much land as possible for African purchase. In particular, it campaigned for the rights of Africans to obtain lease-hold tenure on the Crown lands adjoining the scheduled areas. It was intended thereby to assist 'well-to-do Natives who may wish to better themselves on lines of civilized development'.[53] The NAD was concerned that the pledges of additional land given to the native people at the time of the 1913 Land Act might not be honoured. Moreover, it accused the Lands Department of refusing applications by Africans to obtain land in the dual areas, while at the same time alienating those lands for the use of whites.[54]

In 1922 the Cabinet gave the lead and decided that the land

recommended by the Local Committees was to be regarded as the basis of potential African areas, pending further legislation.[55] The NAD interpreted this decision as a vindication of the right of 'civilised natives' to long leasehold tenure. 'My anxiety', as SNA Barrett put it, 'is to be able to assert that the door has not been barred'.[56] The Department insisted that it would be 'inequitable to place obstacles in the way of Natives acquiring interests in land in the limited areas which are available to them today'. It warned that to deny them this right would be to place Africans entirely at the mercy of white farmers,'thereby virtually enforcing conditions of predial serfdom'.[57]

The position of the Lands Department was somewhat different. In the name of South Africa's 'sound development' it was primarily concerned to advance white interests. Colonel Reitz, then Minister of Lands, paid lip-service to the 'urgent needs of the native population', but said he 'viewed with concern' any scheme which might permanently withdraw presently unknown (mineral) resources from 'advantageous development'.[58] Sommerville, the Lands Secretary, was opposed to the NAD's proposal to settle a class of 'improving' Africans on the Crown lands. He claimed that the sort of tenure proposed by Barrett would 'in effect, be a sale to the natives', and chose to interpret the ministerial conference as stipulating that such sales should not take place.[59]

During the early 1920s the NAD was still attached to the notion of facilitating an African yeoman peasantry on the Crown lands. Yet as moves towards territorial segregation gathered momentum and as the lingering commitment to the 'civilising mission' declined, the NAD's land policies became more defensive. In the mid-1920s the Lands and Native Affairs Department bickered about who should foot the bill for the purchase and development of land reserved for or owned by Africans.[60] After the passing of the Natives Trust and Land Act in 1936, the NAD accused the Lands Department of blocking the purchase of land for Africans in the released areas. It feared that the impression was being given that the government was not genuine in its intention to purchase land and even made suggestions regarding high-level corruption within the Lands Department.[61]

In the mid-1920s the draft Native Administration Bill became the focus of further tension between the two departments, since Chapter 111 proposed to invest native commissioners with the authority to determine conditions of land registration and tenure in the reserves. (This function was traditionally performed by Deeds Registries within the Lands Department, which argued that the NAD's assumption of its duties would lead to wasted governmental expenditure on account of administrative duplication.[62]) The Lands Department suggested that the 1927 Administration Bill was 'a further instalment of the policy of segregation' whereby the NAD would be 'transformed into the executive of a more or less self-contained government having jurisdiction over Native lands within the Union'.[63]

Conflict over jurisdiction between the NAD and the Lands Department smouldered throughout the 1920s and 1930s, at times becoming more heated. There is evidence, too, of occasional flare-ups between the NAD and the veterinary division of the Agriculture Department over the administration of cattle dipping in Natal.[64] These antagonisms were, however, overshadowed by the bitter conflict which existed between the NAD and the Department of Justice over the control of native affairs – a struggle which was intensified by the cuts administered to the NAD after 1922. It will be recalled that these had the effect of virtually eliminating the NAD's effective presence outside the Transkei and the Witwatersrand, thereby further subordinating NAD officials to their superiors in the Department of Justice.

Native Affairs officials bitterly resented their inferior status and registered frustration at the reduction of their powers. They complained that members of the larger and more powerful Department of Justice were able to secure swift promotion, whereas they were left languishing without recognition. For example, Major D.R. Hunt, the Sub-Native Commissioner of Lydenburg, related how the new magistrate and native commissioner, Patrick Dalmahoy, suddenly became his 'immediate boss . . . and would give [him] orders though he admitted ignorance of native matters'. To add insult to injury, Dalmahoy had been Hunt's junior, not only when they were at school together, but in the army, too, and for many years after in the civil service.[65]

T.W.C. Norton, the CNC of the Ciskei, was particularly irked by the fact that he lacked an effective network of Native Affairs officials to execute his instructions. He repeatedly stressed the fact that it was impossible for the NAD to operate through deputies – 'however brilliant' – when they were controlled by another department to whom they looked for commendation. Thus Norton warned that unless the NAD was able to uphold its authority, respect for the government would diminish 'and the people will more easily fall under the influence of glib demagogues posing as the leaders of the ignorant masses.'[66]

Similar complaints over the problems of split jurisdiction were registered by C.A. Wheelwright, the CNC of Natal, who maintained that 'friction' would inevitably develop where Justice and Native Affairs officials operated in the same area.[67] From the Transvaal Major Stubbs stressed the idea that native administration was a unique vocation requiring special talents, and he raised the spectre of inter-racial conflict. According to Stubbs, Native Affairs officials were the 'only body of men in South Africa who can be trusted to hold the scales between black and white . . .' He claimed that Justice magistrates invariably sided with whites and were imbued with colour prejudice. Transferring control of native administration in the Transvaal to the Department of Justice was therefore tantamount to placing 'the fox in charge of the fowl-run'.[68] Stubbs's vision of the NAD's benevolence in contrast to the callousness of the Department of Justice is probably exaggerated on both counts, but it is lent some credence by the attitudes and behaviour of Justice Minister Oswald Pirow himself, who observed in 1927 that 'many people think the Native Affairs Department is too prone to mollycoddle the native'.[69]

The rhetoric which praised the NAD at the expense of the Justice Department was motivated by the NAD's struggle to defend its authority and to reassert its effectiveness as an administrative force. This effort centred on the passage of the 1927 Native Administration Act (subsequently the Black Administration Act), one of the key segregationist measures of the inter-war years. First drafted in 1924, the 1927 Administration Act equipped the NAD with enormous powers. Outside the Cape the governor general was deemed 'Supreme Chief of all natives' – a throwback to the Shepstonian system in colonial Natal – which effectively granted the NAD unrestricted powers to govern the reserves by proclamation. The 1927 Act also represented a major step in the direction of recognising 'native law and custom' and it was responsible for establishing the first commissioner courts in South Africa. In addition, the Administration Act afforded the NAD extensive powers to curb sedition and dissent, and to control the free movement of Africans.

Although the Administration Act had been a political centrepiece of the segregationist (and later apartheid) state, its construction has also to be located – somewhat more narrowly – in bureaucratic terms. To a significant extent the Act must be seen as part of the NAD's attempts to reclaim and extend the jurisdiction which it had lost to the Department of Justice after 1922. The contest between the two departments was essentially a battle for resources and power.[70]

Within the NAD there was a definite appreciation that the draft Native Administration Bill of 1924 would serve to reinstate the Department's authority. Local magistrates and native commissioners appear to have been most enthusiastic about the proposed legislation. The Magistrate of Herschel noted in January 1925, 'It is indeed heartening to find out that at last there are prospects of native administration coming into its own'.[71] Major Hunt was more explicit, arguing that the Bill

> re-establishes & gives a full measure of independent responsibility to the NA Dept., which Department of late years has been emasculated . . . & its officers placed in a position subordinate to the officers of the Magisterial branch of the Dept. of Justice who are not specialised in affairs concerning natives.[72]

The Department of Justice, which stood to lose some of its powers, mounted a sustained attack on the Administration Bill from the outset. Its law advisers greeted the draft legislation with unconcealed disbelief. E.L. Matthews doubted that he could usefully make any comments, dismissing the Bill as 'no more than a preliminary draft or perhaps not more than an outline of proposed legislation . . .' He insisted that the Bill suffered from chronic confusion and a lack of definitional clarity. It was unlikely, Matthews thought, that Parliament would grant 'quite such wide powers to deal with all these matters by regulation or proclamation' even if they were subject to approval by the NAC.[73]

Behind Matthews's contemptuous attitude – he referred to 'that curious Native Administration Bill' prepared by the NAD – lay issues of material consequence to the Department of Justice.[74] W.E. Bok, the Justice Secretary, was concerned with defending the undivided authority of the magistrate. He contended that the magistrate should continue to function as the general district representative of central government and should remain the native commissioner *ex officio*. Where necessary, the NAD could appoint sub-native commissioners for administrative purposes.[75]

Despite these objections the NAD's campaign to reverse the defeat of 1922 gathered force during 1925. It continued to express dissatisfaction with its subordinate relation to the Department of Justice, stressing particularly the removal of sub-native commissioners in the Transvaal. Herbst argued that 'in such circumstances the interests of natives are bound to suffer' and maintained that in spite of the increased administrative cost native affairs officials should be stationed wherever there was 'a considerable resident native population'.[76] Bok responded defensively, claiming that the dual jurisdiction of Justice and NAD officers had 'worked satisfactorily' and that African interests had not suffered in any way.[77]

Despite these protestations the Administration Act was enacted in 1927, and only a year later a number of magistracies in the Ciskei and Zululand were transferred from the Department of Justice to the NAD in terms of the Act. In October 1928 the staff of 17 magisterial districts, comprising about 100 officers, were taken over by the NAD.[78] Although it was reported that the transfers had taken place with the concurrence of the Department of Justice, this does not seem to have been the case. At a local level, a number of magistrates, particularly in Zululand, were fiercely resentful of their transfer to the NAD, fearing that their promotional prospects would be adversely affected.[79] Certainly Justice Secretary Bok agreed to the transfer only under duress. With the 1927 Act a *fait accompli*, he accepted the changes, but he added that he did not 'concur with the policy involved' and affirmed the axiom that the 'administration of Justice is *par excellence* the function of the Department of Justice', to which all magistrates rightfully belonged.[80]

With the passage of the 1927 Administration Act the NAD successfully established the legislative framework for its future expansion within the segregationist and apartheid state. Notably, the PSC reversed its earlier policy. Whereas it had been responsible for stripping the NAD in 1923, it recommended only 5 years later that the NAD's Head Office should be substantially strengthened and upgraded in order to cope with the volume of work generated by such legislation as the 1923 Urban Areas Act, the 1925 Taxation Act and, especially, the 1927 Native Administration Act.[81]

4 'EFFICIENCY', 'ECONOMY' AND 'FLEXIBILITY'

The rejuvenation of the NAD after 1924 was accompanied by the growth of a self-serving 'language of legitimation', stressing the virtues of bureaucratic efficiency.[82] Although never formulated in a rigorous form, the creed of technicism marked a departure from the distinctive Transkeian tradition, with its stress on personalising relations of authority. This departure, however, was never emphasised. On the contrary, the NAD attempted to present the doctrine of 'uniformity' and 'efficiency' as merely the most effective mechanism by which the best aspects of the Union's diverse regional administrative systems could be consolidated and sustained. By presenting new policies in the guise of old, and by appropriating the PSC's celebration of administrative efficiency, the NAD created for itself a dispassionate mask behind which it quietly pursued policies of bureaucratic aggrandisement. Thus measures which by most standards would be considered distinctly contentious were depoliticised by presenting them as nothing more than the working out of a supposedly neutral administrative logic.

The NAD's increasing emphasis during the 1920s on the need for uniformity and efficiency reflects a wider search in society at large for technicist solutions to political problems. In the post-war era the celebration of the 'expert', coupled with a belief in the power of positivist thinking, is a pervasive sub-theme in social thought. G.R. Searle considers that the ideology of 'national efficiency' had become a pervasive political slogan in England at the turn of the century. By the 1930s it evolved into a 'strongly technocratic approach to government' in which science was celebrated as 'a kind of self-sustaining force', providing 'objectively valid solutions to social and political problems, quite independently of the wishes and beliefs of the majority . . .'[83]

In South Africa the need for a solution to the 'native question' embodying the scientific findings of independent experts became a common cry. Leonard Barnes, for example, warned that the 'native question' would end in violence 'unless Science, "the cool, gentle, serious spirit of science", science which alone embodies the maturity of the human mind, takes charge of the situation'.[84] This type of thought was evident too within the field of native administration. An immediate example is the Native Affairs Commission, which was intended by Smuts to be a body of independent experts giving their full attention to the 'native problem'.[85] The NAD's belief in the efficacy of scientific opinion resulted in the creation of an ethnological section in 1925–6 under G.P. Lestrade. In Herbst's view an ethnologist was a necessary acquisition 'both from the point of view of pure scientific knowledge and to serve the more practical ends of native administration'.[86] For a number of years after 1926 the PSC sanctioned the payment of a £50 bonus to NAD officers upon their successful completion of a special diploma course in 'Bantu studies'. These inducements formed part of the NAD's attempts to improve 'the standard of departmental efficiency'. As such, they were also intended to enhance the status and promotional prospects of the Department's officers.[87]

A further index of the drive towards technical efficiency was the appointment in 1929 of R.W. Thornton as the NAD's first Director of Native Agriculture.[88] This appointment represented the beginnings of a strategy to arrest the collapse of the reserves and preserve them as agricultural units. In stressing the need for modern animal husbandry, soil conservation and efficient agricultural techniques, the new sub-department drew on a wider pattern of colonial developmentalist discourse.[89] It is striking how, in South Africa, the ideologies of segregation and conservation proved to be mutually reinforcing. Agricultural policy took shape in the context of segregation, with which it was regarded as being inextricably connected, while the success of segregation was 'in its turn entirely dependent on the agricultural policy in operation'.[90]

As it pursued its course of bureaucratic aggrandisement, the NAD had frequent recourse to the slogans of 'uniformity' and 'elasticity'. These words were invoked in order to justify the coordination and centralisation of regional administrative systems in Pretoria. The goal of administrative uniformity was often presented as a self-evident good. When coupled with the notion of 'compromise', which was a central motif in segregationist ideology, such supposedly neutral formulations made important political changes appear less contentious than they actually were.

The 1925 Taxation Act, for example, sought to consolidate and unify the system and incidence of taxation of Africans in the different provinces. Cape Africans were asked, for the sake of uniformity, to accept higher taxes so that those of their compatriots in the Transvaal could be lowered. In this manner the possibility of generating combined African resistance to what in effect amounted to an increase in the general level of taxation was lessened.[91]

A similar mode of argumentation was employed when African delegates to the 1923 Pretoria Native Conference debated proposed alterations to the pass laws. Africans living in the Cape, where the pass laws were largely inoperative, were asked to accept the proposed Registration and Protection Bill in the interests of uniformity, thereby allowing a fairer system to be devised for their northern compatriots. In discussion, opinion was divided, with a number of African delegates urging acceptance of the pass laws on this basis. Only the incisiveness of Prof. Jabavu and Dr Molema pointed to the trap concealed in the language of uniformity and compromise: 'Uniformity', said Jabavu, 'was a good word' but Cape Africans were 'not prepared to give up anything' for its achievement.[92]

The goal of uniformity was consistently reiterated by the NAD as an ideal during the 1920s. Under Herbst's guidance, the process of welding divergent administrative systems into a coherent yet flexible whole was portrayed as having been the Department's ultimate objective ever since Union.[93] Coordination of 'the main lines of native policy' was therefore presented as an administrative imperative. As proof of this inexorable process both the 1912 Native Disputes Bill and the 1917 Native Affairs Administration Bill were cited.[94] But the truth of Herbst's claim that administrative uniformity had been a goal ever since 1910 is open to doubt. In 1911, for example, M.G. Apthorp (later CNC of the Ciskei) argued that 'while of course uniformity of procedure and administration is an ideal which is never overlooked', it was nevertheless impractical; and he concluded that, given the different conditions and traditions in the various provinces, 'the adoption of what is generally described as a "native policy" is clearly an impossibility at the present time . . .'[95]

Similarly, SNA Edward Dower argued in 1913 that, however desirable it might be to recognise customary law, it would be impossible to render it 'uniformly applicable throughout the Union'. He therefore called for 'elastic power' in order to 'meet the needs in different parts of the Union'.[96] Both Dower and Apthorp were sensitive to the historic and regional differences between the 'advanced' and more 'backward' areas of the Union. Even assuming that they possessed the necessary power, it is unlikely that they would have insisted on retarding the 'progressive' features of the Transkei in order to gerrymander a state of administrative uniformity.

The 1927 Native Administration Act serves as the outstanding example of the drive to 'put on a proper footing the whole administration of Natives throughout the Union'.[97] A lengthy memorandum prepared by the NAD Head Office presented the Bill as a means of consolidating the disparate legislative and administrative systems throughout the Union, and at reconciling their anomalies.[98] The NAD deplored the 'entire absence of uniformity and coordination in the various Provinces of the Union in regard to cardinal principles of native administration', and sought to evolve 'a flexible, homogeneous system of Native Administration for the Union as a whole'.[99] In portraying the proposed legislation as an administrative necessity, great care was taken to conceal its momentous implications. Typically, the Bill was described as little more than

> a general application of principles that have long subsisted and found to work satisfactorily in one or other of the Provinces. It may be regarded as a selective synthesis of existing conditions designed to facilitate and harmonise native administration throughout the Union.[100]

Stressing the Bill's continuity with previous legislation was an essential element of its ideological appeal. Yet the employment of words like 'uniformity' and 'elasticity' and the constant reference to administrative precedent helped to obscure its undoubtedly radical nature. In terms of the 1927 Act the NAD was styled (through the agency of the governor general) 'Supreme Chief of all natives' beyond the Cape, and it was empowered to make or alter any law in the designated reserves by means of proclamation. These sweeping powers were rationalised by reference both to Natalian and Transkeian precedent.[101] The authority of the Transkei was cited most frequently because it was the administrative unit which commanded the greatest degree of acceptance among those most likely to condemn the Bill's autocratic principles. Thus the supposed administrative benefits imparted by edictal legislation were linked to the widely acknowledged success of the Transkei in coping, through Acts of Proclamation, with 'the ever-changing needs of a primitive people rapidly emerging from barbarism and to move step by step with advancing conditions'.[102]

So strong was the ideological purchase of the Transkeian system that anticipated objections to legislation by proclamation were met with the blithe retort that 'almost fifty years of practical experience in the Transkeian Territories clearly demonstrates that no great weight need be attached to them'.[103] What was good enough for the Transkei would be good enough for everyone else. It is ironical therefore that it was the Transkei itself which emerged as the principal opponent of the measure, because of the realisation that the region would thereby be robbed of its coveted administrative autonomy.

Initial drafts of the Administration Bill were met with cautious acceptance by district officials in 1924. As shown above, NAD magistrates and native commissioners welcomed the proposed legislation because it promised to enhance their administrative authority and to free them from subordination to the Department of Justice. T.W.C. Norton, for example, had frequently expressed the need for legislation by proclamation in order to rationalise the legal tangles and administrative 'chaos' in the Ciskei.[104] Thus on receiving the first draft of the Administration Bill he recognised it (somewhat ambivalently) as the 'charter to the Native Affairs Department' which he had been lobbying for.[105]

However, both Norton and Welsh of the Transkei expressed misgivings about the wide powers implied in the draft Bill. Later these fears coalesced into outright opposition when they realised that the Bill would effectively centralise power within the NAD Head Office, and that it implied fundamental refurbishing of chiefly powers.[106] The underlying reason for Transkei's opposition to the Administration Bill is well expressed by A.G. Mcloughlin, an ex-Transkei administrator. Mcloughlin fully recognised the importance of the Bill and accepted that it embodied certain desirable features. Nevertheless, he regarded the Administration Act as a perversion of the Transkeian system, criticising it for

engulfing the [Transkei's] essential features, and carrying with it to sacrifice on the altar of uniformity the soul of the independent system, so patiently, so steadfastly and so excellently created by the long line of able administrators in the Transkei.[107]

It is to the administrative ethos of the Transkei and its relationship to the NAD in general that we now turn our attention.

4   The Ideology of Native Administration

1   THE TRANSKEIAN ADMINISTRATION

The Transkeian administration evolved in the second half of the nineteenth century as a consequence of the frontier wars and the incremental expansion of the Cape Colony. It comprised twenty-seven magisterial districts, each under the administrative and judicial control of a magistrate. Authority was exercised directly by the NAD through the Chief Magistrate of Umtata. Unlike the other provinces, where magistrates were predominantly officials of the Department of Justice, the Transkeian administration was organically linked to the NAD.

The Transkeian corps of native administrators served as the political, ideological and bureaucratic model for native administration as a whole. Its distinctive administrative ethic was widely regarded as the finest example of native administration. Edward Barrett, the outgoing SNA in 1923, rated the Transkeian system the best in the Union;[1] J.H. Hofmeyr referred to it as 'the acknowledged ideal of South African native policy';[2] and the *Cape Times* noted that 'the Transkeian system is considered to be the finest system in the Union by those well able to judge . . .'[3] and urged its general application to the Union as a whole. Similar tributes to the Transkei were recorded by many others, among them C.A. Wheelwright, the CNC of Natal,[4] and even W.M. Macmillan, who referred to it as '. . . the proudest boast of native administration in the Union'.[5]

By the 1920s the 'Transkeian tradition' of benevolent paternalism had acquired a quasi-mythological status. The system had acquired a symbolic value which was attached, like a seal of approval, to a variety of different policies. It was variously portrayed as an original form of 'indirect rule'[6] or as the area 'in which European Trusteeship has been discharged best'.[7] When the notion of 'adaptationism' came into vogue, having been strongly endorsed by the NEC, the Transkei was held up as a successful exemplification of that concept too.[8] The only other administrative tradition which was cited with acclaim was the so-called 'Shepstonian system'. But it was widely considered that this tradition had disintegrated with Shepstone's demise. Indeed, one of its most enthusiastic supporters suggested in 1928 that the Transkei was the true inheritor of the Shepstonian system.[9] But although the NAD grew out of the Transkei, it was at the same time constrained by it. The strengthening and centralisation of the Department which occurred in the 1920s therefore caused an erosion of the Transkei's administrative independence. Thus the eulogies to the Transkei were made in defence of a tradition which was encountering heavy attack.

The view we have of the Transkeian administration in the latter half of the nineteenth century is of a small corps of men operating 'within the framework of social evolutionary theory'.[10] According to Schreuder, the early Cape administrators were strongly committed to the 'Victorian cultural and ideological milieu of Protestantism and Improvement'.[11] Their zealous propagation of the creed of 'progress', 'individualism' and the dignity of labour, drew on a militant evangelical tradition which tended to be contemptuous of the fundamental institutions of African society. But new exigencies brought about by the mineral revolution, as well as the outbreak of rebellions and wars in the 1870s, precipitated a change in this approach. Thus Martin tells us that the 'early sense of robust forward movement', which characterised the 1870s, gave way to a new emphasis in the 1880s and 1890s 'on gradual evolutionary development, within the framework of the "native territorial system", towards goals that [had] almost indefinitely receded'.[12] The Victorian 'civilising mission' was not necessarily renounced. But the force of its cavalier idealism yielded to a distinctive ethos of sober realism and pragmatic conservatism, founded on the assumption that timely political accommodation from above would pre-empt the emergence of powerful social pressures from below.

In the twentieth century the Transkei become synonymous with flexible administration, in which qualities like practical good sense and sound personal knowledge of local conditions were especially esteemed. Like the British administration in Nigeria, the Transkeian administration was said to have emerged organically from local 'men on the spot'. Indeed the system itself, rather than the abstract theories which informed it, attracted the greatest commendation. Typically, A.G. Mcloughlin expressed reservations about the 'ardent Victorian Imperialism' of the early Transkei officials, with their 'profound faith in the efficacy of evangelisation', but he greatly admired the methods, goodwill and sympathy on which the administration was built: 'The system stands today despite their idealism because they dealt with the native on native lines and preserved his customs and social structure'.[13]

The benevolently paternalistic style so strongly associated with the Transkei stemmed in part from the personal histories of its officials. A number of magistrates were second and third generation administrators, themselves the sons of Transkeian officials or missionaries. Names like Stanford, Leary and Brownlee occur so frequently that they are virtually part of the region's iconography. The Brownlees are perhaps the outstanding example. Reverend John Brownlee (1791–1871) was a pioneer of the London Missionary Society, government representative in Kaffraria, and founder of King William's Town. His son, Charles Pacalt Brownlee (1827–90) became the first Secretary of Native Affairs in the Cape Colony in 1872. W.T. Brownlee, son of Charles, became Chief Magistrate of the Transkei. Charles's youngest son Frank (1875–1950) was also a native administrator, as well as being a noted author and collector of Transkeian lore.[14]

Familial ties were considered to be an important asset for the Transkeian officials and were an essential part of the making of its tradition. According to Frank Brownlee, the Transkeian magistrates' unique 'sympathy' towards 'the natives', as well as their knowledge and understanding of African languages and customs, derived from the fact that they were 'unto the manner born'.[15]

In a post-Victorian but pre-democratic age benevolent paternalism was regarded by administrators as an outstanding quality. T.W.C. Norton was fond of remarking that 'the prime necessity of native administration may be expressed in two words "sympathetic contact" '.[16] Walter Stanford spoke approvingly of 'the firm, yet sympathetic personal contact of an administrative official'.[17] For A.G. Mcloughlin, the native administrator's approach to his work followed from a 'fatherly solicitude for the people that may be far short of negrophilism and yet be altruistic enough to spur on the ruler to greater things for the good of the natives themselves and the general good of the people of the Union as a whole'.[18]

The notion of 'personal rule' drew on a conscious paternalism, whereby the function of the native administrator was gradually to wean his subjects over to 'civilisation'. The administrator's role was portrayed in terms reminiscent at once of a chief in traditional society and a Victorian patriarch. For Norton it could 'be confidently stated that in dealing with a people little removed as a whole from barbarism, the personal factor is of supreme importance.'[19]

The individual authority of the Transkeian magistrate and the responsibilities he bore to his wards were strongly associated with the administrative ideal of 'continuity'. Frequent transfers were held to be inimical to the principles of sound administration because they resulted in the loss of local knowledge and experience and destroyed confidence and trust between ruler and ruled. In 1934 Harding Barlow, a veteran native administrator, bemoaned the fact that the old magisterial families had 'died out' as a result of recent changes in the mechanisms for appointment and promotion. As far as he was concerned, 'Natives are very conservative and dislike change . . . They are "Royalists" in that they believe that "blood" tells'.[20]

Above all, native administration was portrayed as a vocation, requiring a detailed and precise knowledge of local customs, languages and traditions.[21] Native administration was considered to be a highly specialised occupation for which an individual had to be uniquely suited. The nature of this specialised knowledge was that it could only be gained through the magistrate's direct experience. It was knowledge acquired 'by the sweat of his brow'.[22]

Two closely linked institutions, the *Bunga* and the annual magisterial conference, were regarded as being central to the Transkei's success. The *Bunga* (Transkeian Territories General Council) emerged out of the network of district councils which had gradually been established throughout the territory in terms of the 1894 Glen Grey Act.[23] These councils (composed of nominated and elected African representatives under the chair of the local magistrate) were invested with a considerable degree of authority in local administrative matters and managed a substantial budget generated by taxation.

The council system was widely studied and frequently applauded. Smuts regarded it as the basis for a policy of differential development; his 1920 Native Affairs Act sought to extend the network of local councils throughout South Africa. Edgar Brookes, in common with many liberal thinkers of the time, hoped that a proliferation of councils as envisaged by the 1920 Native Affairs Act 'was the model which the Union intended to follow'.[24] Hertzog presented a modified council system as the most equitable and practical form of 'native representation' when he introduced his 'Native Bills' in 1926.[25] The annual magisterial conference, which accompanied the convening of the *Bunga*, was a vital mechanism for sustaining the cohesiveness of the Transkei administration and for countering the isolation of individual officials. Chief Magistrate Welsh enthused at length about 'its importance in these territories'.[26] In Rheinallt Jones's words, the conference imparted the sense of 'a corps of magistrates who are really working together. Elsewhere, you feel that there is not that cohesion and the result is that, in other parts, they are dispirited'.[27] The observers and officials who helped to create the mythology surrounding the Transkei were not simply indulging in idle reminiscence: they were deliberately promoting the autonomous tradition of the Transkei at just the time that the Public Service Commission was endeavouring to standardise and centralise its administration. Thus W. Elliot Stanford's 1935 attack on 'the craze for uniformity throughout the Union, which ignored the special requirements for the governance of the natives . . .' was an attempt to prevent further erosion of magisterial authority.[28] Brownlee's stress on native administration as a specialised vocation, as well as his insistence on the efficiency and success of the Transkeian administration, reflected his resistance to low pay, poor recognition and the imposition of magisterial grading.[29] The mechanism of automatic transfer and, in particular, the greater opportunity for promotion in the Department of Justice, were fiercely resented by the NAD. It was this that motivated the insistence by men like Norton and Barlow on the indispensability of 'men of character' who were specially trained for the purpose of native administration.[30]

2   THE ADMINISTRATIVE ETHIC IN OTHER PROVINCES

It is difficult to form an opinion of the nature of other administrative systems in South Africa, since the homogeneity of the Transkei and the immediate links between its officials and the NAD were not replicated elsewhere. In the African districts of Natal, the OFS, the Transvaal or the Ciskei local magistrates were generally attached to the Department of Justice, within which they were regarded as peripheral members with inferior status.

In the Orange Free State, where the NAD presence was confined to the Witzieshoek Reserve and Thaba 'Nchu, the impression one gets of the state of native administration is of almost total neglect. A lengthy report by magistrate R. Colson of Harrismith claimed:

The Magistrate has no special functions in regard to Native Affairs beyond collecting the Native Revenue . . . The Magistrate does not come into contact with the native population at all. He is, naturally, regarded by them as a taxing and punishing instrument whom it is better to avoid as much as possible. Thus there is no official channel of communication between the Government and the Natives.[31]

The Ciskei was nominally administered in the same manner as the rest of the Cape, i.e. by magistrates of the Department of Justice and according to the principles of Roman Dutch law. In reality, however, it was a confused hybrid, resembling the Transkei in many repects. T.W.C. Norton, the first CNC of the Cape (Ciskei), had served as Assistant Chief Magistrate in the Transkei before his appointment to the Ciskei post. Through the 1920s he constantly strove to narrow the gap between the two administrations. The association between the Ciskei and the Transkei was enhanced by the operation of the council system in both territories. The relationship was reinforced after 1928, when a number of the Ciskeian magistracies were transferred to the NAD from the Department of Justice.

The administrative ethic of Natal is difficult to characterise. C.A. Wheelwright, the CNC of Natal, was very much the representative of the NAD and was considered an outstanding administrator by the PSC.[32] However, his effectiveness in coordinating the administration of native affairs was hampered by the presence of magistrates belonging to the Department of Justice and the fact that native commissioners commanded insufficient administrative authority.[33] These problems were to some extent alleviated after 1928 when, in common with the Ciskei, a number of magistracies in Zululand were transferred from the Department of Justice to the NAD. This move, together with Natal's eager emulation of the Transkeian annual magisterial conference in the 1930s, appears to have facilitated a greater sense of unity in native administration.[34]

To what extent did the Shepstonian legacy persist in Natal? According to Nicholas Cope, there was a solid group of officials within the Natal NAD who claimed to 'know best' and 'zealously guarded what was seen as a Natal tradition in "native" administration'.[35] He argues too that the Natal NAD was treated as a 'special case' at Union and that it was allowed a certain measure of independence from the central NAD, in spite of attempts to unify the divergent systems of native administration.[36]

There were undoubtedly individuals within the Natal/Zululand administration who were deeply committed to 'Tribalism and the set of paternal relationships that weaved through it, [which] was deeply ingrained in the Natal system of "Native administration" '.[37] However, there are also strong indications that the Natal administration had lost its essential coherence by the early twentieth century. Edgar Brookes, for example, maintained that following Shepstone's retirement in 1875 the system which bore his name underwent steady decline and fragmentation. In the years after 1912 it had 'by unaccountable neglect, been left, so to speak, to "stew in its own juice" . . .'[38] This view is reinforced by A.G. Mcloughlin's assertion that with the departure of Shepstone 'the system crashed'.[39] Thus, despite retaining an important symbolic and ideological importance in the twentieth century, it appears that Shepstonian principles lacked substantive administrative backing.

The original Natal Native Code of 1878 (as well as the 1891 replacement which was supposed to serve as the basis of the region's administration) appears to have lapsed into confusion and disuse by the early twentieth century. Rivalry between the NAD and the Department of Justice made matters worse. Moreover, the Natal NAD was severely hamstrung by its inability to decide on a unified policy towards the Zulu royal family and the status of Solomon ka Dinuzulu, the Zulu Regent, in particular.[40] In sum it seems that, by the 1920s, Natal and Zululand, despite retaining important features of the nineteenth-century Shepstonian model, was fragmented and lacking in direction. Individual native commissioners and magistrates were strongly imbued with a distinctive Natal identity, but, in contrast with the Transkei, the whole amounted to rather less than the sum of its parts.

In the Transvaal a distinctive tradition of native administration is evident, though it too is associated with the personalities of a number of individuals rather than with any coherent system. Following the Boer War, the Milner administration in the Transvaal established a network of sub-native commissioners (SNCs) who were attached to the NAD. In some cases forceful SNCs were able to extend their network of authority, despite being nominally under the control of a Justice magistrate.

One of the best example of these was Ernest Stubbs, a controversial and maverick administrator of considerable talent.[41] Stubbs was an advocate of total segregation, insisting on the need for a liberal provision of land for Africans. He saw himself, somewhat dramatically, as an arbitrator between the inevitably hostile interests of white and black. In his opinion the reserves were heavily populated with Natives living under varying conditions of society, polity and economy and likely at any time to become disaffected by the Bolshevist propaganda fostered and engineered from time to time by the polyglot crowd in and around the Witwatersrand, and the oncoming evergrowing tide of Pan-Islamism from the North.

The appointed role of the SNC in the Transvaal, Stubbs thought, was to 'hold the balance evenly between white and black' by acting as the mediator between Africans and the government.[42]

Major D.R. Hunt, who had worked with and was influenced by Stubbs, also reflected aspects of the native commissioner as a benevolent autocrat and a grand mediator between hostile races. Like Stubbs, Hunt was one of those 'enthusiastic survivors from the days of Milner'.[43] His brand of sympathetic paternalism is revealed in a nostalgia for the 'olden days' when he used to tour his district in a Cape cart, pausing every few miles 'under a tree for a couple of hours' to talk with 'all the old fellows from the kraals'. Hunt regretted the arrival of the motor car for having fundamentally altered the tone of his pastoral visits. As a result, he had by 1930 'to a very great extent lost touch with all the old fellows in my district . . .'[44]

H.D.M. Stanford, the SNC of Haenertsberg in the Northern Transvaal, was another widely regarded administrator, whose post was one of those threatened with abolition as a result of the PSC's reorganisation proposals for the Transvaal. His impending removal occasioned a storm of protest and a number of testimonials to his unique qualities as a NAD official and his special role in preserving discipline. Stanford was described as possessing that

> rare combination of character and quality that at the same time creates in the natives that feeling of respect, fear and love, that is the proof-stone, and should be the only one, of the native administrator . . . His word is command amongst the natives where-ever he sends it to, and his district is the most extensive one up here. He saves you a lot of police and policing, the man is a commando unto himself.[45]

As in the Transkei, it was especially when retrenchments or administrative changes were in the offing that allusions were made to the ever-present potential for unrest, and the NAD's special role as the arbiter between black and white. Thus W.I.S. Driver, the Sub-Native Commissioner of Nylstroom, whose post was threatened with abolition by the PSC in 1922–3, drafted a letter to Pretoria under the dramatic heading 'Bolshevism in the Bobibidi Tribe'. He recorded a great deal of 'friction' between farmers and Africans in his district, noting too that Sidney Bunting, the communist activist, had recently been in the Northern Transvaal. In these circumstances Driver warned against the 'fatal mistake' of 'swapping horses in the middle of this stream of depression', i.e. handing over full administration to the Department of Justice. To do so would be to throw 'the natives almost entirely upon themselves and into the arms of subversiv: propagandists'.[46]

3 THE 1920 NATIVE AFFAIRS ACT AND ITS DEMISE

To many observers the NAD was a relatively benign and 'sympathetic' institution. This view was especially prevalent in the early 1920s, though it declined markedly during that decade as the Department underwent substantial transformation. Between the two legislative landmarks of the 1920 Native Affairs Act and the 1927 Native Administration Act, however, a profound shift in the NAD's ideological tone took place. Barrett's notion of the NAD as a well intentioned, if faltering, custodian of native interests yielded to Herbst's altogether more purposeful and centralist administration.

A number of contemporary observers noted the way in which the increased bureaucratisation of the NAD had altered its administrative ethos. In 1923 the Archbishop of Cape Town warned against sweeping away 'the last vestiges of Patriarchal Government among native people' and of its replacement by a 'soulless system of the Department of Justice'.[47] By the end of the decade H.M. Taberer reflected on a striking change in race relations over the past 15 years, 'the outcome of the feeling that the Government is no longer their [the Africans'] protector . . . .'[48]

The NAD's ideology of sympathetic paternalism, which had developed in the Cape in the era preceding the mining revolution, was rendered increasingly inappropriate to the harshly anonymous rhythms of industrialisation. In Bradford's words, 'paternalism was losing ground as it was subsumed within an ideology more capitalist in orientation'.[49] Of course the ideology of sympathetic paternalism was never practised in anything like the benign fashion that its champions would have us believe. Conversely, its demise was not as sudden as was indicated by those who feared its loss. Nevertheless, a distinct shift is discernible in the period after 1920, as old-style individualist paternalism gave way to a more corporate or communal style with a harder bureaucratic coin.

Smuts's 1920 Native Affairs Act represents the highpoint of liberal segregation in both its ideological and administrative forms. It was cast in the legacy of the 1894 Glen Grey Act and was seen as a bold and constructive attempt to deal with the 'native question'. The 1920 Act generated a great deal of enthusiasm and secured substantial support among white liberals, African notables and native affairs officials. John L. Dube, for example, considered it to be the 'best attempt yet made to meet the requirements of the bulk of the Native people'.[50] The Act stressed the need to develop mechanisms of consultation between blacks and whites, principally through the creation of local forms of political representation for Africans. One of its main provisions was the establishment of a permanent Native Affairs Commission which would advise the government on proposed legislation throughout the Union.[51]

The first members of the NAC were Senator A.W. Roberts, C.T. Loram and General L.A.S. Lemmer. Initially at least the Commission was regarded with serious interest: its meetings were chaired by the Prime Minister, its early reports were diligent and comprehensive, and membership of the body was eagerly sought after.[52] The Commission's guiding principles, though suitably vague, were couched in the optimistic language of sympathetic consultation. It was conceived of as an expert advisory body which was to be 'primarily and essentially the friend of the Native people . . .', and which should endeavour to win their confidence and to educate public opinion, 'so as to bring about the most harmonious relations possible between black and white in South Africa'.[53]

The spirit of consultation was best exemplified by the series of annual Native Conferences which first met in Bloemfontein in May 1922. Meetings, which were supposed to serve as a 'gauge of native opinion', were attended by a mixture of nominated and elected delegates. Initially the NAC and the NAD regarded the opportunity for consultation as more than just a cynical gesture to the political aspirations of Africans. The *Cape Times*, for example, greeted the Conference as 'the seeds of that system of native representation which will one day blossom into a fully representative native assembly'.[54] However, both the Conference and the Commission were still-born. Their identities and functions were ill-defined, and they were progressively marginalised as the focus of attention fastened upon the vast scheme of social engineering entailed by Hertzog's Native Bills. African delegates soon grew impatient at the failure to make the Conference truly representative or to invest it with meaningful powers. The government had originally intended the Conference as a sounding board and safety valve for African opinion. Increasingly, however, it feared that the Conference would become a radicalising force and that it would be taken over by 'agitators'.

Almost from the start it was apparent that the Conference was not living up to expectations. As early as 1923 the Commission's secretary was moved to comment that the 'atmosphere was rather that of a "parliament" than a "conference" '.[55] Clearly the government was prepared to tolerate 'deliberation' but not 'debate'. The following year Major Herbst found himself wondering publicly about the usefulness of summoning further conferences, and he closed the meeting professing to be 'not quite satisfied with some of the resolutions'.[56] Between 1927 and 1936 (after which it was finally abandoned) the annual Native Conference was summoned only once, in 1930, and again (though by region!) in 1935 to consider Hertzog's Native Bills.

The effective functioning of the NAC was severely undermined, partly as a result of nebulous status, but also on account of disagreements among its members. Only a year after its establishment in 1920 the NAC bemoaned the fact that it was being ignored.[57] Checked on all sides and lacking effective powers, the Commission's strength depended almost entirely on the 'personality and resolution' of its individual members.[58]

The NAC's effectiveness was not enhanced by the fact that its members were divided on a number of key issues. In 1926, for example, both Roberts and Loram disagreed with the principles of the colour bar, whereas General Lemmer supported its application in the Transvaal and the OFS.[59] With the advent of Hertzog's Native Bills, conflict within the Commission intensified. Although it was able to hammer together a shaky consensus 'in favour of differential representation', this failed to obscure the substantial differences between individual members of the Commission.[60] Two years later le Roux van Niekerk failed to agree with Roberts and Loram on the terms of African representation as outlined in the 1929 Franchise Bill.[61]

The failure of liberal hopes for the NAC was reflected in the growing disillusionment of A.W. Roberts, a former teacher at Lovedale, who was steeped in the Eastern Cape missionary tradition. Roberts claimed to have joined the Commission in order to secure reforms, but these hopes had 'withered' as a result of the increasingly 'bureaucratic mode of government'.[62] In a series of letters written to Pim in 1921 Roberts confided his belief that the location system was 'economically and morally unsound' and that the pass laws should be totally scrapped. On the latter point, however, he spoke of his inability to 'carry my colleagues with me', much less the government.[63]

From the mid-1920s the influence and authority of the NAC declined and by 1936 its transformation was complete. Originally conceived of as a body of independent experts, it now confined itself to 'upholding the letter and spirit' of segregation.[64] A place on the commission became a way of rewarding superannuated party politicians. Stripped of its resources and under the overwhelming dominance of Heaton Nicholls, by 1937 it was little more than an official organ for the propagation of trusteeship ideology.[65]

The general extension of native councils envisaged by the 1920 Native Affairs Act also fell victim to the changed political tenor of the Pact years. Notwithstanding the moderate precedent set by the Transkeian *Bunga*, the government became increasingly uneasy about the possibility that the councils would be taken over by 'intellectuals' or 'agitators', who might spur the distintegration of 'tribal' authority.

Despite the much vaunted success of the Transkeian councils as model instruments of local government – W.T. Welsh[66] described them as a 'means of training the Natives in the science and art of local government appropriate to the citizens of a civilised state' – they nonetheless remained conservative institutions. The chief magistrate exercised ultimate control of the *Bunga*'s administrative functions and finances, and the annual magistrates' conference retained the power to review its decisions.[67] This limitation on the councils' autonomy, a restriction which the NAD hierarchy insisted upon, aroused a considerable amount of resentment among many African councillors. The more radical amongst them sought to dispense with white supervision and to increase the councils' executive authority.

As concern within the government and the NAC mounted over the disintegration of 'tribal bonds', the NAD became ever more cautious about extending the council network. Increasingly the view that the *Bunga* would 'break down tribal barriers', and 'tend to produce a bond of interest among the black *vis à vis* the white', gained currency within the administration.[68] This provoked endless debate about the advisability of extending councils to areas where chiefly powers remained relatively intact. Much discussion ensued as to whether representation should be by election or by nomination and whether councils should be constituted geographically or 'tribally'.[69] A number of senior officials within the NAD argued that the provisions of the 1920 Act were 'too advanced' for the 'backward' areas. They insisted, too, that overall magisterial control over the councils was essential to their effective functioning.[70] At the 1923 NAD conference F.S. Malan, the Acting Prime Minister, advised that the council system should not be extended to the Ciskei and the Transvaal, where the 'natives were less advanced in local government'. Although he did not wish the 1920 Act to be altered, he felt it should be kept only 'as an ideal to work up to'.[71]

By the end of the decade the 1920 Act was barely retained even as an ideal. A thoroughly revamped 'tribal' system, recommended by the *Report of the 1932 NEC*, was now recognised as a self-evident necessity. The policies of retribalisation and that of the council system were declared to be 'clearly in conflict'. In these circumstances Major Herbst was able to assert in 1933, 'unless there is a clear majority of the people affected in favour of the council system, we [the NAD] have definitely pronounced against it'.[72]

The growing resistance within the administration to an extension of the council system is reflected by the paucity of councils constituted after 1920. By 1923 the entire Transkei, with the exception of Mount Ayliff, was included in the *Bunga*, and in 1931 a United Transkeian Territories General Council, embracing the Transkei and Pondoland, was established. Nevertheless, no new councils were constituted between 1920 and 1926.[73] Amending legislation was introduced in that year providing for councils with considerably reduced powers. Thereafter, a number of councils were established, principally in the Ciskei and Transvaal.[74]

4 'RETRIBALISATION' AND CUSTOMARY LAW

During the nineteenth century both missionaries and the Cape colonial government sought to break the powers of the chiefs and to suppress African law and custom, on the grounds that these ran counter to the principles of 'civilisation'. However, such attempts were often ambivalent and in any case were often less than wholly successful. Indeed the persistence of customary law is in large measure a testament to the resilience of African societies in the face of the colonial state and the claims of Christianity. From at least the 1880s administrators began to confront explicitly the issue of whether or not to recognise customary law. After Union the dilemma became more acute, not least because of the widely divergent legal systems operative in each of the provinces. In brief, customary law was officially recognised only in Natal, where it was subject to the rigid 1891 Code, and in the Transkei, where a system of case law administered by magistrates had gradually evolved. In the Transvaal customary law was recognised insofar as it was 'not inconsistent with the general principles of civilisation', but traditional marriages were held to offend this proviso. The Ciskei was theoretically part of the Cape, which meant that conventional Roman-Dutch law pertained. In the OFS customary law was recognised to a limited extent.[75]

The discrepancies and anomalies in these divergent systems were aggravated by the fact that the formal legislative systems seldom operated as they were designed to. In Zululand, for example, the old Natal Native Code of 1878 was nominally in force though it was not applied in practice. In the Ciskei an informal court sat at King William's Town and settled disputes arising out of customary marriage, even though 'such alliances [were] regarded as not only illegal but immoral'. Similar courts were operative in the Transvaal. Magistrates therefore functioned as arbitrators, enforcing their decisions through 'judicious bluff', even though their judgments carried no legal sanction.[76] After Union, various attempts were made to regularise the situation; the NAD came under consistent pressure from district officials seeking clarification for administrative purposes, as well as from Africans who continued to practise customary law even where it was outlawed.

The 1913 *Native Laws Commission*, whose underlying intention was to afford magistrates discretionary powers to administer customary marriages – though without either hastening or retarding the gradual drift towards 'civilisation' – reflects the confused state of affairs. At this stage the recognition of customary law was a matter of acceding to popular demand and administrative pressure, in an environment where the ethos of the civilising mission was on the decline.[77] Increasingly, however, the need to recognise customary law was positively asserted. The adoption of a conscious programme to revitalise 'tribal' institutions was given added impetus by growing official concern over the rapid erosion of chiefly structures of authority.

In the first instance the nineteenth-century 'missionary view', which had pronounced against 'heathen customs', came under concerted attack. Edgar Brookes argued in 1924 that there was 'absolutely no reason to discourage *lobolo* [bridewealth] except for the prepossessions of missionaries . . .', and he railed against forms of Christianity which were 'clad in those most horrible of garments – the trappings of mid-Victorian individualism'.[78] The developing discipline of anthropology lent academic credibility to the view that African social structures and cultures were not simply 'barbarous' and that they could, if institutionalised, be utilised for sound administrative purposes.

Within the NAD there was frequent discussion of the need to accord recognition to native law and custom and, in particular, *lobolo*. The failed 1917 Native Administration Bill had been an early attempt at consolidating legislation in this direction. Realising that the measure had foundered because of the 'highly controversial' principle of segregation, E.R. Garthorne proposed the framing of three short acts ('no one of them contentious') in order to give effect to its main intentions.[79] One of these, the Native Marriage Bill, was discussed by senior members of the NAD and NAC at a special conference convened in November 1923.[80]

The Marriage Bill, which was subsequently incorporated into the 1927 Native Administration Act, was principally a technical measure designed to 'afford relief' in *lobolo* cases (especially in the Transvaal and Ciskei). The NAD/NAC conference which met to discuss it was unanimous in recommending that the government make provision for the hearing of cases according to native law and custom in the courts of the Union. The main debate centred not so much on the principle of recognising customary law, which commanded overwhelming acceptance, as on the question of whether the Bill's provisions were sufficiently far-reaching. In discussion there was a concerted attack on the 'missionary view', which opposed polygamy and *lobolo* as immoral and heathenish. As Norton said, it was not the administration's duty 'to help the missionaries in bolstering up their views'.[81]

Similar arguments are to be found elsewhere. With its acute awareness of rapidly deteriorating material conditions in the reserves, the weakening of traditional social structures, and the steady 'drift' to the towns, the 1932 NEC advocated economic development within the reserves and a restoration of 'tribal' authority. It accepted the view that 'the whole social structure of the Abantu rests largely on *lobolo*', an institution which had 'contributed much towards preserving tribes and keeping them intact'.[82] In contrast to earlier views, which saw *lobolo* as a 'barbarous' custom, the commission now identified bridewealth payments in glowing terms as a positive moral agent.[83]

Within the administration, the sense that *lobolo* and customary law possessed a definite utilitarian value was rapidly being crystallised. The goal of social containment, it was realised, could best be achieved through breathing new life into rapidly dissolving 'tribal' institutions. As the Magistrate of Bergville, Natal, said in 1932: 'While the lobolo system tends to involve a large number of moral absurdities which will have to be dealt with sooner or later, its advantages are great'. True, it involved 'the degradation of womanhood and the commercialisation of virtue'. Moreover, it reduced marriage to 'a sort of erotic contract, differing only from recognized prostitution in the question of time'. But, despite these drawbacks, *lobolo* 'served an inestimable cultural purpose. It has been the great schoolmaster who has developed the codes relating to property and enforced their observance . . . it is the builder of legal systems, the germ of trade, the highroad to autonomy'.[84]

It would be incorrect to assume that customary law was foisted unwillingly on Africans on account of the shrewd calculations of white politicians alone. There was certainly an element of such manipulation, but the restoration of customary law was notably also a concession to the demands of significant elements within African society for whom 'tradition' was a means of fending off the demands of a capitalist economy and the incursions of the colonial administration. The 1923 Pretoria Native Conference, for instance, unanimously approved of the principles of the proposed Marriage Bill and went on to ask for the hearing of civil cases in the courts of the Union 'according to Native Law and Custom'.[85] The files of the NAD are full of similar appeals from organisations such as district councils, the *Bunga*, and such major figures as Victor Poto of Pondoland.[86] Recommendations for the institutionalisation of customary law by magistrates and native commissioners are also ubiquitous, though there was disagreement amongst them as to whether such recognition should be permanent or merely a necessary stage in the gradual progress towards 'civilisation'.[87]

The 1927 Native Administration Act marks a decisive moment in the state's attempts to reconstitute and embalm tribal authority. As mentioned previously, its opening chapter established the governor general as 'Supreme Chief of all Natives' beyond the Cape, and it afforded the NAD enormous executive power in all matters of administration. The Act gave implicit recognition to customary marriage by ruling that *lobolo* could not be construed as being contrary to the principles of natural justice. In terms of its provisions, a network of native commissioner courts and divorce courts were established and gradually extended throughout the country. Two Native Appeal Courts modelled on the Transkeian precedent (one for the Cape and OFS, the other for Natal and the Transvaal) were created in 1928. Selected native commissioners were invested with criminal jurisdiction and the governor general was empowered to grant chiefs and headmen rights to administer customary law. The crucial principle of legislation by proclamation generated a constant steam of promulgations after 1928. Moreover, in terms of the 1927 Act, the Natal Native Code was amended and re-enacted in 1932.

These measures indicate the coalescence of administrative opinion in the late 1920s in favour of according significantly enhanced powers to traditional authorities. The development of a retribalisation strategy, however, was not accomplished in as smooth a manner as the official government reports imply. A natural sense of caution as shown by native administrators towards radical policy changes, the persistence of residual traces of the civilisation ideal, as well as differences of approach within regional administrations, all combined to render the process of retribalisation replete with inconsistencies and discontinuities.

Within the NAD it was widely appreciated that 'tribalism' offered major advantages in terms of the maintenance of social control. As H.C. Lugg, Magistrate of Verulam and a prime exponent of the 'Natal' view, put it, 'tribal government . . . enables the people to rule themselves through the medium of their chiefs and headmen . . .'; it is 'most economical and has enabled efficient control over large bodies of natives over extended tracts of country'.[88] Yet officials were also acutely conscious of the steady erosion of chiefly authority, and there was no agreement as to the practicability of arresting its collapse. Magistrate H. Britten, while accepting the need to perpetuate the tribal system 'as long as possible', nonetheless recognised that 'its breakdown is however inevitable and artificial attempts at retardation will be ineffective'.[89] This view was probably shared by most officials in the administration – if indeed a consensus on the issue can be said to have existed at all.

The strongest objections to any increase in the judicial powers of the chiefs came from the Transkei and Ciskei. In 1920 Chief Magistrate Welsh registered opposition to any system of trial by chiefly authorities on the grounds that the 'native people as a whole have advanced beyond the stage of absolute subordination to their chiefs and headmen . . .'[90] During the drafting stages of the Native Administration Act, Welsh, together with Norton of the Ciskei, mounted a formidable campaign against any radical tampering with the 'tribal' system. Norton was of the opinion that 'Tribalism is not a matter of juxtaposition or administration but is a matter of birth and sentiment'. It should therefore not be manipulated at will.[91]

In the Select Committee on the 1927 Administration Bill Welsh and Norton opposed the extension to chiefs and headmen of any judicial capacities 'whether civil or criminal'. They argued that such men were not fitted to exercise these powers and that the traditional Cape policy was to 'foster resort to the magistrate for the settlement of disputes and to encourage the atrophy of the judicial powers originally exercised by chiefs'.[92] This 'desperate opposition', as Garthorne described it, was largely reponsible for excluding the Cape Province from the aegis of the 'Supreme Chief'.[93] As late as 1932 the CNCs of the Cape, Transkei and Natal were united in agreement that chiefly courts should not be invested with criminal, as opposed to civil jurisdiction.[94] The grounds for their opposition were rooted in fears that such courts were prone to corruption and abuses of power.

Despite contradictions and ambiguities, there was a clear and growing acceptance of a 'retribalisation' strategy through the 1920s. This tendency is reflected in the changing views of key administrators. Thus in 1929 Herbst wrote to Welsh confessing that he had 'somewhat modified' his earlier resolution regarding the inadvisability of a 'return to the Transvaal and Natal system in the Cape'. Citing his own experience in the St Marks district of the Transkei, Herbst suggested that chiefs in the Cape Province should be accorded greater powers, though he hastened to add, 'I don't want to create, I only want to recognise existing facts . . .'[95] In reply Welsh admitted that he had for some time given 'anxious consideration' to his opposition to the creation of chiefs' courts in the Transkei. After prolonged discussion and thought he now recommended that Chief

Dalindyebo and Victor Poto Ndamase be authorised to hear civil cases arising out of native law and custom.[96]

The NAD was changing, but it was still somewhat out of step with the more enthusiastic advocates of retribalisation. The Department took strong exception to the NEC Report, for example, which was considered to have been reproachful of its policies. J.F. Herbst emphasised that outside the Cape [Ciskei] there was no area 'in which the powers of the chiefs have in any way been curtailed by any official act . . . The authority of the Chiefs is invariably supported. This will be the policy for many more years to come'.[97] However, the NAD would not lend artificial support to 'tribal administration': 'I do not believe in bolstering up a system once it has led to disintegration and brought the tribe to dissolution, disaster and decay'.[98] One practical consequence of Herbst's caution was his recommendation, with respect to Hertzog's Franchise Bill, not to determine electoral areas on a 'tribal' basis. He considered this proposal to be impracticable, noting that it would cause the 'gravest suspicion' among Africans. 'The advantages', Herbst explained, 'are not commensurate with the distrust and hostility that will be fomented.'[99]

In 1932 an amended Natal Native Code was introduced by proclamation in terms of section 24 of the Native Administration Act. The 1891 Code which it replaced has correctly been described as imparting a 'rigidity to customary law which it had not had in its traditional context'.[100] The same can indeed be said of the new code, which was ostensibly intended to take cognisance of the rapid changes in 'Native family life' since 1891 and to give expression to the 'more important customs which are practised to-day'.[101] In fact the Code's rejuvenation by administrative fiat and without consultation with Africans was a blatantly reactionary move, constituting an almost unparalleled triumph for the exercise of arbitrary power.[102] Though purporting to update customary law, the 1932 Code had the effect of embalming it.

The amended Natal Code aroused strong opposition from African organisations, liberals and parliamentarians such as Payn, Duncan and Hofmeyr.[103] However, since it was promulgated in terms of the Administration Act, it was never submitted to Parliament. Nor was it ever discussed by the annual Native Conference, which was by then effectively defunct. The Johannesburg Joint Council issued one of the most cogent attacks on the 1932 Code, objecting to the fact that it was based on a wholly erroneous conception of the powers of the Supreme Chief in traditional society, that it infringed individual liberty by extending the administration's summary jurisdiction over Africans, and that it afforded the administration total immunity from the courts.[104]

The amended Natal Native Code presents considerable problems of interpretation, even assuming the general trend within the NAD towards a retribalisation strategy; for although the drafting process of the 1932 Code can be traced, it is difficult to determine just where the decisive impetus for its introduction came from. Rheinallt Jones speculated, on the basis of confidential information, that the pressure derived from white Natalians rather than the NAD.[105] Conversely, Clarkson Tredgold thought, on the basis of information from Herbst, that the burden of responsibility lay with the 'NAD in Natal as against the opinion of the heads of the NAD of the Union itself'.[106]

It is quite possible that both Jones and Tredgold were the privileged subjects of calculated disinformation. There is indeed strong evidence to suggest that the Code was drafted furtively and that its content was deliberately concealed from the public.[107] The initial draft of the revised Code was drawn up in February 1928 by a committee consisting of magistrates Farrer and Lugg, and F.B. Burchell, professor of law at Natal University College. It was then referred to the CNC's Office in Pietermaritzburg, where C.A. Wheelwright 'agreed in substance' with the committee's proposals and redrafted the new code (together with N. W. Pringle) to take account of existing legislation.[108] From Natal the Code went back to the NAD Head Office, where it was redrafted by Howard Rogers, assisted by magistrate Barrett of Camperdown. Finally, it was referred back to Natal and revised by officials Lugg, Martin, Hodson and CNC Norton, in association with Howard Rogers.[109]

The fact that Norton and Wheelwright participated in the drafting of the Code appears to be somewhat inconsistent with their earlier views. Norton, as CNC of the Ciskei, had a long record of hostility to the granting of criminal jurisdiction to chiefs and had opposed the codification of customary law throughout the Union.[110] For his part, Wheelwright had been a strong opponent of the application of the old Code in Natal, and a stern critic of the standard of justice dispensed by the Natal Native High Court.[111] Nevertheless, it is possible that Wheelwright viewed the 1932 Code as a substantial improvement on the chaotic Natalian legal system before that date, and it is likely that Norton regarded the administration of the Cape and Natal as separate issues. This certainly appears to have been the view of J. Mould Young, the new CNC of Natal, who confidentially informed Rheinallt Jones in 1932 that he had 'never been in sympathy with many of the Natal methods' and that he had never favoured codification. Mould Young said that he would nevertheless accept the Code, since it has 'been regarded as an integral part of Native Administration in this province for years past . . .'[112]

5 THE LEGACY OF 'PROTECTION'

It has been shown how, after 1923, the trend within the NAD towards increasing centralisation of bureaucratic authority gathered momentum. But although the NAD had campaigned actively for its enhanced powers, it was not unequivocal about their implications. Specifically, the Department was reluctant to abandon its image as the 'protector' of 'native interests'. On a number of important issues there is strong evidence to suggest that the Department attempted to preserve its traditional role, and that it resisted the inevitable decline into a manifestly coercive institution.

Following the electoral victory of the Pact in 1924, the NAD came under sustained pressure to aid in the recruitment of farm labour. In 1925 Oswald Pirow, representing the Tzaneen Agricultural Association, began a campaign against the allegedly favoured position of the mining industry as regards the supply of labour.[113] A year later the Department of Agriculture estimated that farmers' labour requirements fell short by 25 per cent and insisted that it was 'incumbent upon the state to take ameliorative measures . . .'[114] During 1928–9 lobbying by farmers again intensified. Petitions and personal representations asserted farmers' claims to a plentiful supply of cheap labour, and complained of unfair competition with the mines.[115]

This concerted campaign generated a great deal of departmental debate. In response to Pirow, Major Herbst, speaking on behalf of General Hertzog, outlined the NAD's sympathetic attitude towards farmers. But the nub of his argument was that the 'real advantage of the Mining Industry is that it can offer wages which are beyond the means of agriculture, and that it can afford a highly efficient recruiting organisation'.[116] At the 1928 Transkeian magisterial conference a motion was unanimously passed rejecting the concept of using magistrates to recruit farm labour. The proposer, J.M. Young, contended that such schemes would lower the prestige of the magistrate 'by bringing him down to the level of a labour tout'.[117]

On this point the Transkei was not alone. Within the NAD Head Office there was consensus that the poor working conditions of farm labourers were above all responsible for the labour shortage. The Director of Native Labour, Major H.S. Cooke, detailed various administrative attempts to facilitate a supply of farm labour and reiterated the governments's desire to assist this supply 'by all legitimate means'. But he stressed that farmers would have to come 'into line to some extent' with other industries, where labouring conditions were vastly better.[118]

As an outcome of these deliberations, an article by Herbst appeared in *The South African Farmer* on the subject of 'Native Farm Labour'. Herbst proposed the establishment of a semi-official representative body which would undertake the responsibility for recruitment, while ensuring that the conditions of contract were adhered to. The NAD could not, however, be a direct participant: 'It is regarded as the protector of the Native', reminded Herbst. 'This is its primary function. Can it therefore be both recruiter and protector?'[119]

The reluctance of the NAD to take an active part in farm labour recruitment appears to be at odds with its long-established cooperation with the recruiting organisations of the mines. But this does not imply any inherent bias on the part of the NAD in favour of mining capital. The NAD preferred to deal with the mines because it was able, through the offices of the Director of Native Labour and the CNC Witwatersrand, to guarantee wage rates and oversee conditions of contract. With Hertzog as Minister, the NAD was especially concerned not to be seen as antagonistic to farming interests. In 1924, for example, E.R. Garthorne expressed the NAD's willingness to cooperate should a farm labour bureau be established under the auspices of the Department of Agriculture.[120] Yet the NAD was not prepared to intercede on the behalf of farmers without adequate controls, and if this entailed artificially cheapening the price of labour. To do so would be to risk being seen by Africans as a ruthlessly oppressive insititution rather than as an agency of protection.[121]

The Native Service Contract Act was a draconian piece of legislation governing master and servant relations on the farms of the Transvaal and Natal.[122] Its main objects were to prevent the desertion of labourers from service, to discourage rural labour from migrating to the cities, and to force squatters into relations of labour tenancy. In order to give effect to these intentions the Act introduced measures which would drastically reduce labour mobility. It sought to enchance parental authority by forbidding the employment of Africans under the age of 18 without the consent of their guardian and employer. Contravention of the law by minors was made punishable by whipping. A further section of the Act imposed a punitive tax of £5 on landowners for every African on a farm who was not in employment.[123]

The Native Service Contract Act was passed in the House of Assembly with the support of Nationalists and SAP members from Natal. But it was vigorously opposed by the Cape members of the SAP as well as by the Labour Party – Cabinet Minister F.H.P. Creswell was forced to admit that it was 'a piece of barbaric legislation'.[124] The Act aroused fierce opposition from a range of opposition groupings,[125] and although it was intended to be in the direct interests of farmers, section 9, which imposed the £5 squatter tax, was rejected by a number of farmers' organisations as well as by the influential Transvaal Landowners' Association.[126]

The Contract Bill was introduced by the Minister of Justice, Oswald Pirow, rather than by the Minister of Native Affairs. This constitutional anomaly was seized upon by those opposing the Bill, though they failed to make much headway. The Bill, which the *Cape Times* sarcastically referred to as 'Mr Pirow's Little Joke', was the direct responsiblity of the Minister of Justice himself.[127] Without doubt, it was strongly resisted by the NAD. There is abundant evidence to show that district native commissioners and magistrates of the NAD were unreservedly antagonistic to the proposed legislation. It was greeted with much scepticism and its enforcement was considered to be utterly impracticable, if not impossible.[128] Concern was also registered by NAD officials, who feared the social consequences of the eviction of thousands of squatters with their cattle. H.C. Lugg, the CNC of Natal, warned that the application of section 9 in Natal would be 'little short of calamitous', given the enormous number of Africans who would be forcibly displaced. It was 'a picture that the Department dare not contemplate with passivity or equanimity'.[129]

Major Herbst contended that there was insufficient ground available to accommodate the thousands of Africans who would be rendered homeless should the Act be enforced. He appealed to the Department of Justice to ensure that no released land be proclaimed under section 9. 'The Natives' he said, 'would regard any such step as a breach of faith on the part of the Government', and this would give rise to a 'most undesirable state of affairs'.[130] So strong was the NAD's resistance to the Contract Act that the Department effectively refused to administer its provisions: the NAD regarded the Act as having been 'promulgated under the aegis of the Minister of Justice', whose department would therefore have to bear the burden of its administration.[131]

It has already been demonstrated, in the case of the 1927 Native Administration Act, how the NAD's attempts to extend the range of its authority conflicted with its espoused beliefs. One of the important elements in this legislation enabled native commissioners to be invested with criminal jurisdiction. In support of their claims to exercise such powers many members of the Department invoked the doctrine of paternal protection. It was argued that Africans should be tried by 'officers who have special knowledge of their habits and mentality'. Moreover, many administrators claimed their exercising of criminal jurisdiction was 'essential to effective native administration'.[132] As Major Hunt expressed it in 1927, the maintenance of 'direct visible power over the natives' was a vital prerequisite of effective administration.[133]

With regard to the police, who also came under the Department of Justice, NAD officers argued in similar fashion. In his capacity as Director of Native Labour, A.L. Barrett attempted to extend the authority of native commissioners in tax and pass cases, claiming that the police were 'unduly heavy-handed in making arrests for trivial offences'.[134] Generally speaking, it may be surmised that native commissioners enjoyed a better reputation among Africans than the police.[135]

Thus, according to one interpretation of the doctrine of paternalist administration, NAD officials should be invested with as much power as possible, since they would naturally exercise it in a sympathetic fashion. An alternative outlook took the view that the NAD could not afford to sacrifice its credibility as 'guardian of the native races' by accruing punitive powers to itself. In 1924, for instance, T.W.C. Norton had warned that to combine the powers of a police officer with those of a civil administrator was 'objectionable'. Although the civil authority might have to enlist the aid of the police on occasion, nevertheless 'an administrator should not be a policeman'.[136]

Norton's cautious attitude was probably a minority one within the NAD. After 1927, however, the NAD was flooded with applications from district officials requesting to be invested with powers of criminal jurisdiction; and by the early 1930s the Department was becoming increasingly concerned at the tendency for relatively minor officials to accumulate substantial judicial powers. SNA Douglas Smit finally dismissed the persistent demands of the native commissioner of Pietermaritzburg for such powers by referring to 'an underlying difference between your conception of the true functions of a Native Commissioner and that of this office'. He rejected the idea that 'administrative control to be effective must carry with it criminal jurisdiction'. Instead Smit conveniently resorted to the NAD creed, asserting that the essential function of the Department was 'to assist, guide, protect and generally to subserve the interests of the native population', whereas 'the administration of the ordinary criminal law of the land is essentially the function of the Department of Justice'.[137]

The moderating influence of the NAD on segregationist policy may be further illustrated by reference to urban areas legislation between 1923 and 1937. The original 1923 Urban Areas Act was a curious measure, whose objective of extending social control embraced both welfarist and authoritarian elements. Through its pass provisions the Act sought to regulate the flow of African labour to the cities. But it was also designed to improve the living conditions of Africans by decisively shifting the responsibility for providing adequate housing and sanitation on to the municipalities. (It was as a result of the 1919 influenza epidemic that the appalling slum conditions under which urban Africans lived became a matter of general public concern.[138])

The 1923 Act may therefore be said to have embodied two distinctive approaches to urban policy. Its 'liberal' incorporationist component may be traced back to the 1919 Godley Commission, which was dominated by senior NAD officials, and tended to the view that 'suitable accommodation' had to be provided for a growing and inevitably permanent urban African population. This Commission had also recommended, unsuccessfully as it turned out, the repeal of all existing pass laws, which were held to be both ineffective and unnecessarily restrictive in terms of personal liberty, and the adoption instead of a single 'Native Registration and Protection Act'.[139] However, the 1923 Act also bears the imprint of the 1921 Stallard (Transvaal Local Government) Commission, which regarded African urbanisation as fundamentally undesirable and took the position that Africans had no right in urban areas other than to 'minister' to the need of whites.[140]

In later years this ambivalence in the 1923 act was progressively settled in favour of Stallardist principles. Whereas the 1923 Act had attempted to stabilise and regulate existing conditions in the urban areas, it proved wholly unable to retard the urbanisation process. Between 1921 and 1936 it was calculated that the urban African population had almost doubled from 587 000 to 1 150 000.[141] Particular concern was registered at the rapid urbanisation of African women, whose presence in 'white' towns was estimated to have increased by 50 per cent between 1911 and 1921, and by at least that amount again between 1921 and 1926.[142]

In 1927 an Amendment Bill to the 1923 Act, drafted and discussed by municipal representatives and the NAD, had the 'primary object' of introducing 'greater powers of control over the influx of Natives into urban areas . . .'[143] This Amendment Bill, which eventually passed into law as Act 25/1930, permitted municipalities to restrict the numbers of Africans in urban areas, but failed to have much effect.[144] A further Amendment Bill to the Urban Areas Act circulated in 1932 was intended to 'secure closer control over Natives in urban areas and to give a more definite impetus to the policy of segregation . . .'[145] After lengthy consideration by a Parliamentary Commission, the Joint Select Committee on the Native Bills as well as the NAD and NAC, it was ultimately enacted as the Native Laws Amendment Act of 1937.

In language, tone and intent, the Native Laws Amendment Act marked a significant departure from its predecessor of 1923. It increased the obligation upon local authorities to restrict the entry of a 'redundant native population', aimed at preventing the further influx of African women, and provided for the taking of a biennial census of labour needs in order to facilitate the repatriation of 'surplus' Africans. The genesis of the 1937 Act can be traced back to Colonel Stallard's submissions to the 1930 Joint Select Committee on the Native Bills – indeed Heaton Nicholls portrayed it as an integral part of the 1936 Hertzog legislation.[146]

The NAD's position in this changing political environment is intriguing, for although the Department followed the general trend towards centralised authoritarian control of Africans in the urban areas, and in some respects was responsible for having initiated the process, it nevertheless attempted to modify the terms of the 1937 legislation. Just as the Godley Committee exerted a moderating influence on the 1923 Act, so the NAD's Young-Barrett Committee of 1935–6 (which considered the proposed amendments to the Urban Areas Act) provided a 'liberal' input.[147] The Committee gave detailed consideration to the Stallardist doctrine that Africans should only be present in the cities to 'minister' to the white man's needs, and rejected each of its assumptions in turn. It declared that a significant number of Africans 'have definitely divorced themselves from the tribal life of the Reserves' and would not be persuaded to return under any conditions. Thus the Committee felt unable to subscribe to a policy which would mean 'the wholesale eviction or expulsion of numbers of families who have been resident in the urban areas for generations'.[148]

The extent to which the Young-Barrett Committee was representative of mainstream NAD opinion remains uncertain. It is particularly difficult to square the relatively enlightened wartime views of SNA Douglas Smit on the question of African urbanisation with his support of the 1937 legislation.[149] But despite the increasingly authoritarian and bureaucratically centralised character of the NAD through the 1920s and 30s, the Young-Barrett Committee indicates that elements of the NAD's assimilationist and protectionist ideology remained intact. Perhaps it was for this reason that Smuts predicted that the 1937 Act would be carried out in a 'milder and fairer form than many people think', considering that the 'Native Affairs Department is on the whole wiser than the legislators of this country'.[150]

6 CONCLUSION

The unprecendented degree of social ferment during the decade following the First World War raised the alarming spectre of racial conflict taking on a powerful class dimension. In this situation the NAD was vitally concerned to preserve its reputation as the 'protector' of African interests, rather than be seen as the naked agent of white domination. Thus it defined its function in terms of providing 'a just and equitable balance where the interests of one race impinge upon those of the other'.[151] The NAD's identity as a benevolent institution with specialist functions was essential to its task as the official mediator between black and white; moreover, it underpinned the basis of the Department's separate existence within the state as a whole.

In the post-Union era the NAD was politically weak and administratively fragmented. Outside the Transkei, which formed its primary administrative and ideological reference point, the Department lacked cohesion, and it remained subordinate in crucial respects to the Department of Justice. The NAD's predicament was exacerbated after 1922, when it underwent substantial reorganisation as a result of recommendations made by the Public Service Commission.

Segregationist policies, which were promoted with increasing intensity after 1924, provided the political environment within which the NAD began to rebuild its administrative power-base. In this context the 1927 Native Administration Act may be interpreted not only as a major triumph for segregationism, but also as the mechanism by which the NAD attempted to recapture the authority it had lost to the Department of Justice after 1922. Segregation should therefore be seen not only as an ideology within which different material interests resolved their contradictions, but also as a site of contest for competing arms of the state. Likewise, the manner in which intra- and inter-departmental conflict was settled exerted an appreciable influence on the introduction and implementation of segregation.

In the struggle over access to resources and the extent of its jurisdiction, the NAD came to restate its administrative and ideological objectives in closer accord with segregationist discourse. The Department's commitment to 'personal rule' and the primacy of the 'man on the spot' yielded to an increased emphasis on technocratic ideals such as 'uniformity', 'efficiency' and administrative centralisation. Paradoxically, however, the NAD continued to lay claim to an idealised conception of the 'Transkeian tradition', even though the expansion and centralisation of its authority was achieved at the expense of the Transkei's regional autonomy.

During the 1920s the fluid and implicitly incorporationist brand of segregation proposed by Smuts gave way to a sterner and more exclusionist interpretation in the hands of Hertzog. Administratively this may be seen in the demise of the 1920 Native Affairs Act and the declining powers of the consultative mechanisms established within the terms of that legislation. Moreover, the 1927 Native Administration Act served to consolidate and centralise the authority of the NAD. It entrenched the principle of government by executive proclamation and actively embraced a strategy of 'retribalisation'.

The NAD responded ambivalently to these developments. It supported the general trend of segregationist legislation, but by no means always led the way. For example, whereas the Department welcomed the restitution of chiefly authority and customary law as a useful means of retarding the process of 'detribalisation', it recognised that capitalist penetration of the reserves was inevitable, and was anxious not to engage too overtly in an artificial bolstering of chiefly powers. The NAD also made various attempts to modify the implementation of segregationist measures. Thus it resisted taking part in the recruitment of labour for white farmers in the 1920s, refused to sanction the Native Service Contract Act, attempted to secure as much territory as possible for African usage within the limits imposed by segregation, and continued to favour a mildly welfarist and incorporationist strategy with respect to urban policy.

In the wider context of state policy during the 1920s and 1930s, and in comparison with its behaviour during the apartheid era, the NAD may be regarded as a relatively benign institution. This does not mean, however, that the NAD was opposed to segregation, much less that it rejected the essential precepts of white supremacy. On the contrary, the Department may be said to have taken the long view, viewing segregation as a means by which the harsh conditions occasioned by South Africa's process of industrialisation could be ameliorated.

The NAD was part of, and responsible to, an unashamedly white supremacist government which placed a premium on securing a reliable supply of cheap labour for capitalist industry and agriculture. But it was also aware that the rapid disintegration of the reserve economies and the uncontrolled influx of an African proletariat into the cities posed a major threat to continued white supremacy. The processes of capital accumulation had to be squared with the demands of ideological legitimation. Though receptive to the needs of capital, and by extension the maintenance of white domination, the NAD was not simply the crude tool of the ruling classes it is sometimes assumed to be.

Part III

5   The Passage of Hertzog's Native Bills, Part One

1   INTRODUCTION

As Prime Minister, General Hertzog is usually credited with having made two fundamental policy initiatives. The first relates to his role as an Afrikaner nationalist leader seeking to establish parity between English- and Afrikaans-speakers; while the second is commonly accepted to be his 'native policy'. At first sight there appears little to connect these political programmes, but the relationship is in fact a close one: the creation of a unified 'white nation' under the rubric of 'South Africanism' was the mirror image of the subordination and exclusion of Africans from civil society. Indeed the success of each was conditional, to at least some extent, on the fulfilment of the other.

Stanley Trapido has shown that the non-racial franchise of the mid-nineteenth-century mercantile Cape served as a useful device for the incorporation of privileged Africans within colonial society.[1] But the feasibility of this option declined with the mineral revolution of the 1870s and 1880s. In the mercantile era it was plausible to found a political strategy upon the gradual co-optation of an 'improving' African peasantry or mission-educated elite. Access to citizenship could be, and was, controlled by manipulating the property and educational qualifications necessary to attain the franchise. Under conditions of industrial capitalism, however, this was no longer the case. The growing presence of a large African proletariat in the urban areas had the contradictory effect of emphasising Africans' social and economic power while highlighting their lack of political rights.

This paradox was clearly understood by George Heaton Nicholls, whose ideas strongly informed the thinking of the powerful Joint Select Committee on the Native Bills between 1930 and 1935. Above all, Nicholls stressed the threat to continued white supremacy posed by a disenfranchised African proletariat. It was for this reason that he hoped, through the policy of 'trusteeship', to redirect the political

131

development of Africans away from 'communism' by the revival of what he termed 'communalism'. The apocalyptic vision which accompanied Nicholls's radically conservative analysis was not always shared by his more pragmatic political contemporaries, but it resonated strongly with white fears of 'swamping' at the polls and of the 'rising tide of colour'.

Argument about the political aspect of segregation centred on the question of the non-racial franchise. When one considers that the Cape African vote had declined by 1933 to a mere 1.2 per cent of the Union total, it may be wondered why this was so divisive an issue. As a first response it should be noted that the non-racial qualified franchise in the Cape was of great symbolic significance. It represented a direct continuity with the Victorian 'civilising mission', which promised that at some point in the future, however remote, at least some Africans could participate as equals in a common political society. The mere existence of this possibility drove a wedge between the political aspirations of the upwardly mobile African elite and the mass of African workers and peasants.

Constitutionally, too, the Cape franchise was of great importance. Having been entrenched in the 1909 Act of Union, its removal could only be effected by means of a two-thirds majority of both Houses of Parliament. Moreover, so long as it stood intact, the non-racial franchise posed formidable legal obstacles to the imposition of formal land segregation in the Cape. In 1917 the judgment of the Appeal Court in the case of Thomson and Stilwell v. Khama resulted in the 1913 Land Act being declared *ultra vires* in the Cape. This was so because the Land Act was considered to infringe the constitutionally entrenched Cape franchise by interfering with the ability of Cape Africans to qualify for the vote on the basis of property held. The implication was that so long as the Cape franchise continued to exist, it would be impossible to establish a uniform policy of land segregation throughout the Union.

Party political considerations also had a bearing on the issue of the non-racial franchise. The African vote was widely perceived to be crucial to the SAP's electoral prospects in a number of Cape constituencies, whose sitting MPs were amongst its prominent defenders. On the other hand, a strong element of the SAP in Natal, whose loyalty to the Party was in any case in doubt, remained implacably opposed to the continued existence of the Cape franchise. General Smuts's evasive and contradictory stance on the Native Bills reflected these rifts in the SAP, as he desperately tried to prevent the party's fragmentation over the vexed issue. In narrow parliamentary terms then, the political significance of the African vote is reflected in the SAP's determination to delay the enactment of the Native Bills for a full decade.

The basis of Hertzog's political strategy flowed from his insistence on the interdependence of the four Native Bills. He presented segregation throughout as a grand compromise (or *quid pro quo*) in which a range of interested constituencies, black and white, were invited to participate. Within the major white political parties segregation became a consensus ideology, notwithstanding differences on points of detail. Although the passage of the Native Bills required a decade to be enacted, the underlying tendency saw the SAP and the Nationalists drawing steadily together on the 'native question', a process which was greatly facilitated when they merged in 1934 to form the United Party.

Those critics of segregation who hoped to procure material advantages for Africans strove to separate the more acceptable provisions of the Land and Council Bills from those dealing with the franchise. But the opposition of key individuals and organisations was often confused and ambivalent. The contradiction between public avowals in favour of the non-racial franchise and private attempts to negotiate its abolition highlights the confusion and powerlessness of the extra-parliamentary opposition. It also reflects the success of segregation as an ideology with a remarkable capacity for drawing a wide range of political opinion within the terms of its discourse. White liberals sought constantly to soften the impact of segregation by seeking to negotiate honourable compromises with the government. Similarly, a number of key African leaders, trapped by the acute need for land and struggling to defend traditional resources, frequently found themselves forced to trade their claims to political citizenship for a greater share of their territorial birthright.

General Hertzog's Native Bills finally became law in 1936, a full decade after their initial introduction. During this time the Bills underwent substantial changes, having been subject to a myriad of detailed amendments, each of which was accompanied by intense lobbying amongst the major parties in the parliamentary system. Ultimately the original four Hertzog Bills of 1926 were distilled into two: the 1936 Representation of Natives Act and the 1936 Native Land and Trust Act.[2] The Representation Act was chiefly concerned with the removal of the Cape African franchise, which had been a feature of South African political life since 1853, and its replacement by a complex system of indirect representation.[3] The Cape African franchise had been firmly entrenched in the Union constitution of 1909, so that its abolition could only be secured by means of a two-thirds majority of both Houses of Parliament. Four electoral areas were established in terms of the Representation Act, each of which returned one representative to the Senate.[4] By law only whites were eligible to become 'native senators'. They were chosen by an intricate system of communal voting, comprising 'tribal' chiefs, representatives of local councils, native advisory boards and specially constituted electoral committees. The means by which senators were elected differed from province to province, but the general effect was to fragment political constituencies and to weight representation away from the urban centres and towards the rural areas.

In terms of a late legislative twist introduced by Hertzog in 1936, elements of the Cape franchise were purportedly retained. Africans on the existing voters' roll were transferred to a special 'Cape native voters' roll', which elected three members to the House of Assembly and two representatives to the Provincial Council. Like the senators, these representatives had to be white. A further section of the Representation Act provided for the establishment of a Natives' Representative Council, comprising six officials of the Native Affairs Department, four nominated and twelve elected members – a total of twenty-two. The nominated members were appointed by the government, while the elected representatives were to be chosen through regional electoral colleges. The Representative Council was permitted to deliberate upon any issues affecting Africans, but its powers were purely consultative.[5]

The 1936 Native Trust and Land Act completed the process of spatial segregation which the 1913 Land Act had initiated. It promised, but did not guarantee, to supplement the 'scheduled areas' (which had been set aside in 1913 for exclusive African occupation) with an additional 7.25 million morgen (1 morgen = 2,116 acres). This land was made available for purchase either by individual Africans or by a statutory 'Native Trust' established, on the model of the former Natal and Zululand Native Trusts, as a corporate body under the control of the governor general. Parliament was to make funds available to the Trust Fund, whose function was to acquire and develop land within the enlarged reserves for communal African usage.

The 1936 Land Act also dealt with the position of Africans living outside the scheduled or released areas, i.e. Africans living on white farms. Thus Chapter IV prescibed the conditions under which those Africans who were not yet full-time employees of white farmers could continue to live in the white-owned rural areas. Farm-owners were required to register all labour tenants and squatters resident on their land.[6] In the case of labour tenants, the fee per tenant was the nominal sum of sixpence, though farmers were normally entitled to have only five labour tenant families living on their land without special permission.

In terms of the Land Act, squatters had also to be registered and licensed by the government. Unlike labour tenants, however, the licence fees for squatters were punitive, rising from 10 shillings for the first year to a crippling £5 for the tenth and each subsequent year that the squatter remained. The clear intention of this section was (i) to restructure the relations of production in the countryside by encouraging direct forms of labour service (ultimately full wage-labour), and (ii) to redistribute African labour more evenly among white farmers. The section of the 1936 Land Act governing conditions of contract was highly contentious. Within the white farmers' community, particularly in those regions considered to be 'backward', immediate enforcement of its provisions would have resulted in widespread squatter evictions as well as fundamental economic and social dislocation. In the face of such pressures the government therefore decided that Chapter IV could only be applied gradually, and until at least the end of the Second World War it was not in force anywhere.[7]

Lack of space precludes any detailed discussion of the complex legislative evolution of the 1936 legislation, whose history (in the case of the Land Act) has to be traced back to the 1913 Land Act, the 1916 Beaumont Commission, the failed 1917 Native Administration Bill and the five 1918 Local Land Committees. The 1936 Representation Act had an equally complex history and underwent substantial modification by various parliamentary select committees during the decade following its initial introduction in 1926. The tortuous amendments to which it was subjected in this period had an important bearing on the changing character of political segregation, but these cannot either be treated here in a systematic fashion.

2   SMUTS AND HERTZOG, 1925–9

General Hertzog used to claim, with some justification, that he was committed to a policy of segregation as early as 1912.[8] In the run-up to the 1924 General Election he made repeated references to the need for segregation, but it was only after becoming Prime Minister that year that he began to concentrate on segregation as a major political priority. His first major statement on the proposed Native Bills occurs in a speech delivered to his Smithfield constituents in November 1925.[9].

Hertzog began his address with a lengthy attack on the Cape African franchise. The burden of his argument was that the number of enfranchised African voters in the Cape was likely to exceed the number of white voters within 50 years and that it would therefore be impossible to withhold the franchise from Africans in the northern provinces. This was a potentially disastrous state of affairs which could only be averted by abolishing the Cape franchise as soon as possible. The alternative was 'either civil war or the white man's ruin and that of European civilisation in South Africa'.[10]

To compensate for the loss of the Cape African franchise Hertzog offered an historic *quid pro quo* which was intended to solve the native question as a whole. Firstly, he proposed that provision would have to be made for the granting of further land to Africans as promised by the Land Act of 1913. Secondly, he suggested alternative forms of political representation for Africans. In the reserves Africans were to be encouraged to govern themselves as far as possible through the creation of many more local and general councils. Further, the annual Native Conference was to be transformed by statute into a Union Native Council. Its elected and nominated members would ultimately exercise both advisory and legislative functions. To compensate for the loss of their parliamentary vote, Africans throughout the country were to be offered the opportunity to elect seven white representatives to the House of Assembly.[11]

The major proposals outlined at Smithfield anticipated the form of the four 1926 Native Bills and established the terms of segregationist discourse during the era of the Pact Government. Notably, Hertzog was able to provoke hysterical white fears about the future of 'European civilisation', while at the same time maintaining the balanced tone of the even-handed statesman: he proved adept at portraying the native question as a problem particularly susceptible to manipulation by 'agitators' and communists, and therefore requiring an immediate solution, while at the same time appealing to whites to suspend party political and personal prejudices in the interests of national (white) solidarity.[12]

These themes remained a consistent feature of Hertzog's rhetoric for the next decade, though they were couched in terms sufficiently ambiguous to permit significant differences in emphasis. For example, when in December 1925 Hertzog addressed the annual Native Conference in Pretoria on the theme of segregation, he adopted a conciliatory tone – dealing first with the creation of a Union Native Council and the provision of more land, while leaving the issue of the franchise for last. Hertzog took particular care to emphasise that segregation was a natural desire compatible with the mutual protection of both black and white, invoking an innocent pastoral metaphor to illustrate his point: 'I hope you will agree with me that there is no injustice done when different grazing is given to sheep than that given to the cattle'.[13]

By contrast, Hertzog's Malmesbury speech of May 1926 placed a more strident emphasis on the need to preserve white supremacy. On this occasion Hertzog repeated his familiar warnings about the numerical superiority of Africans and the threat posed by the common franchise, clothing his arguments in the explicit language of biological racism. 'The native', Hertzog declared, 'stands in relation to the European as a child in religion and moral conviction, lacking any art or science . . .' The cause of the colour bar was not colour itself so much as 'a profound decisive difference in nature, development and civilisation . . .'[14] So long as Africans remained in an 'inferior' stage of development talk of political equality was impossible:

> he will have to be told in the most unequivocal language that the European is fully determined that South Africa shall be governed by the white man, and that the white man will not tolerate any attempt to deprive him of that task.[15]

With the parliamentary tabling of the four Native Bills in 1926 segregation became declared government policy. The response of the official opposition South African Party was outlined in a comprehensive statement written by Smuts in 1926.[16] Like so many of his pronouncements on the 'native question', Smuts's memorandum was first and foremost an attempt to postpone the imposition of segregation. The technique he adopted amounted to spoiling tactics, whereby he defended the *status quo* by representing Hertzog's proposals as a potentially dangerous 'leap in the dark'. In his convoluted way Smuts appeared to criticise Hertzog's proposals both for being segregationist and for not being segregationist enough.

Smuts was most favourably disposed to the Land and Council Bills, which, he said, offered distinct possibilities for advance even if they were flawed. He tacitly accepted the need to reserve more land for Africans, but criticised the proposals to throw open the released areas to competitive purchase by whites and Africans. This, he suggested, amounted to a reversal of the segregation policy, since it would open the door 'to all the evils of mixed or piebald landholding against which the Act of 1913 was intended to provide.'[17] Moreover, the 'ferocious licensing system for farm squatters and labour tenants' would encourage a dangerous influx of Africans into the towns.[18] Smuts was amenable to the Union Council Bill, claiming it as an extension of his own 1920 Native Affairs Act and therefore worthy of support. Nevertheless, he warned that a General Native Council might easily become a 'hot-bed for agitation and bolshevism amongst the natives, who [were] at present orderly and law-abiding'.[19]

Smuts's strongest opposition was reserved for the Franchise Bills. On the one hand, he criticised the proposal to remove Africans from the electoral roll, since it amounted to a 'direct violation of the spirit and intention of the Constitution'.[20] On the other hand, he warned against the supposed dangers inherent in the alternative schemes for African representation. Smuts questioned whether Africans in the northern provinces were ready for the exercise of political rights, and threatened that the seven white representatives to Parliament might constitute a 'native block vote' with the potential to hold the balance of power.[21]

The English press acclaimed Smuts's memorandum as a vitally important contribution to the segregation debate.[22] Yet, however clever he had been in exposing the weakness of the Hertzog proposals, the document amounted to little more than a sophisticated attempt at political procrastination. Smuts's only positive recommendation was to organise a national convention for the purpose of discussing political segregation. Meanwhile, the prudent step would be to devote a 'few years of serious public thought and inquiry' to its consideration.[23] Delaying tactics such as these characterised Smuts's approach to the Native Bills over the next decade. As a strategy it failed, for Smuts was left carping and sniping defensively, while

Hertzog retained the political initiative and pressed remorselessly ahead.

The public debate between the two generals extended also to the private sphere. Between December 1925 and January 1926 Smuts and Hertzog entered into a correspondence (in Afrikaans) on the 'native question'. Hertzog proposed that Smuts and other members of the SAP should cooperate with him in an attempt at a solution outside the arena of party politics.[24] Smuts's response was hostile. He accused Hertzog of having misrepresented his position in the past, refused to discuss a solution on the basis of the Smithfield proposals, and suggested instead calling a National Convention.[25] Smuts subsequently became more conciliatory, but he nevertheless remained intent that consultation be carried out in public and that the Smithfield proposals could not serve as the basis of discussion.[26] Beyond the vague suggestion of a National Convention, which he frequently returned to, Smuts was unable to formulate a constructive policy alternative to Hertzog's proposals.

Patrick Duncan, Smuts's close political associate, realised that the SAP was unable to gain the political initiative on the 'native question' and advised him in December 1927 to cooperate with Hertzog.[27] In February 1928, probably as a direct result of this suggestion, the two party leaders met a number of times to resolve the issue. According to Smuts's detailed notes of the 1928 meetings, Hertzog expressed a desire to press on with the segregationist legislation before rising black expectations (fuelled, so he claimed, by Communist agitation) made further progress impossible.[28] On the franchise issue Hertzog indicated a willingness to compromise, suggesting indirect mechanisms whereby Africans in the three northern provinces and the Cape could elect white representatives to the Senate and the House of Assembly respectively.[29] This offer was clearly intended as a concession to the SAP, but Smuts responded only by raising problems about the growing political claims of women and Indians. He proposed a more comprehensive solution, embodying a common Union-wide qualified franchise based on occupation and income, which would be sufficiently high to exclude most Africans while not high enough to exclude whites.[30]

During a further conversation Hertzog informed Smuts that he was not in favour of a general, i.e. non-racial, franchise reform; Smuts's response indicated that he was in any case not much committed to the idea himself. Returning to Hertzog's original proposals, Smuts quibbled about the amount of representation Africans should be entitled to; insisted that existing African voters should retain their rights for the rest of their lives; informed Hertzog that he was 'not enamoured' of the idea of a General Council, on the grounds that such an institution might 'collect all the Kadalies and Communist agitators in South Africa' into a single body; criticised the Coloured Representational Bill as unworkable; and argued that the Land Bill was far too complicated. Smuts closed by saying that he was not making any definite proposal, but was only trying to induce Hertzog to put forward a reasonable scheme.[31]

On 27 February 1928 the two leaders met once again. Hertzog opened the discussion, noting that 'real progress' had been made in their talks. Without committing himself, Hertzog appeared to take on board some of Smuts's suggestions. He thought it might be possible eventually to have five representatives from the Cape and considered that the General Council proposal might be postponed while the conference system was developed . On the Land Bill Hertzog agreed that simplification was possible and he suggested that the released areas might serve merely as an indication of the areas within which Africans would in future be free to purchase land.[32]

The 1928 discussions appear to have been conducted in a better spirit than the Hertzog-Smuts correspondence of 1926. On the whole they reveal two leaders whose substantive differences on 'native policy' were relatively minor. Hertzog's conciliatory spirit was probably motivated by a desire to achieve inter-party consensus so as to press ahead with the Native Bills. But Smuts continued to prevaricate and persisted in raising a myriad of objections to Hertzog's proposals – while evading the major issues of principle. His disagreement with Hertzog was primarily motivated by a reluctance to countenance major policy changes and, as a matter of political style, by a concern to soften the impact of segregation.

There was an important additional reason for Smuts's delaying tactics. In the Cape a number of SAP MPs were resolute supporters of the existing African franchise, partly out of a genuine ideological commitment to the principle of non-racial representation, but also on account of the fact that the African vote was believed to be decisive in a number of SAP-held Cape seats. Estimates varied. In 1929 Howard Pim claimed that at least eleven SAP seats in the Cape were held on account of the African vote; Charles Crewe calculated in 1926 that the abolition of the Cape franchise would entail the loss of about six SAP seats in the Eastern Cape, and would result in a substantial reduction in the parliamentary majorities of five other constituencies; while Oswald Pirow argued that the SAP was dependent on the African electorate in seventeen Cape constituencies.[33] To a significant extent therefore, the African vote was an important feature of the SAP's hopes for electoral victory.

By contrast, a number of Natal MPs, led by George Heaton Nicholls and J.S. Marwick, were strongly opposed to the existence of the Cape franchise. On the question of political representation they often stood to the right of Hertzog, and their loyalty to the SAP was frequently called into question. By 1929 it was clear that Smuts was beleaguered within his party. There were strong rumours that the Natal section of the party was urging him to accept Hertzog's Bills, failing which, the SAP might break up. But Smuts could not accede to Natal's demands without seriously alienating his support in the Cape. According to Howard Pim, he was merely 'drifting' in the hope of keeping the SAP intact.[34]

Throughout the decade during which the Native Bills were debated Smuts's position was notoriously inconsistent. At times he appeared as an embattled defender of the African franchise, whereas on other occasions he was perceived as a prime conspirator in its demise. A number of writers have attempted to unravel these contradictions by casting a sympathetic light on Smuts. Alan Paton cites Smuts's complex personality and his inability to reconcile his world reputation as a champion of freedom with his blindness to many domestic South African issues. Paton even goes so far to suggest that Smuts's procrastination and his eventual support of the Native Bills in 1936 are to be explained by his realisation of the need to keep the United Party government intact in the face of the growing Nazi threat.[35] J.T. Cameron ascribes predominantly positive motives to Smuts in his adoption of what she calls a 'Fabian policy' between 1926 and 1936. This 'dilatory policy of attrition', she argues in her master's thesis, was determined by his complex view of the 'native problem' and his attempt to preserve peace and conciliation between all the peoples of South Africa.[36]

Such attempts to explain the puzzling contradictions in Smuts's personality – the conflict between the 'old boer' and the 'British liberal' attitudes, as J.H. Hofmeyr put it – are far from convincing.[37] They rely on two equally unsatisfactory legends, which merely serve to shift the burden of historical explanation on to the mystery of 'Smuts the man'. The key to Smuts's mercurial behaviour is more prosaic: on the 'native question' he was a pragmatic politician whose prime motivation was the prerogative to maintain unity in a party which was fundamentally divided on the issue. Bernard Friedman is therefore correct in his observation that Smuts could not offer an alternative to Nationalist Party policies because he too stood for white supremacy. Nor could Smuts propose a substitute, because he was unable to persuade the electorate that his own method of ensuring white supremacy would be more effective than Hertzog's.[38]

The 1929 general election provided a revealing example of Hertzog's capacity to outmanoeuvre Smuts politically on this issue. Popularly dubbed as the 'black peril' election, it was notable as the first occasion since Union that the 'native question' emerged as the foremost issue during a national poll. In January 1929 Smuts alluded in a speech at Ermelo to the formation of a 'great African federation of States' to unite British Africa. This curious vision, reminiscent of Rhodes's empire stretching from the Cape to Cairo, was seized upon and skilfully manipulated by the Nationalist Party leadership. A document known as the 'black manifesto' branded Smuts as the determined 'apostle of a black Kafir State' stretching from the Cape to the Sudan.[39] South African whites, it declared, were 'entitled to know whereto South Africa is destined – to be a white man's country or a kafir land?'[40] Smuts's attempts to repudiate this allegation were ineffective however much his words had been deliberately misquoted. Needless to say, he was not, as accused, an advocate of 'equal political rights' for all men.[41]

As expected, the Native Bills failed to gain the necessary two-thirds majority of both Houses of Parliament during the Joint Session of 1929. Nevertheless, this did not constitute defeat for Hertzog. Indeed the *Round Table* observed astutely that Smuts's election speeches and his Oxford addresses suggested that 'he and the rank and file of his supporters do not stand so very far apart from the Nationalists in the matter of the franchise'.[42]

3   THE JOINT SELECT COMMITTEE AND FUSION, 1930–5

In January 1929 the Native Bills (minus the Union Native Council Bill, which had been dropped) were introduced at a Joint Sitting of both Houses of Parliament. At its third reading, however, the Natives' Representation Bill failed to secure the requisite two-thirds majority and Hertzog, who insisted on the interdependence of the Bills, therefore withdrew the others. The Representation Bills were introduced again in 1930 to a combined sitting of the House of

Assembly and the Senate, which in turn referred them to a Joint Select Committee of both Houses.

This Committee, which sat from 1930 to 1935 was a powerful body consisting of major political figures on both sides of the House; the *Cape Times* regarded it as the most powerful Select Committee that had 'ever been appointed in South Africa'.[43] The proceedings of the Select Committee were conducted in secret, so that little is known of its deliberations, aside from relatively skimpy official reports and suggestive material located in various collections of private papers.[44] According to George Heaton Nicholls, one of its most influential members, the Joint Select Committee worked on the basis that there 'should be no party line. The whips were off'. It was further accepted that 'the whole native question should disappear from the party political arena until the Committee reported back to the House'.[45] These conditions worked to Hertzog's advantage, for, in the absence of public debate, consensus on the Native Bills was able to coalesce. As Hancock explains, Hertzog used the Joint Select Committee as an 'instrument for crushing the SAP facade of unity'. The suspension of party loyalties meant that Smuts 'sat powerless while Heaton Nicholls and the Natal contingent with strong support from Stallard and other SAP men on the Rand, did Hertzog's work for him'.[46]

From late February through to April 1930 the Committee considered Hertzog's Native Representation Bill. A reading of Smuts's notes on these meetings reveals that the early discussions were dominated by debate over such issues as what form the qualified franchise should take, how much representation Africans should be accorded, whether this should take place in the Senate or the Assembly, and how the Cape franchise should be altered.[47] In the welter of detail the fundamental principles underlying the Bill were lost.

On 9 May Hertzog moved that 'the Committee disapproves of the principle of common representation in Parliament for Europeans and natives'.[48] Amendments forwarded by F.S. Malan and J.H. Hofmeyr proposing to retain elements of the common franchise were defeated by 18 votes to 8. Thereafter, Hertzog's original motion was put and passed.[49] 'It was decisive', Nicholls later recorded. 'Never again was there any question raised of retaining the Cape franchise.[50]

The Joint Select Committee reconvened on 14 May, and it was resolved to accept an alternative Representation Bill (forwarded by Heaton Nicholls, with additions by Colonel Stallard, on 2 May) as the basis of discussion.[51] Nicholls's Bill proposed to substitute the existing Cape franchise with African representation in the Senate; and Stallard suggested the creation of a powerful 'Senatorial Grand Committee' – on which Africans would have direct representation – with substantial powers to review and initiate 'native' legislation. He also proposed mechanisms to limit the influx of Africans into the urban areas and to expel any in 'excess of the number required to minister to the wants of the non-native population'.[52] The Nicholls-Stallard scheme remained at the heart of the Committee's deliberations until the advent of Fusion and substantially shaped the character of the 1936 Hertzog legislation.

In his speech to the Select Committee on 2 May 1930 Nicholls sought to devise a native policy which would be 'in consonance with all the modern ideas of native Government in Africa'. He began by proclaiming two fundamental principles which should underwrite African parliamentary representation. These were (i) the need to ensure the 'dominance of the European', and (ii) recognition of 'the native's rights to his own development in such a way as to win his approval'.[53] Nicholls dismissed the Select Committee's deliberations up to that point as 'mere juggling with the representations proposed by the Prime Minister'. They were based neither on 'any logical plan', nor were they 'rooted in any principle' – and would therefore ensure neither white domination nor meet with African approval.[54]

Nicholls attacked James Rose Innes, who championed a non-racial qualified franchise, for 'completely turning his back upon the Bantu as a race, with all its traditions, feelings and customs . . .' The effect of such a policy would be no differentiation of any kind and rapid 'detribalisation', with Africans driven swiftly along 'the road of Europeanisation'.[55] Nicholls argued that the alternative to such a scenario, namely Hertzog's policy of placing Africans on a separate register, was just as illogical. It aimed at the 'democratisation of the native just as surely as the scheme proposed by Rose Innes', because African voters would be set completely apart from their compatriots, thereby creating 'in the minds of the mass a belief in the voter class superiority'.[56] For Nicholls, it was imperative to deny Africans any form of representation in the Assembly, even by means of a quota, since this amounted to a recognition of 'democracy'. Once established, the course of democracy was unstoppable and would ultimately remove 'all obstacles to the political equality of man'.[57]

Nicholls's 'native policy' was rooted in the need to recognise and protect the distinctiveness of a separate 'Bantu ethos' as the basis of a 'Bantu Nation'. It was vital, he said, to 'go back to the native kraal, to the native family, to the tribe, to the tribal council, before we arrive at representation in Parliament'.[58] All Africans – whether 'detribalised', 'civilised' or 'uncivilised' – should be recognised as belonging to the 'mass of the Bantu Nation'. There should therefore be no African voters in the House of Assembly; instead they should be given rights in the Senate, which, by its constitutional nature, was not a 'democratic' institution.[59]

Nicholls recognised that Africans would not be satisfied with the right to elect only four senators who had already been nominated by the government. In order to function as a credible 'Forum of the Nation' it was therefore essential that the Senate be accorded a higher status and that Africans should be directly represented on it.[60] To enhance the attractiveness of his scheme, Nicholls proposed to set aside a large sum of money – some £30 million spread over a number of years – to purchase and develop additional land for Africans. The effect of this financial provision would be 'to create in the native reserves a counter attraction to the lure of the towns', thereby helping to solve the problem of the 'redundant native' in the cities.[61]

Conjointly with his Representation Bill Nicholls proposed a Native Land Development Bill which would empower the governor general to acquire land for communal use by Africans, as well as the establishment of a 'Natives Land Bank' to develop communal or 'tribal' land.[62] When, in 1931, the Committee began work on the Land Bill, Nicholls succeeded in having the first chapter redrafted to incorporate the concept of a 'Native Trust' (adapted from the old 'Natal Native Trust').[63] In a major public statement delivered in 1935 Nicholls described trusteeship as the antithesis of the 'Cape idea of universal Parliamentary democracy' or of 'common citizenship'.[64] Trusteeship envisaged 'areas where native interests will be paramount, where native institutions will have liberty to evolve in consonance with the growth of the native people, and where the indigenous tribal government through chiefs and Councils, modified to suit local needs, must be encouraged and developed'.[65]

Nicholls was careful to disclaim personal responsibility for the formulation of trusteeship ideology, so as to ensure the widest possible political acceptance of its principles. He insisted that 'trusteeship' and 'adaptation' reflected the current policy in all British African states, claiming that it had been the unconscious guiding principle of Sir Theophilus Shepstone in Natal and that it was also present in Transkeian and Transvaal native policy.[66] When a newspaper editorial referred to him as 'Public Omniscient No 1', Nicholls coyly protested that he was thereby 'raised to a pinnacle' far beyond his 'wildest dreams'; he could not claim parentage of the trusteeship doctrine because it had been defined by Hertzog in an address to the Transkeian *Bunga* in 1925, and again by Smuts in his celebrated 1929 Oxford lectures.[67]

Despite these disclaimers, Nicholls's reinterpretation of trusteeship ideology, and the brand of biological racism with which he invested it, were of vital importance in crystallising the ideological character of the Native Bills. Within the SAP contingent on the Joint Select Committee, Nicholls was an outsider and he frequently felt isolated during its sessions. Even when confiding to his wife Ruby, 'I feel I am making history', his confidence was complicated by a sense of embarrassment that he was becoming the darling of the Nationalists and increasingly 'estranged from the Smuts Crowd'.[68] He feared that he was 'making more and more of an enemy of Smuts' on account of the independent position he adopted on the Select Committee.[69] That rift was greatly exacerbated by Nicholls's stand in favour of Natal separatism, for which he was publicly repudiated by Smuts in 1932.[70]

In November 1932 the Joint Select Committee unanimously adopted a Natives Parliamentary Representation Bill (providing for African representation in the Senate) and parts of the Native Trust and Land Bill (only Patrick Duncan dissenting).[71] The acceptance of these measures represented a major victory for the Nicholls-Stallard position, though it was agreed that certain outstanding details required further attention. The Joint Select Committee was reappointed in 1933–4 but it made little progress because of the fundamental restructuring of white parliamentary politics which was then in process.

Coalition talks had begun in early 1933 between the SAP and the Nationalists. The major cause of this initiative was that both parties had been severely weakened as a result of the crippling world depression of 1929–32. With the fragmentation in 1928–9 of its governmental partner, the Labour Party, the Nationalists' parliamentary majority was reduced. Hertzog's stubborn refusal to abandon the Gold Standard until December 1932 prolonged the economic depression in South Africa and further threatened his support base. His problems were exacerbated when Tielman Roos re-entered politics in December 1932, opportunistically demanding that South Africa leave the Gold Standard, in the hope of forming a National Government with himself as leader. Like the Nationalists, the SAP was also experiencing grave difficulties: in Natal, MPs were seeking devolution, while in the Transvaal the Party's rural base demanded reunion with the Nationalists.

To cope with these problems the SAP and the Nationalists formed a coalition in 1933. In the May election of that year they won an overwhelming 136 of 150 seats. In June 1934 they merged, by an act known as 'fusion', to become the South African National Party (subsequently the United Party). Hertzog retained the post of Prime Minister in the new government, with Smuts acting as his deputy and Minister of Justice.[72]

The private discussions held betwen Smuts and Hertzog in 1925–6 and 1928, the 1930–35 Joint Select Committee on the Native Bills, coalition in 1933 and fusion in 1934, have together fuelled speculation that the dramatic *rapprochement* between the two major political parties was part of a covert attempt to get rid of the Cape African franchise. As early as 1928 Lord Olivier wrote to W.M. Macmillan about rumours that Smuts and Hertzog were 'agreeing to reform the Cape franchise into nullity'.[73] And in 1930 the generally well informed *Round Table* suggested that the Joint Select Committee might be 'a treaty between the two European parties to deprive the Bantu of all real substance of political influence'.[74] More recently Marian Lacey has argued that the 1930–5 Joint Select Committee was a secret forum wherein the ruling classes collaborated to sink their differences on the Native Bills in the combined interests of all capitalist sectors.[75]

This assessment is a vast oversimplification of a complex process. Although Lacey is correct when she suggests that 'the idea of scrapping the African vote was widely accepted long before the SAP and NP fused in 1934', it is wrong to infer that the terms of fusion had been settled in advance by the Joint Select Committee.[76] Neither coalition nor fusion were merely convenient pretexts for the passing of the Native Bills. Indeed it was precisely on the issue of a political deal on the 'native question' that the coalition talks came closest to foundering. Whereas Hertzog insisted that the terms of coalition should make explicit reference to the need to abolish the African franchise, Smuts refused, probably because it would have been personally humiliating to renege on his public support of the existing Cape franchise. In the end Hertzog conceded the point, aware that he could afford to allow Smuts to save face without jeopardising his chance of securing a two-thirds majority on the Native Bills. Thus the terms of coalition revealed close agreement on constitutional, economic and general political principles, but on the 'native question' there was only a vague agreement to make an 'earnest effort' to find a solution along lines which guaranteed the paramountcy of 'European civilisation' without depriving Africans of their rights of development.[77]

In sum, while fusion was not predicated on a conspiracy to pass the Native Bills, it did offer an unprecendented opportunity to do so. For the SAP, the emergence of a new governing party meant that the Cape franchise was now dispensable in electoral terms. For the Nationalists, Hertzog's elusive two-thirds majority was finally a real possibility, since the support of those members of the SAP who had hitherto opposed the abolition of the Cape franchise as a matter of party loyalty could now be relied on. By the 1930s segregation was a consensus ideology within white society; to a large extent it was only the ritualised conflict characteristic of the two-party system and the contest for immediate political advantage that kept Nationalists and SAP apart.

6 The Passage of Hertzog's Native Bills, Part Two

1 REACTIONS TO THE SEGREGATION BILLS, 1926–36

From the start Hertzog's Native Bills were extensively discussed within extra-parliamentary political circles. A range of white and African political groupings gave evidence to specially constituted Select Committees, produced memoranda and submitted countless representations to government. Certain common themes are discernible in this plethora of evidence. For the most part the response of the extra-parliamentary opposition was to (i) welcome the Native Council Bill (with amendments), (ii) insist on a more generous land provision for Africans and (iii) reject the proposed abolition of the Cape African franchise. Hertzog was repeatedly asked to abandon his insistence on the interdependence of the Bills so as to consider them on their individual merits. However, segregation was rarely rejected out of hand. Far more often, groups and individuals argued within the parameters of segregationist discourse in the hope of securing an amenable compromise. The stress laid by most political groupings on maintaining responsible dialogue with the government meant that by 1936 very few organisations, either white or black, could claim not to have participated in the segregationist process.

One of the first discussions of the Native Bills took place at the 1925 Native Conference in Pretoria. In the first place the Conference requested Hertzog to drop the clause making the Bills interdependent. The franchise Bill was rejected and the government was requested instead to initiate a 'small beginning' in the way of franchise rights for the northern provinces, while leaving the Cape African franchise intact.[1] The Conference registered strong opposition to the proposed extension of the Land Act to the Cape. It recommended either that the whole country be released from the operation of the Land Act, or else that the Beaumont and 1918 Committee areas be adopted as the minimum areas for exclusive African purchase. Finally, the Conference resolved that the principle of the Native Council Bill be accepted with certain amendments.[2]

149

Consideration of the language and tone of the conference deliberations reveals a somewhat more ambiguous approach to the Native Bills. The proceedings were heavily impregnated with a sense of gratitude that the government had entered into dialogue with African spokesmen, with delegates assuring Hertzog of their 'willingness to cooperate with him in the adjustment of the racial relationship between the Black and White races . . .'[3] This may plausibly be interpreted as a diplomatic effort to manipulate the government by the avoidance of strident language, which might be understood as a direct challenge to its authority. Even so, the force of apparently strong statements was vitiated by political timidity and a pronounced willingness to arrive at a compromise.

A similar tendency is evident in the proceedings of the 1927 Select Committee on the Native Bills.[4] The representatives of the Transkei Native General Council (*Bunga*) began by expressing appreciation of the 'grave responsibility' placed upon their Committee, and recorded their 'earnest desire to find a via media' acceptable both to the government and to their own constituents.[5] On the question of the Land Bill the *Bunga* felt that its whole tenor was 'marked by a tendency to give with one hand and take away with the other'. Any merit it contained was therefore 'nullified by the disabilities it imposes'.[6] The *Bunga*'s representatives were more favourably disposed towards the Council Bill, but wanted an extension of its powers and emphasised that commitment to the principles of the measure could not be construed as a tacit acceptance of the surrender of the franchise.[7] They expressed their absolute and entire opposition to the withdrawal of the Cape franchise, saying that they knew of no precedent in history whereby a government had deprived a section of its law-abiding citizens of their citizenship rights.[8]

In the Cape a number of small, elite organisations, such as the Cape Native Voters' Convention and the Cape Native Rights Protection Association, came out in strong defence of the Cape franchise.[9] These groupings tended to be marginal and politically weak, but their office-holders were often men of considerable personal standing. Prof. D.D.T. Jabavu, who gave evidence to the Select Committee on behalf of the Cape Native Voters' Association, as well as a host of other organisations, was perhaps the best known and most widely respected of these figures. His learned arguments in favour of common citizenship epitomised the universalist aspirations of many of the mission-educated African intelligentsia.

For Jabavu the franchise question resolved itself into a problem

of two competing traditions: 'the historical conflict between the ideals
of the liberal Cape and the inflexible Northern Provinces habituated
to governing the subject races on the principles of so-called
"firmness" '.[10] Jabavu ceaselessly expressed his commitment to the
meritocratic Christian values of the late Victorian era, in which race
was supposedly no criterion for citizenship. He assembled meticulous
and detailed arguments repudiating the position of those who
intended to remove the Cape franchise. Thus he denied, *inter alia*,
that the Cape African vote was a menace to 'European civilisation',
that whites would be swamped by the numerical preponderance
of Africans, that political equality would inevitably lead to 'social
equality', and that the Cape vote was 'obnoxious' because it placed
Cape Africans on a 'higher footing' than their northern compatriots.[11] In considering and rejecting each of these propositions in
turn, Jabavu repeated his central theme that the Cape franchise was
a vital symbol of political equality. It was an unparalleled encouragement for Africans to break free from the forces of 'barbarism' and
join in the march towards 'civilisation'; conversely, removal of the
vote would 'block the progress of those who like to advance and . . .
dam them back to the slough of ignorance'.[12]

Segregation for men like Jabavu, Selope Thema, or Sol Plaatje,
was condemned first and foremost on the grounds that it negated
the universalist principles associated with mid-Victorian liberalism.[13]
However, this perspective was frequently marked by a reluctance,
or inability, to understand the wider threat posed by segregation to
the mass of ordinary Africans. Though Jabavu did address himself
on occasion to more general matters affecting Africans, such as
taxation, wages and living conditions, he concentrated his attention
on defending the rights of a relatively small group of privileged
individuals.[14] His vision primarily reflected the upwardly mobile
aspirations of a Christian 'improving' elite whose ideological roots
were deeply embedded in nineteenth-century liberal ideology.
According to Jabavu,

> Every black man who is a voter has *ipso facto* abandoned the
> position of barbarism. We are ranged on the side of civilization.
> Our interests are interwined with civilized interests. We would not
> like to go back naked to the Kraals and live a barbarous life. We
> have renounced that life once and for all. In fact, if to-day there
> were a war between barbarism and civilization, we would be on
> the side of civilization.[15]

Statements such as these did not always resonate with the demands of the emerging popular classes who, in confronting the harsh realities of capitalist industrialisation, gravitated towards embryonic trade-union organisations like the ICU or sought refuge in the millenarian promises of Africanist and Garveyite thought. In their recent major study of rural politics in the Transkei, Beinart and Bundy draw attention to the complex and contradictory forms in which popular consciousness was expressed. They employ the term 'rural Africanism' to characterise the amalgam of Garveyism, nationalism and independent Christianity which emerged during the 1920s. Rural Africanism was both a manifestation of the reassertion of traditionalist values and an attempt to defend communal resources, as well as a response to a segregationist state which 'no longer rewarded loyalism and progressivism as they once had'.[16] Beinart and Bundy argue further that the implementation of segregation in the Transkei was facilitated by the fact that 'parts of the rural population were formulating demands . . . that actually accorded with some of the new segregatory institutions and policies'. At least some of the wealthiest 'school' families saw in the council system 'a possible avenue to local political power and accumulation', while traditionalist elements would 'support measures to "reserve" rural lands and to entrench communal tenure, and also welcomed the restoration of status to popular representatives of hereditary chiefs'. Thus, among certain agents within the rural areas, 'it was possible for the state to find acquiescence in or support for some of the measures it introduced . . .'[17]

Within the state archives there is substantial evidence of active African support for Hertzog, though it is difficult to evaluate how representative this was. It is uncertain, for instance, whether the telegram from Chief Maitse Moloi to General Hertzog, which read 'Message from Transvaal and Free State chiefs. Away with franchise. Give us Land', was genuinely reflective of a wider constituency, or whether it was merely an isolated instance of rank opportunism.[18] An area requiring further research might look at the extent to which Africanist elements detected in segregation the possibility of special forms of economic and political advance. Consider the case of S.M. Bennet Ncwana, at one time an ICU leader and founder of the newspaper *The Black Man*, and the Rev. James A. Rune of the 'Bantu League of Economic Independence', who expressed gratitude to Hertzog for 'pointing out the way of economic salvation and independence for the Native races of South Africa in his Native

Bills'. The League dismissed the Cape African franchise as 'a mere political farce', explaining,

> We believe that the abolition of the Cape Native vote, for something more substantial, would give our intellectuals nobler opportunities afforded to us by complete segregation of the races . . . wild agitation, intemperate declamation will never get the Natives anywhere. The White man is morally justified in looking after the interest of his own people first. The Native must learn like all other nations to steer his own boat, and not quarrel with other people because they won't look after their interests.[19]

Similar undertones are detectable in the evidence given by Meshach Pelem, a prosperous and influential Eastern Cape figure, to the 1927 Select Committee on the Native Bills. Speaking on behalf of the Bantu Union, though in his personal capacity and without a mandate, Pelem challenged the idea that 'native opinion was unanimous in its sweeping disparagement and condemnation of the Prime Minister's Bills . . .' He personally thought they contained 'some very excellent provisions' and declared himself in favour of segregation in representation, suggesting that Africans could represent their own views in Parliament more effectively than whites.[20] Pelem's views were somewhat contradictory, but they seem to be founded upon the notion that Africans were best advised to take cognisance of the reality of their inferior status, and make the best of whatever openings were available to them.

In his study of African nationalism Peter Walshe describes the ideological tension that existed within the ANC after 1913 on the issue of segregation. He argues that some groups came out strongly against the principle of segregation because it 'ran counter to what was seen as the whole tradition of Victorian Government in South Africa'. Others accepted the necessity of defined rural areas, though wishing this to go 'hand in hand with common political institutions', while a third approach 'involved theoretical acceptance of territorial segregation but a concomitant realisation that no just solution was available on these lines'.[21] Walshe claims that the ANC's opposition to segregation solidified during the 1920s in reaction to the unfolding of Hertzog's Native Bills. But even during this, its most radical period until the 1940s, the organisation's rejection of segregation was less than resolute.

At its 1926 Bloemfontein Convention the ANC, probably influenced by the speech of Clements Kadalie, the specially invited ICU representative, declared itself 'opposed to any form of segregation', resolved to ignore the annual government conference in Pretoria, demanded an extension of the Cape African franchise thoughout the Union, and called for a round-table conference with the government.[22] This militancy was carried through to the 1927 Select Committee, where the tone and language employed by the Congress representatives was equally forthright. President Z.R. Mahabane went further than most other African groups in expressing opposition to the Native Bills, declaring that it was the 'decided view' of the ANC that both the Native Council and Representation Bills should be dropped. It was preferable to abandon plans to extend political rights to Africans in the northern provinces than to tamper with the existing Cape franchise.[23]

Mahabane's calls for a universal (presumably male) education-based qualified franchise throughout the Union; his suggestion that it would be best to return to the system of land tenure prior to 1913; and his proposal for the convening of a round table conference (where there would be a free exchange of views between whites and blacks) to settle the land franchise questions, were radical demands by the standards of the day.[24] But, despite this forthright approach, Mahabane did not entirely break with the concept of segregation itself. He did not present universal adult male suffrage as a non-negotiable position, nor did he dismiss the idea of territorial segregation out of hand. On the contrary, he repeated a suggestion made in 1923 that he would be amenable to segregation subject to the land being divided equally between white and black.[25] Some years later Pixley Seme, the conservative President of the ANC, reiterated these sentiments when he stated that a 'fair distribution of land' within which Africans could 'develop' would 'go a long way towards solving our trouble'.[26]

Colin Bundy points out that once the fact of territorial segregation had been established in the 1913 Land Act, the ANC sought to 'amend the terms of land allocation rather than dispute the principle'. Similarly, the ANC's hostility to the Land Act during the 1920s continued to be expressed in terms of the inadequacy of its provisions. Bundy observes that this 'somewhat abstract commitment to an ultimately satisfactory allocation of land was not easily translated into support for rural movements concerned with the immediate burdens of stock dipping, evictions, higher rents, declining market opportunities and the like'.[27] But the urban-based ANC leadership, concerned above all with access to civil and political rights, largely failed to integrate organised opposition to segregation with the trajectory of rural resistance movements. Thus the opportunity to build a popular campaign based on bread-and-butter issues against Hertzogite segregation was missed.

Aside from the ANC the only African organisation which appeared to reject the Native Bills completely was the ICU. In 1927 its leader, Clements Kadalie, forwarded to Hertzog a number of resolutions on the government's native policy which were 'unanimously adopted' by all branches of the organisation.[28] The proposed legislation was condemned because it refused Africans any real participation in government within the land of their birth, it discouraged the progress of 'the more enlightened section of the people' and it would inaugurate, through forced labour conditions, 'a fresh era of slavery'.[29] The ICU therefore resolved to oppose the Native Bills 'strenuously and unconditionally' and requested Hertzog to drop his proposals 'in *TOTO*'.[30] Yet even this unequivocal stand did not constitute a total break with segregation. For example, the detailed ICU resolutions called for the allocation of territories 'specifically for native occupation' as well as the extension of the franchise throughout the Union with considerably raised qualifications.[31] Clements Kadalie had himself made political overtures to Hertzog in 1921 and again in 1924.[32] It was probably the hope that segregation would entail a more equitable division of the country (as well as disillusionment with the SAP) which led him to support Hertzog publicly in the 1924 election and to declare that 'segregation was natural'.[33]

Mainstream liberal political thought was represented by the Joint Councils of Europeans and Natives and its umbrella organisation, the South African Institute of Race Relations. This organisational network played a key role in orchestrating opposition to the Native Bills through a process of insistent, but non-confrontationary, lobbying. The Joint Councils owe their immediate origin to the visit to South Africa in 1921 of the Rev. Thomas Jesse Jones and Dr James K. Aggrey on behalf of the Phelps-Stokes Commission of Enquiry to Africa. As champions of Booker T. Washington's methods in the American South, they preached a conservative ideology of moderation, gradual reform, political compromise and Christian moral uplift. In South Africa the Phelps-Stokes Commission worked closely with C.T. Loram and Rheinallt Jones, and they persuaded Howard Pim, then President of the Johannesburg Native Welfare Society, of the need to include both blacks and whites in a single organisation. As a result, the first Joint Council of Europeans and Natives was established in Johannesburg in 1921. Within a decade some twenty-six Joint Councils had been formed in towns and cities throughout South Africa.

The Joint Councils' primary interest was in matters concerning social welfare. But they also attempted, through a process of discussion and research, to 'build bridges' between whites and blacks, on the one hand, and influence government policies, on the other. In the absence of statutory bodies which could effectively mediate between whites and blacks, the politically centrist Joint Councils occupied a special position. Their members comprised prominent liberal professionals, African politicians, academics, churchmen and welfare workers, who were dedicated to the fostering of inter-racial 'understanding' and gradual political reform. Richard Elphick has rightly drawn attention to the Christian and international mission framework into which inter-war liberalism was locked, suggestively referring to this network as 'the benevolent empire'.[34] In 1929 an attempt was made to establish a single institution to coordinate the activities of the Joint Councils throughout South Africa. With funding from the Phelps-Stokes Foundation and the Carnegie Corporation, this emerged as the South African Institute of Race Relations (SAIRR).[35]

In 1927 the influential Johannesburg Joint Council published two lengthy memoranda on the Hertzog Bills.[36] Like the Joint Council/SAIRR publications which followed, these memoranda placed a premium on sound logic and empirical accuracy in their detailed analysis of the proposed legislation. While adopting a critical standpoint, the Joint Councils' publications were conceived of as 'positive' contributions to the political debate. Much emphasis was therefore placed on the proposal of 'constructive alternatives' to the Bills, rather than rejecting them out of hand.

In 1927 W.M. Macmillan, R.V. Selope Thema and Howard Pim gave evidence to the Native Bills Select Committee on behalf of the Johannesburg Joint Council. The Council devoted the bulk of its attention to the Land Bill. To a considerable extent this reflected the fact that in 1927 many liberals remained ambivalent about the utility of the non-racial franchise and retained a considerable sympathy towards some form of equitable territorial separation. The essence of the Council's criticisms was that the Land Bill departed from the principle of the 1913 Act by proposing to throw open the released areas to competitive purchase. It therefore urged that an amount of land equivalent at least to the extent of the 1918 Committee areas should be set aside for exclusive use by Africans; it would be their *'minimum security'*.[37]

The Johannesburg Joint Council also suggested a number of 'constructive' alternatives to the Land Bill's provisions. Its major proposal was to allow African squatters and tenants to lease land in white areas, noting that this did not necessarily mean the abandonment of segregation. Leasehold tenure would encourage both the development of wage labour and the emergence of 'progressive native farming'.[38] Macmillan spoke of the need to create 'two different classes of natives, that is, the essential labourer who lives in [the] reserves and goes out to labour, and the native who will live on leasehold tenure'.[39] The concept of leasehold tenure in the released areas, which was frequently compared with the development of the crofting system in Scotland, was for a number of liberal commentators an attractive proposition. It was presented as a highly flexible policy which would afford security to Africans, allow a measure of segregation, and facilitate African advancement at one and the same time. Not only would leasing help to solve the land problem, but it would provide concrete opportunities for an improving class of African cultivators. Moreover, raising the efficiency of African agriculture would in turn provide a necessary boost to the national dividend.

The Johannesburg Joint Council also proposed complementary measures to facilitate the economic development of the reserves more generally. It recommended the establishment of a central Land Board to govern the demarcation and acquisition of land, as well as the creation of a 'Native Bank' which would provide finance for land purchase and permanent improvements, such as fencing, irrigation and housing. Other development projects embracing agricultural shows, education and training were also advanced.[40] A comprehensive policy along these lines would 'promote the progress of the native people in civilisation, and thereby make them better fellow-citizens of the White people'.[41]

On the issue of the franchise, and to a lesser extent the Council Bills, the Joint Councils were ambivalent. The Johannesburg Joint Council took the view, as expressed by Howard Pim, that while it was not in favour of differential political treatment for Africans, partial and differential representation might be necessary in the interim.[42] But the Pretoria Joint Council, under the leadership of

Edgar Brookes, James Lang and Frederick Livie-Noble, declared itself in favour of the principle of the Representation Bill, provided that an adequate *quid pro quo* for the abolition of the Cape franchise was provided.[43] In general the Joint Councils supported the Cape African franchise (and ultimately its expansion) during this period, on the grounds that Africans had never abused their voting rights, that there was no evidence to support the notion of a 'native menace', and that the existence of the Cape franchise was widely regarded by Africans as the 'touchstone' of good faith on the part of whites.[44] But they failed to commit themselves to an unequivocal statement of principle on the matter. In part this was due to the fact that many of their most prominent members, e.g. Edgar Brookes, Rheinallt Jones and Howard Pim, had in the recent past been partly responsible for the formulation of segregationist ideas. Moreover, the Councils were pragmatic in their attempt to steer clear of outright political confrontation with the government.

In their attempt to maintain a low profile and to increase their influence the Joint Councils often sought to work through other groups. One of the best illustrations of this strategy was the series of European-Bantu conferences which were convened during the 1920s and 1930s under the auspices of the Dutch Reformed Church. Black and white members of the Joint Councils formed the core element at these conferences, although the attendance of various Christian, Afrikaner and government delegates lent a more representative feeling to the proceedings. Segregation was explicitly discussed at the first DRC Conference held in 1923. Edgar Brookes proposed a resolution in favour of the 'differential development of the Bantu, so far as differentiation is based on Bantu traditions and requirements, and is not used as a means of repression'. But the resolution does not appear to have been voted on.[45] At the 1927 European-Bantu Conference the Native Bills emerged as a major point of discussion. The occasion proved to be an important moment in the developing liberal critique of segregation and the exposure of differential development as a myth: one of the major resolutions declared that the cooperation of both blacks and whites was 'necessary for the material welfare and progress of South Africa' since they were 'comprised in the same economic system'.[46] But resolutions were also passed expressing qualified support for the Land and Council Bills, subject to certain amendments.[47] Press reports on the Conference were generally favourable and spoke enthusiastically of a remarkable display of unanimity on most issues. On the question of the franchise, however, no resolution was arrived at, and the Conference was reported to be 'hopelessly divided '.[48]

The political moderation and welfarist orientation of liberals grouped around the Joint Councils may be contrasted with an older strand of liberalism often associated with the nineteenth-century Cape. In 1929 Sir James Rose Innes, together with such other noted Cape liberals as Henry Burton, J.W. Jagger and Sir Clarkson Tredgold, founded the Non-Racial Franchise Association (NRFA). These men had all played prominent roles in public life and were strongly committed to upholding entrenched constitutional principles.[49] For the most part they exemplified the remnants of what Stanley Trapido has referred to as the 'great tradition' of Cape liberalism. Together with similar organizations, such as the Cape Native Franchise Vigilance Committee and the National Franchise League, the NRFA focused its attentions almost exclusively on the question of the franchise. Its declared objects were to resist any differentiation of franchise rights on the grounds of colour and to make a 'civilisation test' the sole criterion of eligibility for the franchise. But there was an important rider to this declaration: if fears of black domination proved real, the franchise qualification could always be raised.[50]

Unlike those liberals who had been influenced by the cultural relativism of contemporary anthropological thought, the NRFA had no doubts about the universality of western civilisation. For Rose Innes the 'ideals of freedom and justice and ordered government for which the white man stands' should unquestionably prevail. In fact he believed that those standards would be most effectively maintained by 'admitting every race to our policy so far as it is civilised'.[51] This was the authentic voice of nineteenth-century Cape liberalism, with its confident belief in the capacity, indeed the advisability, of colonial societies to incorporate individual Africans into its social and political hierarchy.

The NRFA's belief in the value of common citizenship was unyielding. It defended the Cape franchise on the grounds that Africans had never abused the vote and that it was fundamentally unjust to tamper with entrenched constitutional rights. Implicit in these beliefs was the notion that traditional liberal values constituted the best guarantee of social order: the dangerous possibility that class might become identified with race would be diminished by the inclusion of 'civilised' Africans within the white body politic. As

J.W. Jagger noted, 'there is wisdom in providing a safety value [sic], in allowing a free outlet for the expression of opinion'.[52]

The patrician liberals of the NRFA were never able to command significant influence, partly because they were something of an anachronism, but also because their support was mainly confined to the Cape. Described by Ross Frames as 'extinct South African Party volcanoes', they are mostly noteworthy for the way in which they challenged the political pragmatism of the SAP and the Joint Council movement.[53] In 1929, for example, the NRFA refused to meet the SAP to discuss opposition to the Native Bills, explaining that they were a non-party body devoted to 'spreading the gospel' of the common franchise. The NRFA was convinced that it should 'not appear to weaken by one iota' from its policies – there would be time enough to accept compromises 'when we find the big thing cannot be got'.[54] Indeed the NRFA publicly challenged Smuts to clarify his views on the franchise question during the 1929 election campaign, declaring that the country was 'bewildered'.[55] In private Henry Burton confessed that he actually feared a SAP return to power even more than the Nationalists, for whereas Hertzog 'would simply plunge along with his bills again and be defeated', Smuts might hold his promised national convention and concede 'goodness only knows what compromises . . .'[56] As it turned out, the Nationalists made substantial political capital through representing the NRFA's stand on the franchise as official SAP policy; on the eve of his 1929 electoral defeat Smuts complained bitterly that the NRFA's manifestos had 'been a godsend to Hertzog'.[57]

From 1930 to 1935 when the Native Bills were being secretly discussed by the parliamentary Joint Select Committee, the intensity of public opposition to segregation declined. During these years much of the extra-parliamentary protest was characterised by confusion and personal recrimination. The failure of opposition groups to agree on a united plan of action, their inability to formulate unequivocal demands, and the general lack of knowledge about the Joint Select Committee's private deliberations, were all contributory factors. Despite their apparent renunciation of segregation in the late 1920s, liberal groupings still clung to the illusion that patient, responsible and discreet political lobbying would ultimately secure an acceptable compromise. Hancock draws attention to the timidity of liberal protest, noting that many defenders of the Cape franchise frequently argued that the franchise made no difference, and would never be allowed to make a difference, to white political supremacy.

'A liberalism so lacking in self-confidence could not inspire a strong fighting spirit: in substance it had capitulated to its enemies before the battle opened.'[58]

By the late 1920s the focus of liberal attention began to shift from a consideration of the land question to the issue of the franchise. This reflected both a growing disillusionment with Hertzog's segregationist vision and a reaction to the principled challenge posed by the NRFA. Nevertheless, most liberals grouped within the SAIRR and Joint Council network remained willing to arrive at some sort of political accommodation with the government. As a result there was a yawning disparity between their private and public statements, and accusations of betrayal were frequently traded back and forth.

In 1928 it appeared that the Joint Councils and the SAIRR were about to confirm their position in favour of the retention of the Cape franchise. Rheinallt Jones, one of the leading tacticians of the SAIRR, wrote an article in *The South African Outlook* in which he argued that once the central principle of common citizenship was abandoned, 'we are forced into a quagmire of difficulties'. The force of this statement was somewhat weakened, however, by his qualification that the Cape franchise would be defended 'until the country offers some other alternative that does not endanger the status of the Bantu people and the safety of the State'.[59]

In the same year the Johannesburg Joint Council published a pamphlet expressing explicit support for the Cape franchise.[60] But this public commitment was brought into question in January 1930 when Rheinallt Jones submitted a confidential memorandum to the Council movement. Noting the 'distinct feeling' amongst SAP supporters in Natal and the Cape that Smuts 'should be pressed to take a more active line' in support of the Franchise Bill, and also that Hertzog might well secure his parliamentary majority, Jones argued that the opponents of the Bill should organise closely and effectively. He suggested that discussion on a 'second line of defence' should be continued, though with the 'utmost secrecy to avoid any suggestion of a weakening of our forces'. The central principle of a common franchise, he said, should be upheld until 'the time is right' to put forward constructive alternatives.[61]

This notion of a 'second line of defence' remained the sub-text of much liberal pronouncement in favour of the common franchise. It was criticised by James Rose Innes, who informed Jones that it was impossible for him 'at any stage of the struggle which is yet in sight to advise the natives to make the best of things and save something out of the wreck'. That time might come, but in the mean time the wise course was to 'stand upon the principle of no colour differentiation'.[62]

Like Rheinallt Jones, Edgar Brookes, though renouncing segregation after 1927, remained constantly on the lookout to play the honest broker and secure a compromise. In 1929, noting the dissension within the SAP and the possibility that Hertzog was only some fifteen votes short of a two-thirds majority, he advised Pim not to ask the SAP to 'nail their colours to the mast of the Cape franchise at the present juncture'. Claiming to have been in close touch with Hofmeyr on the matter – Hofmeyr apparently discussed it with Smuts – he suggested that the franchise be played down so as to ensure an 'adequate equivalent'.[63] Brookes followed this up in 1930 with a series of four articles published in the *Cape Times*. He proposed a compromise solution to the franchise question based on a highly complex scheme whereby 'the mass of natives' would be given separate representation in the Senate, while 'those few who can really be called civilised' would be accommodated on a common register.[64]

In June 1928 the Eastern Cape missionary publication *The South African Outlook*, under the editorship of J.T. Henderson, came out in favour of a differential franchise roll for whites and blacks.[65] This provocative piece unleashed a flurry of protest in the journal's columns, largely organised by Rheinallt Jones, with Howard Pim, Selope Thema and Jones himself rallying to the defence of the common franchise.[66] One of the most prominent respondents was the respected African leader D.D.T. Jabavu, who claimed, not entirely convincingly, that the attitude of the 'whole Bantu intelligent population' was unanimous in its determination to leave the Cape franchise untouched.[67] Only 2 years later, however, Jabavu was himself accused of having been prepared to compromise the franchise.

At the 1930 Pretoria Native Conference Heaton Nicholls and J.S. Marwick, both of whom were SAP members of the Joint Select Committee from Natal, called Jabavu aside for a 'private talk'. Reportedly they told him that the Joint Select Committee had virtually reached agreement on the Native Bills. They urged Jabavu to agree to the proposal that Parliament would vote £30 million for native land and development on the basis that this would be the last chance to secure such a large-scale concession.[68] Nicholls subsequently attempted to use this conversation as evidence that the African leadership was prepared to compromise on the Native Bills.

Rheinallt Jones wrote to Jabavu in March 1931 informing him that the private conversation with Nicholls and Marwick was 'known to others' and that it could be used to the disadvantage of Jabavu and his cause.[69] On Jones's advice Jabavu wrote to J.H. Hofmeyr to scotch rumours of any compromise, so that Hofmeyr could convey this information to the Joint Select Committee. Jabavu therefore assured Hofmeyr that he had totally rejected the Nicholls-Marwick offer and that he preferred 'to die holding the fort of non-discrimination beween citizens on grounds of race alone until the forces of Christianity, justice and civilisation become strong enough to overpower mutual suspicion'.[70]

Heaton Nicholls enjoyed more success in his attempt to draw African support for his trusteeship bribe when he approached the veteran Natal leader John Dube. In 1931 Nicholls wrote to Dube outlining the proposals he had made to the Select Committee to 'build up a real native economy in the Native Reserves' and to substitute the Cape franchise for a uniform system of senatorial representation. He asked Dube to report on African opinion throughout the Union for the benefit of the Select Committee.[71] Dube undertook to travel to Johannesburg, Kimberley, Bloemfontein, the Transkei and Ciskei. He reported that 'all the leaders in the Transkei' were prepared to accede to a compromise, saying that 'land and development measures are more acceptable to them than the vote'. In the Ciskei Meshach Pelem was apparently prepared to compromise. Dube even suggested that 'Jabavu himself would be willing' were it not for his fear that he would encounter opposition and thereby 'lose his influence'.[72] In a further document Dube claimed to have procured the signatures of Chief Gilbert Majozi and W.W. Ndhlovu in Natal, R.V. Selope Thema and H. Selby Msimang in the Transvaal as well as T. Mapikela and E.K. Royne of the OFS, in support of a compromise solution.[73]

Dube's claims are partially corroborated elsewhere. In a letter to Jabavu Rheinallt Jones claimed that Selope Thema had admitted to having signed an acceptance of the Nicholls-Marwick proposals together with Selby Msimang and a number of others. Jones accused Thema of 'a grave betrayal of the interests of the Bantu' and 'a most unfriendly action' towards those whites who had 'stood by the Bantu on the question of the common franchise'. When told what use was being made of his signature, Thema was reported to be 'generally

distressed'.[74] Jabavu's response to Rheinallt Jones gave no indication
that he too might have been sympathetic to Dube's approaches. On
the contrary, he declared that Dube had no authority to 'cadge
for Cape signatures', noting that the whole business of confidential
discussions was a 'confidence trick'. But he acknowledged that 'the
enemy' had 'got the better of us because we are now divided into
two camps . . .'[75]

The significance of these intrigues lies in the extent to which
many of the most prominent defenders of African political rights –
Brookes, Rheinallt Jones, Jabavu, Selope Thema, John Dube,
etc. – were at various times accused, as often as not by each other,
of having been prepared to abandon the Cape franchise. While they
upheld the principle of common citizenship and rejected Hertzogite
segregation in public, privately they took part in a succession of
clandestine attempts to secure what they considered to be a reasonable compromise. Having abandoned the principled stance adopted
by such organisations as the NRFA, other groups opposed to segregation waited for the most propitious moment at which to arrive at
a political settlement. But on account of their manifest inability to
agree on the timing of such an accord, their ranks were left danger-
ously divided.

In April 1935 the Joint Select Committee reported for the last
time and presented the Representation and Land Bills to Parliament.[76] From this moment, and until their consideration by Parliament in February 1936, public debate intensified markedly. Z.R.
Mahabane, A.B. Xuma and Selope Thema immediately began planning a broadly representative national convention of African leaders.
In December 1935 over 400 delegates converged in Bloemfontein to
inaugurate the All-African Convention (AAC). Prof. D.D.T. Jabavu
was elected President and Dr Xuma Vice-President. The AAC functioned as a political forum rather than an organization, and its 1935
meeting was perhaps the most representative gathering of African
political figures ever convened.[77]

A series of strong resolutions were carried at Bloemfontein by a
convincing majority. The Convention rejected the concept of
trusteeship, arguing that the inextricable interdependence of all races
implied that only the 'adoption of a policy of political identity' would
ensure the ultimate creation of one South African nation.[78] It opposed
the abolition of the Cape franchise and went so far as to demand
the immediate granting of franchise rights to Africans throughout
the Union, subject, if necessary, to some form of 'civilization test'.[79]

The proposed Union Representative Council was rejected, since it was intended as a substitute for the existing Cape African franchise.[80] At the next day's meeting of the AAC Z.R. Mahabane predicted that the 'trend of native legislation' was going to lead to 'revolution' in South Africa.[81] A resolution welcoming the establishment of a 'Native Trust' was passed, though it criticised the 'gross inadequacy' of land set aside for African occupation.[82] A further resolution stated that the Convention could be called together again should any 'emergency' arise with respect to the draft Segregation Bills.[83]

Meanwhile, other attempts were being made to mobilise opposition to the draft Bills. Rheinallt Jones and Alfred Hoernlé of the SAIRR approached the government in an attempt to postpone the introduction of the measures to Parliament. Noting that the annual Native Conferences in Pretoria had lapsed, they asked Richard Stuttaford, the acting Minister of Native Affairs, and D.L. Smit, Herbst's successor as SNA, to consider convening a special conference at which the government could present the Bills to African representatives.[84] Stuttaford and Smit agreed with the principle of explaining the proposed legislation, but expressed their preference for a system of 'sectional conferences' to a single 'Union-wide' conference, which 'would include certain obnoxious "agitators" '.[85]

Five such regional conferences were held under the government's auspices in September 1935. Their conclusions were not entirely uniform. Nevertheless, familiar resolutions were passed in defence of the Cape franchise, extending a cautious welcome to the proposed Natives' Representative Council, and calling for the provision of additional land. All the conferences requested that the government postpone the introduction of the Bills, pending their translation into the vernacular and the summoning of a further Union conference. Reviewing the series of conferences, the *Cape Times* commented that their 'outstanding feature [was] that they did not categorically reject the Bills with that contumely and scorn that was prophesied in some quarters'.[86] Whereas Cape Africans concentrated on the franchise issue, in other areas the Bills met with greater receptiveness. The Maritzburg conference of Zulu leaders appeared to accept the proposed Representative Council in place of representation in the Senate and failed to condemn the abolition of the Cape Franchise.[87]

Throughout this period the SAIRR and the Joint Council movement kept exceptionally busy, mobilising whatever opposition to the Segregation Bills it could. In August 1935 the Institute published a lengthy description and analysis of the Bills, which explained their workings clause by clause.[88] Typically, it was intended to be 'as impartial and objective as possible' and to serve as the basis of future public criticism.[89] The Institute's activities received a major boost with the anonymous donation (from a Colonel Donaldson) of £500 for the purposes of preparing propaganda against the Native Bills. Two Continuation Committees were established in Cape Town and Johannesburg to organise the campaign against the abolition of the franchise. In January 1936 a large 'European-Bantu Conference' was convened in Cape Town under the auspices of the Joint Councils at which some forty organisations were represented. Sir James Rose Innes delivered the key-note address and proposed a motion which declared that the abolition of the Cape franchise was 'an unmerited and flagrant injustice to the interest of South Africa'.[90] The SAIRR was in one way or another a leading agent in all these initiatives, though it was anxious not to be seen as the source of all protest. But, through various satellite organs, it kept up a steady stream of letters and pamphlets, lobbying MPs, newspapers and prominent individuals.[91]

2 THE 1936 'COMPROMISE' AND THE ENACTMENT OF THE NATIVE BILLS

The climax of this drawn-out process was the controversial 'compromise' of 1936. Following the meeting in Bloemfontein of the AAC in December 1935, a deputation under Jabavu was sent to Cape Town where it met Hertzog on a number of occasions. At one of these meetings, in early February, Hertzog indicated that he was prepared to make fundamental changes to the Representation Bill, providing that the AAC would agree that 'a change in the present system is necessary'.[92] This dramatic offer presented the AAC with a new set of options. Jabavu and Msimang felt unable to accept the compromise offer without a mandate, and a meeting of the entire AAC executive was therefore summoned.

There was wide speculation that Jabavu and others were about to capitulate on the principle of the non-racial franchise, which the AAC had been so firm about at its inaugural meeting just a few weeks before. Rheinallt Jones reported from Cape Town that 'the Natives were weakening on the vote question'.[93] In the Transvaal the *Rand Daily Mail* suggested that the new proposals were about to be accepted by the AAC 'with some of whose leading members the proposed compromise was framed'.[94] Hoernlé, Ramsbottom and Schreiner sent a telegram to Cape Town expressing disbelief at the possibility that 'Natives seriously contemplate any such compromise'. A cable from Ballinger to Xuma read, 'No Compromise Dont let your European Friends Down Africans also anxious'.[95]

On 12 February the augmented AAC executive met Hertzog to discuss the compromise, but they failed to reach an immediate decision. After a tense few days of discussion, and amid much public speculation, the AAC formally presented its reply to Hertzog on Saturday, 15 February. Its unanimous decison declared that the Convention 'would not bargain or compromise with the political citizenship of the African people by sacrificing the franchise . . .' Common citizenship alone was acceptable.[96]

Despite the AAC's ultimate rejection of Hertzog's offer, a great deal of controversy surrounded the negotiations, particularly with regard to Jabavu's role in the affair. In Parliament Hertzog disclaimed responsibility for the compromise, while Smuts suggested that the proposals derived originally from the AAC itself.[97] The most probable explanation is that the idea of a compromise originated during informal discussions between Jabavu and a group of Eastern Cape MPs in early February. A further meeting was arranged between the MPs and members of the Cape AAC delegation on 7 February. According to Alfred Payn, one of the Eastern Cape MPs party to the negotiations, the AAC representatives 'wholeheartedly gave their support to the proposed compromise . . .'[98] During the recriminations which followed the Eastern Cape MPs insisted that it was Jabavu who initiated contact with them and that they had acted in good faith in supporting the compromise along the lines suggested by the AAC delegation.[99] Jabavu's version of the events differs slightly, in that he denied having suggested the terms of a settlement to the MPs. He also denied having proposed the compromise to Hertzog, claiming that the suggestions originated from Hertzog himself, who wished the AAC to 'accept paternal responsibility' for them. This the AAC Committee refused to do.[100]

It seems certain that Jabavu *did* inform the Eastern Cape MPs at their first meeting that he remained opposed to the abolition of the Cape franchise. He qualified this, however, by saying that, were the principle of common representation defeated in Parliament, the MPs 'would be doing a service' if they were able to retain the individual vote in the Cape.[101] This rather ambiguous statement appears to have been the source of the subsequent confusion. It is likely that Jabavu and the AAC delegation were initially sympathetic to some form of settlement, but that they distanced themselves later when its practical implications became clearer. For their part, the MPs understood Jabavu to be fully supportive of a compromise and they subsequently became committed to it themselves as a means of resolving the franchise issue.[102]

Despite their public rejection of the compromise, similar fractures are evident within the white liberal community. Thus Edgar Brookes made a 'provisional' decision not to reject the compromise, while Alfred Hoernlé admitted that the suggested alternative seemed to 'have merits'.[103] By contrast, O.D. Schreiner and Ramsbottom were 'not in the least inclined to bother their heads' about amendments to the compromise Franchise Bill, believing that once the Cape Franchise was lost, it made little difference whether the Act was 'a little better or worse'.[104]

The final Joint Sitting of both Houses of Parliament had just convened to enact the Native Bills when the AAC delegation declined Hertzog's offer of a compromise. But on 17 February Hertzog announced to an astonished Parliament that he would discard the Representation Bill in any case and replace it with a new measure embodying the compromise. According to the *Cape Times*, Hertzog's announcement was met with 'a gasp of surprise, followed by cheering'.[105] The new measure, which was referred to as Bill No. 2, purported to save the individual Cape franchise by transferring existing African voters on to a special register. These voters 'would be entitled to elect three members to the House of Assembly'.[106] It seemed that the arduous work of the Select Committee was to be ignored, as the new Bill was in many respects similar to the long-abandoned measure of 1929.

It is not clear why the Representation Bill was altered at the last moment; Hertzog himself admitted that he was more in favour of Bill No 1. Moreover, many believed that he would have attained a two-thirds majority without any changes to the 1935 Bill, which had been produced by the Joint Select Committee. The most plausible explanation is provided by Patrick Duncan, who believed that the compromise was intended to attract the support of 'Cape members and of a large section of the public, including natives'. Without the support of Malan's Purified National Party, Duncan feared that Hertzog might fail to attain the necessary majority. This would have precipitated a major political crisis and the United Party would have had to go to the country 'completely divided'.[107]

Hertzog's last-minute concession had the intended effect of persuading many opponents of the Bill to give it their support. The *Cape Times*, which generally took a centrist SAP position, welcomed the compromise with some relief. After paying lip-service to the principle of common citizenship, it suggested that 'the Cape Native vote had reached a dead end'. In the context of the 'generally liberal nature' of the provisions of the Land and Representation Bills and the unprecedented opportunities for Africans to 'work out their destiny under the white man's guidance', it concluded that 'the faith which animates the bills' might ultimately be far more valuable to Africans 'than the fading glamour of the Cape native franchise'.[108]

The new Bill departed from the Nicholls-Stallard measure's stress on the necessity to abolish the 'democratic' Cape franchise and to restrict African representation to the Senate alone. The alteration was bitterly resented by Nicholls, who later claimed that Parliament was 'bull-dozed by a back-stairs intrigue with Cape members'.[109] Nicholls kept relatively quiet during the proceedings of the 1936 Joint Sitting, though he swallowed his pride and voted with the government.[110] Stallard actually voted against the government on the grounds that the principle of the Senatorial Grand Committee had been abandoned; however, it is likely that this decision had at least as much to do with the fact that he had left the SAP in 1934 to form the opposition Dominion Party.

Debate during the lengthy 1936 Joint Sitting was, for the most part, unremarkable. Malan's Nationalists steadfastly opposed the new Bill on the grounds that it departed from essential segregationist principles, though indicating that they might have supported Hertzog had he stuck with the original measure. Smuts joined the debate on 27 February. Having opposed the Representation Bill through most stages of the Joint Select Committee, he now welcomed the compromise as a reasonable settlement. While perhaps not ideal in all respects, he believed it to be a fair solution of the Cape franchise problem and of 'native policy' as a whole.[111] For those ex-SAP MPs who remained equivocal, Smuts's endorsement of the new Bill proved decisive; they took their lead from him and elected to support it.[112]

Perhaps the most famous speech was delivered by J.H. Hofmeyr. During the third reading of the Representation Bill he stood up and refused to vote with his cabinet colleagues in its support, protesting that the Bill had become steadily more retrogressive since it was first introduced in 1926.[113] Hofmeyr emphasised the injustice of removing the entrenched constitutional rights of Africans, adding, however, that he did not 'necessarily stand or fall by the ideal of common citizenship as an absolute thing'.[114] The 'fear of race mixture and miscegenation', he continued, was largely unreasoning and illogical.[115]

Largely through the efforts of Alan Paton, Hofmeyr has entered the pantheon of South Africa's liberal mythology. We are told that his words had the effect of turning 'despondency into resolution' and that his 'great speech' represented a brilliant triumph of the liberal spirit; it was an affirmation of values which history would condone.[116] Phyllis Lewsen remarks on Hofmeyr's 'brilliant speech opposing any curtailment of the voting right cherished by Africans'.[117]

In reality Hofmeyr's speech was more remarkable for the fact that it ran counter to so many of his earlier statements on the franchise question. If it was representative of inter-war liberal thought, this was simply in virtue of its vacillating inconsistency. In 1929, for example, Hofmeyr delivered a speech at Rivonia where he was reported to have endorsed segregation. This was followed by a letter to a Dr F. Stohr in which he argued that the only way to prevent the government attaining their two-thirds majority was to re-establish a 'spirit of cooperation', and he suggested that, as a basis of further discussion, the SAP should indicate that it was 'not wedded to the Cape Native Franchise *on its present basis*'.[118] Significantly, Hofmeyr had proposed to the 1930 Joint Select Committee that the common franchise should be restricted to the Cape and that the number of Africans on the Cape voters' roll should never exceed one-tenth of the total.[119] Furthermore, he had supported the 1936 Representation Bill at its first reading.

Hofmeyr's defiant speech in 1936 was thus something of a departure from his original position. There can be no denying that it was courageous, for, in opposing both Hertzog and Smuts, his loyalty to the government was called sharply into question. The burden of Hofmeyr's 1936 speech was that it was wrong to deprive Africans of a constitutionally entrenched right, yet he did not commit himself to a positive affirmation of common citizenship. In 1936 Hofmeyr was still temperamentally inclined towards a policy of 'constructive segregation', though he believed that this was no longer practical in the light of the unwillingness of whites to make the necessary 'sacrifice' in terms of land and labour which was demanded of them. [120]

It remains to be said that probably the only prominent member of the SAP and Joint Select Committee who consistently stood by traditional Cape liberal principles was the veteran politician F.S. Malan. Indeed *Imvo* declared that Malan would 'go down in history as the only voice that cried in the wilderness against the massacre of Cape Native political rights', a sentiment which was echoed by Alfred Hoernlé and the historian Eric Walker.[121]

3 CONCLUSION

It is striking how much the rhetoric of those wishing to remove the Cape African vote changed over the years. Initially Hertzog's scheme for segregation was firmly predicated on the idea that within 50 years white voters would be 'swamped' by a rapidly increasing African electorate. These fears were fuelled by the prevailing climate of social Darwinism, which made it easy to blur any strong distinction between common citizenship, 'swamping' at the polls, the 'rising tide' of nationalism, and 'miscegenation'.

The response of Hertzog's critics was to demonstrate that his projections were wholly unsupported by the facts concerning the proportion of African to white voters.[122] After 1929 the notion of a proportionate increase in African vote became even more implausible. Act No. 18 of 1930 conferred the franchise on adult white women throughout the Union, and Act No. 41 of 1931 extended the franchise to all adult white men. Thus the total white vote almost tripled from 300 860 in 1927 to 886 592, while the combined Coloured and African vote actually declined from 40 860 in 1927 to 36 098 in 1933. Of the latter figure, Africans comprised only 10 778 votes in 1933. This meant that Africans constituted a mere 2.7 per cent of the Cape electorate and 1.2 per cent of the Union total in 1933.[123]

The realisation that the existing African vote could not be considered a serious threat to the white electorate was accompanied by a change in the ideological justification for abolishing the Cape franchise. Whereas in the 1920s the African vote was perceived as a potential menace, in the 1930s it was dismissed as a useless institution. Patrick Duncan, for instance, acknowledged that the franchise was 'to the educated native a symbol of equality . . . and to take it away will be felt as an assertion of his perpetual inferiority'. But he considered that the existing franchise was 'not of much practical use' and that the new schemes of African representation were 'the only way of progress'.[124]

This line of argument was an essential element of Heaton Nich-olls's concept of 'trusteeship', which maintained that the develop-ment of African agriculture and 'traditional' political institutions was of far greater practical value to Africans than the dubious advantage of common citizenship. According to Nicholls, the Cape franchise was 'a sham' because it advanced the interests of a tiny educated African minority while condemning the mass to a state of wretched poverty.[125] It was essential to abolish the Cape franchise because only by ending white fears of the African electorate, could 'native development' proceed.[126]

In many respects these ideas reflected Hertzog's idea of a *quid pro quo*, whereby land was to be offered to Africans in return for the abolition of the Cape common franchise. This coupling remained at the heart of segregationist discourse, enabling Hertzog to draw a wide range of politically interested groupings within the ambit of its ideology. By defining the range of political alternatives, segregation became a hegemonic ideology within white South Africa. The agree-ment between the SAP and the Nationalists that the 'native question' should not become 'a political football' is an indication of this consensus, even though the arrangement was broken as frequently as it was invoked.

The difference between Hertzog and Smuts was more a matter of style (relating to the differing orientations of the Nationalists and the SAP, respectively) than of political substance. Both major parties were unshakeably committed to the maintenance of white supremacy and both embraced the central tenets of segregation. Their disagree-ments centred on the manner in which segregation should be implemented and were exaggerated by the codes and rituals of the parliamentary system. But these artificial barriers were for the most part removed after 1933–4, when the Nationalists and the SAP fused to form the governing United Party.

The response of African organisations and individuals to the Native Bills was a great deal more ambivalent than is sometimes supposed. Karis and Carter, for example, convey the impression that Africans were unanimous in their rejection of Hertzog's Bills. [127] By contrast, Richard Haines highlights the 'rather uninspiring perform-ance of African protest bodies in their opposition to the Segregation Bills', ascribing this, *inter alia*, to organisational shortcomings; the lack of a strong, cohesive African leadership; the tendency of some leaders to establish personal fiefdoms, resulting in 'regionalism'; and the fact that land hunger and poverty muted opposition. Thus Haines concludes that the extra-parliamentary opposition to the Hertzog Bills was 'not a coherent movement, but rather a series of reactive and *ad hoc* responses. For the entire period 1925–36, the various protest movements were on the defensive'.[128]

There were a variety of strands within African opposition forces. One tendency, epitomised by D.D.T. Jabavu and R.V. Selope Thema, vigorously defended the universalist principles of common citizenship and took as their reference point an idealised notion of the non-racial Cape tradition. On this account the common franchise was of enormous symbolic significance, representing the achievement of political and moral equality and the progress from a state of 'barbarism' to that of 'civilisation'. Conversely, a greater, if less articulate, body of African opinion was receptive to a reformist position, hoping that concessions could be won on the land issue and that indirect forms of political representation could be extended. Moreover, the development of separatist and Africanist sentiment during the 1920s resonated with certain segregationist precepts and encouraged a measure of susceptibility to the language of segregation. A more militant tradition of rejecting segregation can be traced through elements within the ICU and among such leaders of the ANC as the Rev. Z.R. Mahabane. However, it was rare to hear segregation condemned outright, as J.T. Gumede did in 1926, when he declared, 'The Natives recognise no good in any of General Hertzog's four Bills which are framed in connection with his native policy'.[129]

Opposition to the Native Bills, so often expressed by reference to the sacred principles of common citizenship and the legitimacy of the British Crown, was inherently contradictory. At one and the same time an idealised colonial system was called to account for not living up to its promise, but in so doing the system was itself legitimised. It is notable that whatever criticisms were mounted against the trend of government legislation and administration, the fundamental legitimacy of the state was rarely questioned. In an age where individual rights and justice were claimed, but before 'democracy' became a popular demand, the African elite wanted access to citizenship rather a radical redefinition of the scope of political sovereignty.

Acquiescence in segregation should not be confused with support; it therefore seems inappropriate to blame those who, by today's standards, may be regarded as having collaborated with white supremacists. In a recent work whose central theme is 'ambiguity' Shula Marks analyses the fragile position of the petit-bourgeois African leadership in a colonial situation, having to negotiate 'the politics of the tightrope'. She argues,

> a concept of ambiguity is crucial to any understanding of domination; even while demanding obedience, and provoking resistance, domination operates not simply through coercion but also through concessions that themselves are shaped by the nature of resistance. These in turn become the basis of consent as well as of further struggle by the dominated.[130]

This is certainly true of segregation, an ideology whose material existence was called forth by the dynamics of minority domination in an industrialising society, and whose particular form was modified by the forces which it sought to contain.

A major failure of African resistance to segregationist ideology and legislation was its inability to translate such opposition into a populist idiom. The work of such writers as Bradford, Beinart and Bundy has shown that there was during the 1920s an intense, if not always clearly directed, popular upsurge at a local level. However, there was a disjuncture between the groundswell of popular feeling in the countryside and the form in which opposition to the Land and Franchise Bills was expressed. There is a sense in which segregation, conceived of in abstract ideological terms, remained largely the political preserve of a narrow African leadership, whose aspirations as a class were predominantly bourgeois. Margaret Hodgson (Ballinger) complained in 1933 of the African elite's complacency, fearing that in spite of the impending 'repressive legislation', 'the Natives are going to take it lying down as they have taken all the rest':

> The only thing we can see is an increasing stratification of Native society – the consolidation of a middle class, quite considerable in extent, and in some strange way apparently quite comfortably off, a class which knows less about other classes of the people to whom it belongs than we do and apparently cares less . . . . It makes me very anxious that they should have so little consciousness of the insecurity of the foundation of their present pleasure and that the hopelessness of the future, not only for their race but for themselves as individuals if they cannot fight for some basic human rights now.[131]

The other major focus of this study has been the activities of white liberals, grouped around the Joint Council/Race Relations nexus. Attention has been drawn to the publicly expressed opposition of several prominent political figures to segregation in contradistinction to their private willingness to secure a settlement. This equivocation was the source of a great deal of confusion and mutual mistrust. It has been suggested, most notably by Martin Legassick, that these liberals acted to defuse potential militancy on the part of Africans by directing activity towards welfarist rather than political concerns.[132] While there is a strong element of truth in this view, it remains a moot point whether in the absence of political clearing houses like the SAIRR African opposition to the Segregation Bills would have been more radical or effective than it actually was.

Leading liberal spokesmen such as Alfred Hoernlé, Edgar Brookes and J.D. Rheinallt Jones, were all amenable at various times to arriving at a compromise settlement, though they were by no means agreed on the terms or timing of such an agreement. From 1928 the Joint Councils and later the SAIRR maintained a public front of commitment to the Cape franchise. But, in private, reformism and accommodation were to the fore. Edgar Brookes stressed his intention both in his many press articles and in the important 1935 memorandum which he drafted on the Institute's behalf 'to advocate careful consideration, not mere opposition, and to advise against all policies of non-cooperation'.[133] This sort of talk reflected the political orientation of the SAIRR no less than its much publicised protestations in favour of a non-racial civil society.

A small liberal sub-grouping, based predominantly in the Cape, attempted to maintain continuity with classic nineteenth-century liberal principles. Such individuals as James Rose Innes criticised the 'impartiality' of the SAIRR, warning of the danger of 'becoming all things to all men' at the risk of 'holding up a candle to the devil'.[134] The commitment of Rose Innes and his colleagues in the NRFA and the Native Franchise Vigilance Commitee to the non-racial franchise was a matter of conviction. But their criticisms of the SAIRR's pragmatism, though couched in ethical terms, were more than mere claims to moral superiority. Their ideology was grounded in an alternative liberal strategy of social co-optation which sought the gradual political incorporation of a 'civilising' African elite. To the leaders of the NRFA maintenance of the 'fundamentals of liberty' was essential to the future stability of South Africa. In their terms the main social threat posed by the proposal to abolish the franchise was that it would inevitably 'drive all Bantus – civilised or uncivilised, educated or uneducated – into one camp by giving them a common grievance'. Far from being politically dangerous, extension of the qualified franchise on a non-racial basis was essential, for to deny full civic rights to 'civilised Bantu people' might 'precipitate a racial struggle the possibilities of which are too dreadful to contemplate . . .'[135]

Conclusion

Apartheid is undeniably an ideology in decline. Indeed it is now widely apparent, not only in the opinion of its critics, that apartheid is suffering from a fundamental crisis of legitimacy. The State President himself has admitted that apartheid is 'outmoded'. Those who were once true believers openly acknowledge their doubts. White supremacy can no longer be justified in terms of 'separate development' or 'national self-determination'; the state virtually admits that its sole claim to rule rests in its capacity to maintain 'law and order'.

Apartheid is not merely an extension of segregation, as some have argued; nor does it represent a fundamental rupture from the past, as others have supposed. Indeed it is inconceivable that apartheid could have been imagined, let alone implemented, had it not been able to build on segregation. At no point did even the most passionate Afrikaner nationalist proponents of apartheid in the 1950s and 1960s renounce segregation. Rather, they sought to reformulate it in a more consistent and radical form. Just as segregation was a response to vastly changed social conditions in the first two decades of this century, so apartheid emerged out of the massive social, economic and political dislocation of the 1940s and 1950s. Segregation, like apartheid, was adopted in the aftermath of world war, industrial expansion, and a profound resurgence in African political resistance. In both cases this provoked a fundamental reassessment of the 'native question': just as segregationists of the 1920s criticised the South African Party's 'drift' on the issue, so the champions of apartheid deplored the 'drift' of the United Party's segregationism.

There are clear ideological links between segregation and apartheid. It is notable, for example, that segregationists of the inter-war era, such as Ernest Stubbs and George Heaton Nicholls, saw their work being resurrected in support of apartheid during the 1950s. We have seen that the terms of segregationist ideology were in large measure worked out by English-speaking liberal paternalists, many of whom rejected segregation when its true character became apparent. In the 1950s a number of leading Afrikaner nationalist intellectuals, grouped together in organisations like the South African Bureau of Racial Affairs, likewise conceived of apartheid as a fair and legitimate solution of the intractable 'native question'.[1] In the same way that segregationists such as Maurice Evans and Jan

Hofmeyr argued that whites would have to make economic concessions in order to secure their survival, so the advocates of full territorial separation indicated their preparedness to grant more land to Africans and, even, to dispense with their labour. The reality of economic integration convinced liberal segregationists in the late 1920s to reconsider their position. Similarly, the failure of the Nationalist Party under Verwoerd to carry its policies through to their theoretical conclusion led former Afrikaner proponents of total separation such as Nic Olivier to reject apartheid, from a liberal perspective, by the 1960s.

Despite these resemblances, segregation and apartheid cannot be conflated. Important similarities in the structure of apartheid and segregationist ideology should not obscure very real differences in the content and tone of their respective discourses. Apartheid was largely based on Christian-Nationalist ideology which sought to justify, by means of tortuous Biblical exegesis, the 'sacred mission' of Afrikanerdom and the need for racial and cultural separation. But there was no theological equivalent of Kuyperian neo-Calvinism in the segregationist era. A notion of cultural relativism derived from contemporary anthropology served as an important organising principle for segregationist ideology. Under apartheid cultural differences were greatly rigidified and 'ethnos' theory was developed to legitimise the administrative entrenchment of separate ethnic identities. In this matter, as in others, apartheid was qualitatively distinctive in virtue of its dogmatic intensity. Whereas the hallmark of segregation was its ambiguity and ideological flexibility, apartheid ideology was unremitting in its zeal and logic.[2]

A further difference between apartheid and segregation arises out of the distinct historical contexts in which they arose. Segregation drew on the example of Jim Crow in the American South and on the policies of indirect rule in British colonial Africa. To this extent segregation was broadly comparable with similar tendencies in the rest of the world. By contrast, apartheid was elaborated directly after the Second World War, just as the triumph over fascism was being celebrated and as the principles of universal human rights were endorsed by the Atlantic Charter. Moreover, the implementation of apartheid in the 1950s and 1960s coincided with the anti-colonial struggle in Africa and Asia as well as the civil-rights movement in the United States. Apartheid therefore ran against the tide of international opinion, and South Africa became a pariah state as a result. The same cannot be said of segregation.

In the field of 'native administration' there is both continuity and disjuncture in the transition from segregation to apartheid. I have argued in this book that the structure and ideology of the NAD was inextricably linked to segregationist policy. During the inter-war years the NAD was strengthened and unified in important respects. The Native Administration Act played a key role in the implementation of segregation and, later, apartheid. It was also vital to the clarification of the NAD's enhanced position within the state as a whole. But despite its increasing importance within the state during the 1920s and 19230s, the NAD had maintained a relatively low ideological profile so far as *political* segregation was concerned. It played a negligible role, for example, in the passage of the 1936 Representation of Natives in Parliament Act. And although the idiom of sympathetic paternalism declined during the segregationist era, elements of that legacy continued to moderate the manner in which segregation was applied.

By contrast, the Native (or Bantu) Affairs Department underwent vast expansion after 1948. Building on the already existing framework of legislation, the scope of its activities was substantially enlarged. In particular, the NAD extended its control over Africans in the urban areas. Under the stewardship of Verwoerd and Eiselen the department became a crusading political bureaucracy, and it undertook a programme of social engineering which would have been inconceivable in earlier times. In constructing grand apartheid the NAD encroached ever more into the daily lives of Africans. Whatever residual traces of benevolent paternalism remained were remorselessly submerged within an ethos of authoritarian rigidity and repression.

By the 1960s, then, the NAD was irrevocably linked, both administratively and symbolically, with apartheid. However, this direct association became increasingly embarrassing during the 1970s and 1980s as the state was faced with an unprecedented popular challenge to its authority. In 1985 the Department of Cooperation and Development (the old Native Affairs Department) was renamed once again, and most of its functions were transferred to the Department of Constitutional Development and Planning. It is safe to assume that the dismantling of this administrative empire had much to do with the state's 'reform process' and the retreat in the 1980s from old-style apartheid.

In its political aspects segregation underwent a major transformation in the post-1948 era. The Nationalist government inherited

Hertzog's 1936 Land and Representation Acts, but these soon became inadequate to its needs. In 1951 it abolished the Native Representative Council and in 1960 the system of indirect parliamentary representation of Africans by whites was ended. The assault on non-white political rights continued when 'coloureds' were removed from the voters' roll in 1956, after the state had packed the Senate in order to get its requisite two-thirds majority.

Whereas segregation sought to establish a system of differential sovereignty wherein Africans were excluded from direct participation in central government, apartheid has attempted to remove even their citizenship. The struggle against political segregation in the inter-war years was largely a question of preserving common citizenship rights and individual liberties. But with the possible exception of Africanist or separatist movements, the legitimacy of the state itself was barely called into question at this time. Demands were couched in terms of the inclusion of 'qualified' Africans within existing structures of power. It was only in the 1940s that the call for democratic rights became widespread – as expressed in the contemporary demand for majority rule in a unitary state and the insistence that political rights cannot be separated from access to economic wealth.

This book has pointed to two major themes with regard to the analysis of segregation in its political, ideological and administrative forms: first, the idea that segregation was primarily a defensive strategy aimed at consolidating white supremacy in the face of the challenge posed by the emergence of an African proletariat; and, second, that segregation, rather than being a simple rationalisation of white domination and capitalist exploitation, was an umbrella ideology which included a wide range of different interests in its consensual orbit. Segregation's success as a political ideology relates to the fact that it managed to conceal to a large extent the level of repression which underwrote it. According to John Cell, segregation 'must be recognised as one of the most successful political ideologies of the past century. It was, indeed, the highest stage of white supremacy'.[3] When the apartheid state is finally replaced, historians will have to explain not only why it was overthrown but also why the process took so long. Part of the answer to the regime's longevity surely relates to the profoundly ambiguous character of segregation and the way in which it succeeded, for a considerable period of time, in defining the range of feasible political alternatives.

Notes and References

Introduction

1. M. Legassick, 'South Africa: Forced Labour, Industrialization and Racial Differentiation', in R. Harris (ed.) *The Political Economy of Africa* (Massachusetts, 1975), p. 250.
2. H. Wolpe, 'Capitalism and Cheap Labour-Power in South Africa: From Segregation to Apartheid', in *Economy and Society*, I, 4, 1972.
3. M. Lacey, *Working for Boroko. The Origins of a Coercive Labour System in South Africa* (Johannesburg, 1981).
4. S. Marks, *The Ambiguities of Dependence in South Africa. Class, Nationalism and the State in Twentieth-Century Natal* (Baltimore and Johannesburg, 1986), p. 38.
5. M. Legassick, 'The Making of South African "Native Policy", 1903–1923: The Origins of "Segregation" ' (seminar paper, Institute of Commonwealth Studies, London University, 1973), p. 1.
6. It should be noted that to say that segregation provided the political and social conditions for the long-term reproduction of capitalism as a system begs several questions. How long is the long-term? Is capitalism a single system, or does it make more sense to speak of capitalism as embracing varying systems of accumulation, all of which involve different degrees of exploitation?
7. S. Marks, 'Natal, the Zulu Royal Family and the Ideology of Segregation', in *Journal of Southern African Studies* (Henceforth JSAS), IV, 2, 1978, 177.
8. J. W. Cell, *The Highest Stage of White Supremacy: The Origins of Segregation in South Africa and the American South* (Cambridge, 1982), p. 3.
9. P. B. Rich, *White Power and the Liberal Conscience. Racial Segregation and South African Liberalism 1921–60* (Johannesburg and Manchester, 1984).
10. G. H. Nicholls, *South Africa in My Time* (London, 1961), p. 277. While substantially true, this statement should also be seen in terms of Nicholls' desire to prove the importance of his own contribution to 'native policy' in the period after 1920.
11. N. L. G. Cope, 'The Zulu Royal Family Under the South African Government, 1910–1933: Solomon kaDinuzulu, Inkatha and Zulu Nationalism' (PhD thesis, Natal University, 1985), pp. 151–2.
12. W. K. Hancock, *Smuts, Vol.II. The Fields of Force 1919–1950* (Cambridge, 1968), p. 21.
13. A. J. Barnouw, *Language and Race Problems in South Africa* (The Hague, 1934), pp. 57–8.
14. S. G. Millin, *The South Africans* (London 1926), p. 94.
15. N. E. Dubow, *Irma Stern* (Cape Town, 1974), pp. 16–17.

181

182   *Segregation and Apartheid in South Africa*

16. M. Perham, *African Apprenticeship. An Autobiographical Journey in Southern Africa 1929* (London, 1974), p. 143.
17. L. Barnes, *Caliban in Africa. An Impression of Colour-Madness* (London, 1930), p. 70.
18. In 1929 Margery Perham observed: 'It is rather interesting that, parallel with all the new anthropological appreciation of the native, there has gone an artistic interpretation. They are closely linked'. See her *African Apprenticeship*, p. 143.
19. A. Ashforth, 'On the "Native Question": A Reading of the Grand Tradition of Commissions of Inquiry into the "Native Question" in Twentieth-Century South Africa' (DPhil thesis, Oxford University, 1987), pp. 92–3.
20. The phrase 'differential sovereignty' is Ashforth's.
21. Cell, *White Supremacy*, p. 18.
22. On the link between South Africa and the United States, see Cell, *White Supremacy*; also G.M. Fredrickson, *White Supremacy. A Comparative Study in American and South African History* (Oxford and New York, 1981).
23. H. A. Shannon, 'Urbanization, 1904–1936', *South African Journal of Economics*, V, 2, 1937.
24. *House of Assembly Debates* (1930), vol. 14, col 230.
25. H. Bradford, 'The Industrial and Commercial Workers' Union of Africa in the South African Countryside, 1924–1930' (PhD thesis, University of the Witwatersrand, 1985), pp. 232–3.
26. J. Lonsdale, 'Classes and Social Process in Africa: A Historiographical Survey', in the *African Studies Review*, XXIV, 2–3, 1981, 187.
27. In 1985 the Department of Cooperation of Development (the direct descendant of the Native Affairs Department) was renamed and most of its functions were transferred to the Department of Constitutional Development and Planning.
28. N. Poulantzas, *State, Power, Socialism* (London, 1978).
29. W. Beinart, *The Political Economy of Pondoland 1860–1930* (Cambridge, 1982), pp. 164–5.
30. Perham, *African Apprenticeship*, p. 178. Perham mistakenly ascribes too much importance to the 'Afrikanerisation' of the state in explaining this transition.
31. Hertzog papers, A32 vol. 173, J. Albert Coetzee to General Hertzog 3/2/33, enclosing 'Nation Building in South Africa'.
32. W. G. Ballinger, 'All Union Politics are Native Affairs', in *Cape Times*, 27 February 1930.
33. D. E. Kaplan, 'Class Conflict, Capital Accumulation and the State: An Historical Analysis of the State in Twentieth Century South Africa' (PhD thesis, Sussex University, 1977), pp. 12,14,15.

1 The Elaboration of Segregationist Ideology, c. 1900–36

1. M. Lacey, *Working for Boroko. The Origins of a Coercive Labour System in South Africa* (Johannesburg, 1981), pp. 14–17; R. Parry,

' "In a Sense Citizens, But Not altogether Citizens . . ." Rhodes, Race, and the Ideology of Segregation at the Cape in the Late Nineteenth Century', *Canadian Journal of African Studies*, XVII, 3, 1983.
2. See, for example, Paul B. Rich, *Race and Empire in British Politics* (Cambridge, 1986), p. 21; E. H. Brookes, *The History of Native Policy in South Africa from 1830 to the Present Day* (Cape Town, 1924), pp. 99–107. Note that the Chairman of the SANAC report was Sir Godfrey Lagden, a former Resident Commissioner of Basutoland. In arguing for segregation Howard Pim (see below) often cited the Basutoland precedent.
3. D. Welsh, *The Roots of Segregation. Native Policy in Colonial Natal, 1845–1910* (London and Cape Town, 1971), p. 322.
4. Marks, *The Ambiguities*, p. 5 and Chapter 1. See also S. Marks, 'White Supremacy. A Review Article', *Comparative Studies in Society and History*, XXIX, 2, 1987.
5. C. W. de Kiewiet, *A History of South Africa, Social and Economic* (Oxford, 1941); E. A. Walker, *The Frontier Tradition in South Africa* (Oxford, 1930); C. M. Tatz, *Shadow and Substance in South Africa. A Study in Land and Franchise Policies Affecting Africans, 1910–1960* (Pietermaritzburg, 1962)
6. G. Leach, *South Africa. No Easy Path to Peace*, 2nd edition (London, 1987), pp. 36, 40.
7. A. N. Pelzer's authorised history of the Afrikaner Broederbond, *Die Afrikaner-Broederbond: Eerste 50 Jaar* (Cape Town, 1979), pp. 163–4, quotes an official Broederbond document dated 1933 as reflecting the organisation's basic creed on native policy – adding that it appears to have been forgotten since that date. The document calls for the imposition of total segregation as the immediate, practical policy of the state, and seems to foreshadow a policy of 'tribal' balkanisation.
8. M. Legassick, 'The Making of South African "Native Policy", 1903–1923: The Origins of "Segregation" ', seminar paper, Institute of Commonwealth Studies, London University, 1973, p. 2.
9. Cell, *White Supremacy*, p. 211.
10. *South African Native Affairs Commission 1903–5. Vol. I*, (Cape Town, 1905).
11. Rich, *Race and Empire*, p. 56.
12. *Cape Argus*, 20 August 1902. Note that the governor general was not talking of territorial segregation, he was referring to the creation of special urban 'locations' for Africans in the wake of the bubonic plague. My thanks to Christopher Saunders for this reference.
13. Pim papers, A881 Hb8.16, 'The Native Problem in South Africa', by J. H. Pim, 1905. J. H. Pim (1862–1934) was born near Dublin and educated at Trinity College, Dublin. He came to South Africa in 1890 as a chartered accountant with Rhodes's British South Africa Company. In 1894 he established his own practice and became an auditor to De Beers Consolidated Mines Ltd. He was a member of Milner's nominated Johannesburg Town Council of 1903. On account of the principled stand he took against the importation of Chinese labour in 1904, the Chamber of Mines and Rand Mines Ltd refused to

reappoint him as their auditor. He recovered from this boycott (to be 'Pimmed' became a colloquial expression in Johannesburg) and served on a number of important government commissions. Pim was a committed Quaker, who increasingly devoted himself to a variety of social welfare activities. Through his connection with the Joint Councils and the Institute of Race Relations, he became a prominent figure in liberal circles, and functioned as a theorist, organizer and patron. Various obituaries testify to Pim's humanitarianism and refer to him as a champion of 'native rights'.

14. *Ibid.*, p. 9.
15. P. Rich, 'The Agrarian Counter-Revolution in the Transvaal and the Origins of Segregation: 1902–1913', (African Studies seminar paper, University of the Witwatersrand, 1975) p. 15; M. Legassick and D. Innes, 'Capital Restructuring and Apartheid: A Critique of Constructive Engagement', in *African Affairs*, LXXVI, 305, 1977, pp. 465–6.
16. Pim, 'The Native Problem', p. 9,
17. *Ibid.*, pp. 7, 10.
18. Pim papers, A881 Fa 3/2 Abstract of paper for British Association, p. 2. For more on Pim's interpretation of American History see his paper 'The Question of Race', delivered to the Fortnightly Club, 15 November 1906, in Pim papers, A881 Hb 17.
19. Pim papers, Fa 1/3, 'A Note on Native Policy', p. 7.
20. *Ibid.*, p. 7.
21. *Ibid.*, pp. 7–8.
22. Pim, 'The Question of Race', p. 2.
23. *South African Native Affairs Commission 1903–5. Vol I* (Cape Town, 1905), p. 895.
24. Pim papers, A881 Fa 9/7, 'Memorandum re "Segregation" ', 1914, p. 2.
25. Stanley Trapido has pointed out to me that Pim's ideas about the functions of the reserves appears in Appendix VIII, p. 111 of Cd 7707, *Dominions Royal Commission. Minutes of Evidence Taken in the Union of South Africa in 1914, Part II*.
26. M. S. Evans, *Black and White in South East Africa. A Study in Sociology* (London, 1911). Maurice Smethurst Evans (1854–1920) went to Natal in 1875 and became a member of its Legislative Assembly in 1897. He served on the 1906–7 *Natal Native Commission* and published a pamphlet, *The Native Problem in Natal* (Durban, 1906). Evans travelled to the United States, after which he published a second volume *Black and White in the Southern States. A Study of the Race Problem in the United States from a South African Point of View* (London, 1915).
27. See, for example, Sarah Gertrude Millin in her *The South Africans*, p. 279, where she describes Evans as the 'soundest and fairest observer of black and white inter-relationships in South Africa'.
28. Evans, *Black and White in South East Africa*, p. 276.
29. *Ibid.*, p. 277.
30. *Ibid.*, p. 310.

31. *Ibid.*, p. 153.
32. *Ibid.*, p. 316.
33. *Ibid.*, p. 177. See also pp. 149–50.
34. C. T. Loram, *The Education of the South African Native* (London, 1917). Charles Templeman Loram (1879–1940) was born in Pietermaritzburg and educated at the universities of Cape Town and Cambridge. He completed a doctorate at Columbia University in 1916. The thesis was published as *Education of the South African Native*. Between 1906 and 1920 he worked within the Natal Education Department. He left in 1920 to take up a position on the newly created Native Affairs Commission, in which capacity he served until 1929. In 1930 he rejoined the Natal Education Department as its Superintendent of Education. Loram was part of the Phelps-Stokes Educational Commission to Africa during 1921–24, and played a key role in allocating funds for research projects. He was closely involved in the Joint Council movement and became the first Chairman of the South African Institute of Race Relations in 1929. In 1931 Loram left SA to become Sterling Professor of Education at Yale University. He became Chairman and Director of Studies in the Department of Culture Contacts and Race Relations at Yale in 1933.
35. *Ibid.* See chaps. IX and X.
36. *Ibid.*, pp. 17–25.
37. E. H. Brookes, *The History of Native Policy in South Africa from 1830 to the Present Day* (Cape Town, 1924).
38. *Ibid.*, p. 501.
39. *Ibid.*, p. 343.
40. *Ibid.*, p. 504.
41. This section is a condensed version of a paper entitled ' "Race, civilisation and culture": the elaboration of segregationist discourse in the inter-war years', in S. Marks and S. Trapido (eds), *The Politics of Race, Class and Nationalism in Twentieth-Century South Africa* (London and New York, 1987).
42. Jones, *Social Darwinism*, p. 147.
43. Jones, *Social Darwinism*, p. 103.
44. Rich, *Race and Empire*.
45. Parry, 'In a Sense Citizens', pp. 384–8.
46. S. J. R. Martin, 'Political and Social Theories of Transkeian Administrators in the Late Nineteenth Century' (MA thesis, UCT, 1978), p. 82.
47. R. Hyam, *Elgin and Churchill at the Colonial Office 1905–8* (London, 1968), p. 539.
48. *Ibid.*
49. P. Rich, *White Power*, p. 5.
50. On the prevalence (in the pre-Nazi area) of theories of racial superiority in South Africa derived from the biological sciences, see J. M. Coetzee's brilliant essay, 'Blood, Flaw, Taint, Degeneration: The Case of Sarah Gertrude Millin', *English Studies in Africa*, XXIII, 1, 1980.
51. C. T. Loram, *The Education*, pp. 9,11. See also Brookes, *History*, ch. XVIII. On p. 403 Brookes states that 'The native . . . is not naturally a town-dweller or an industrialist'.

52. See Rich, *Race and Empire*, chap. 6, which investigates the anti-miscegenation movement in inter-war Britain, centring on the presence of black seamen in ports like Cardiff and Liverpool.
53. E. Stubbs, *Tightening Coils. An Essay on Segregation* (Pretoria, 1925); G.H. Nicholls, *Bayete!* (London, 1923).
54. M. Evans, *Black and White in South East Africa*, p. 223.
55. See, for example, Hertzog's Smithfield and Malmesbury speeches in *The Segregation Problem. General Hertzog's Solution* (Cape Town, n.d., [1926]).
56. C.M. Tatz, *Shadow and Substance* On pp. 41–5 Tatz isolates and evaluates the validity of twelve arguments advanced by Hertzog for the removal of the Cape African franchise.
57. De Kiewiet, *A History of South Africa*, p. 181.
58. See, for example, J. E. Duerden, 'Genetics and Eugenics in South Africa: Heredity and Environment' *South African Journal of Science* (henceforth SAJS), XXII, 1925.
59. See, for example, M. L. Fick, 'Intelligence Test Results of Poor White, Native (Zulu), Coloured and Indian School Children and the Educational and Social Implications', in *SAJS*, XXVI, 1929; Loram, *The Education*, chaps, IX-XI.
60. Rheinallt Jones, 'The Need'; Loram, *The Education*; Evidence of Prof. & Mrs Hoernlé to Native Economic Commission (henceforth NEC), 13 June 1931, pp. 9183–5.
61. Union Government, Pretoria, U.G. (henceforth UG), 14 – '26, *Report of the Economic and Wage Commission (1925)*, p. 326.
62. S. M. Molema, *The Bantu – Past and Present* (Edinburgh, 1920), p. 328.
63. W. Eiselen, *Die Naturelle Vraagstuk* (Cape Town, 1929), pp. 3–4.
64. On Eiselen's retirement the Bantu Affairs Department's official journal *Bantu*, VII, 8, 1960, devoted an entire issue to him. A lengthy eulogy to Eiselen quoted extensively from the 1929 address cited above. It was represented as a direct antecedent to his views on apartheid.
65. On the material basis of Cape liberalism, see Stanley Trapido's pioneering essay ' "The friends of the natives": merchants, peasants and the political and ideological structure of liberalism in the Cape, 1854–1910', in S. Marks and A. Atmore (eds) *Economy and Society in Pre-Industrial South Africa* (London, 1980).
66. On the institutionalisation of anthropological studies in South Africa and its relationship to segregation see my ' "Understanding the Native Mind": Anthropology, cultural adaptation and the elaboration of a segregationist discourse in South Africa, c.1920–36' (seminar paper, University of Cape Town, 1984). For a discussion of the impact of anthropology on liberal thought in the 1920s and 1930s, see Rich, *White Power*, ch. 3.
67. Loram, *The Education*, pp. vii-viii; J. D. Rheinallt Jones, 'Editorial' in *Bantu Studies*, I, 1, 1921, p. 1; J. E. Duerden, 'Social Anthropology in South Africa: Problems of Nationality', *SAJS*, XVIII, 1921, pp. 4–5. According to Adam Kuper, *Anthropologists and Anthropology* (London, 1973), p. 62, Smuts, in consultation with Haddon of

Cambridge, was personally responsible for inviting Radcliffe-Brown to UCT.

68. A. R. Radcliffe-Brown, 'Some Problems of Bantu Sociology', *Bantu Studies*, I, 3, 1922, p. 5.

69. See my ' "Understanding the Native Mind" '.

70. See Rich, *White Power*, ch. 3, especially pp. 54–63; also Rich, *Race and Empire*, chap. 5.

71. G. W. Stocking, *Race, Culture and Evolution. Essays in the History of Anthropology* (New York, 1968). This is supported by Newby's view that the impact of Boasian thought in the United States led to a precipitous decline by 1930 in the 'amount of scientific literature purporting to prove the Negro's alleged inferiority '. See Newby, *Jim Crow's Defense*, p. 51. For an assessment of the impact of Boasian thought, see also M. Harris *The Rise of Anthropological Theory* (London, 1968) chaps IX and X.

72. Stocking, *Race, Culture and Evolution*, pp. 199–200. See also the entry on 'culture' in R. Williams's *Keywords. A Vocabulary of Culture and Society* (London, 1976), pp. 78–9. Williams describes how 'culture', understood as a unilinear concept, became separated from 'civilisation' through a 'decisive change of use in Herder', and how this plural sense became common in twentieth-century anthropology.

73. J. C. Smuts, *Africa and Some World Problems* (Oxford, 1930).

74. *Ibid.*, p. 77.

75. *Ibid.*, p. 77.

76. *Ibid.*, p. 84.

77. Evidence of G. P. Lestrade to NEC, Pretoria 9 June 1931, p. 8787.

78. Lestrade papers, BC 255 K1. 11, 'Statements in Answer to General Questionnaire Issued by the NEC'.

79. UG 22-'32, *Report of the Native Economic Commission 1930–32*, p. 31, para. 200. Note that Dr Roberts of the Native Affairs Commission and NEC, dissented from this view, adding, '. . . the way of progress for the Native lies along the path of the Native assimilating as rapidly as possible the European civilization and culture'. p. 31, para. 201.

80. J. E. Holloway, 'The American Negro and the South African Bantu – A Study in Assimilation', *South African Journal of Economics*, I, 4, 1933, p. 422.

81. Schapera, *Western Civilisation and the Natives of South Africa. Studies in Culture Contact* (London, 1934). See also his 'Changing Life in the Native Reserves', *Race Relations*, I, 1, 1933. See Max Gluckman's paper 'Anthropology and Apartheid: The work of South African Anthropologists', in M. Fortes and S. Patterson (eds) *Studies in African Social Anthropology* (London and New York, 1975), p. 36. Gluckman credits Schapera as the dominant figure in reorientating British anthropology towards the idea that Africans and whites were 'integral parts of a single social system, so that all had to be studied in the same way'.

82. W. M. Macmillan, *My South African Years. An Autobiography* (Cape Town, 1975), pp. 194, 214–219. Macmillan criticised Rheinallt Jones, the Hoernlés and especially Loram for their involvement in anthropological research. For details of his failed attempt to subvert Jones's

course on native law and administration, see Wits. Arts Faculty Minutes, vol. VIII pp. 38–40b (Wits. archives).
83. W. M. Macmillan, *Complex South Africa. An Economic Footnote to, History* (London, 1930), preface, p. 8.
84. Heaton Nicholls papers, KCM 3323 file 3. Handwritten memo. on Native Policy, n. d., p. 1.
85. Records of the South African Institute of Race Relations (henceforth 'SAIRR') AD 843 72. 1. Unmarked newspaper clipping, 10 May 1929 (CPA). For the full Afrikaans version, see Eiselen, *Die Naturelle Vraagstuk*.
86. Smuts, *Africa*, p. 96.
87. SAIRR papers, AD 843 B53. 1, *Natal Advertiser*, 15 May 1935.
88. *Ibid.*
89. Rich, *Race and Empire*, chap. 2.
90. M. Perham, 'A Restatement of Indirect Rule', *Africa*, VII, 3, 1934, p. 326. See also B. Porter, *The Lion's Share. A Short History of British Imperialism 1850–1983* (London and New York, 1975), p. 293.
91. L. Mair, *Native Policies in Africa* (London, 1936), pp. 261–9.
92. Hancock, *Smuts Vol. II*, p. 116.
93. UG 7-'19, *Report of the Native Affairs Department (NAD) for the Years 1913–1918*, p. 16. This periodisation differs from John Cell's, who argues that the essential institutions of segregation were in place by 1924 and that its principal architect was Smuts, not Hertzog. See his *White Supremacy*, pp. 58, 216.
94. See, e.g. *The Round Table*, no. 44, 1921, p. 945; GG 1435 50/865, Governor-General Buxton to Viscount Milner, 21 July 1920, 'Native Affairs Bill (Confidential)'; J. H. Hofmeyr, *South Africa* (London, 1931), pp. 170–1.
95. Lestrade papers BC 255 K1. 8, Memo. by C. L. R. Harries 'Relating Chiefly to Native Political Affairs on the Witwatersrand', 14 May 1919, pp. 1–2
96. See, e.g. W. K. Hancock and J. van der Poel (eds), *Selections from the Smuts Papers*, 7 vols (Cambridge, 1966, 1973) V, Document 89, p. 54, Smuts to Bishop Talbot, 5 December 1922; GG 1435 50/853, Buxton to Viscount Milner 'confidential', 2 June 1920.
97. UG 34-'22 *Report of the NAD for the Years 1919–1921*, p. 4.
98. *Ibid.*, pp. 1–4. See also *Rand Daily Mail*, 21 February 1923.
99. P. Walshe, *The Rise of African Nationalism in South Africa. The African National Congress 1912–1952* (London, 1970), pp. 70–71, 89 and *passim*. See also H. J. and R. Simons, *Class and Colour in South Africa 1850–1950* (Harmondsworth, 1969), ch. 11; E. Roux, *Time Longer than Rope. The Black Man's Struggle for Freedom in South Africa* (London, 1948), p. 143.
100. P. Bonner, 'The Transvaal Native Congress 1917–1920: the radicalisation of the black petty bourgeoisie on the Rand', in Marks and Rathbone (eds), *Industrialisation and Social Change: African Class Formation, Culture and Consciousness, 1870–1930* (London, 1982).
101. H. Bradford, 'The Industrial and Commercial Workers' Union', p. 1.
102. *House of Assembly Debates*, vol. 9 1927. See Second Reading of Native

Administration Bill, esp. cols. 2997, 3016, 3032–4, 3045–6; *Cape Times* (editorial), 20 August 1927.

103. R. A. Hill and G. A. Pirio, ' "Africa for the Africans": the Garveyite Movement in South Africa, 1920–1940', in Marks and Trapido (eds), *The Politics of Race, Class and Nationalism.* Robert Edgar's work on Wellington Butelezi is a notable exception with respect to the comment about 'earlier scholarship'.

104. Bradford, 'The Industrial and Commercial Workers' Union', p. 188.

105. Simons and Simons, *Class and Colour*, ch. 17; E. Roux,*Time Longer than Rope*, chaps. XII-XXI.

106. GG 1435 50/854, Buxton to Viscount Milner, 3 June 1920, 'Report on the Native Affairs Bill', p. 1. See also Herbst Papers BC 79 D24, Memo. by E. R. Garthorne on Native Segregation, 7 October 1924. Garthorne said that while segregation was 'freely advocated in general terms, there has as yet been no very precise or authoritative exposition of its implications . . .' p. 1.

107. *The Round Table*, no. 57, December 1924, p. 192.

108. Cape Times (editorial), 3 May 1924. See also 11 and 12 June 1924, 17 September 1924 and 18 October 1924.

109. Hancock, *Smuts Vol. II*, p. 163.

110. For an account of this lineage, see *Cape Times* (editorial), 22 October 1924; 7 April 1936 (editorial); 1 May 1935 (editorial); 22 August 1936 (editorial). Also Smuts, *Native Policy*, pp. 78–85; Hancock, *Smuts Vol. II*, p. 227; Hofmeyr, *South Africa*, pp. 313–15.

111. *Cape Times*, (editorial) 23 January 1925; 11 May 1926 (editorial); 17 February 1925 (editorial).

112. J. H. Pim, 'General Hertzog's Smithfield Proposals', *The SA Quarterly*, VII, 3–4, 1926, 6. 'I have no quarrel with the native colour bar formed by public opinion' but the proposed legislation 'will have grave reactions upon the relations between Europeans and Natives throughout the Union. It protects the inefficient white against the efficient native'. See also Brookes, *The Colour Problems of South Africa* (Lovedale, 1934), p. 9.

113. See e.g. *Cape Times*, 3 April 1922, 29 June 1927 (editorial); UG 36-'23 *Report of the Native Affairs Commission for the Year 1922*, pp. 4–5; *The Round Table* no. 53, 1923, p. 174.

114. Hofmeyr, *South Africa*, pp. 311–2.

115. Cell, *White Supremacy*, p. 221.

116. Diary of F. J. Bagshawe, Mss. Afr. S. 288, Rhodes House, Oxford, vol. XI, 2 March 1929.

117. Rich, 'The Agrarian counter-revolution', p. 19.

118. NTS 8623 41/362, Memo. by Roberts to PM 12 June 1925, 'Certain Reflections on the Existence of a Native People in South Africa, and of the Need for a Clear Policy in dealing with them', pp. 17, 35. Roberts's participation is intriguing. He generally adhered to a more traditional brand of 'Cape' liberalism and was probably politically to the left of Loram.

119. Hertzog papers, A32 vol. 112, Hertzog to Brookes 25 March 1924. A

thousand copies were published at a cost of about £360. Hertzog
personally disposed of fifty-six complimentary copies to his associates.
120. *Ibid.*, Hertzog to Brookes, 23 March 1924.
121. *Cape Times* (editorial), 21 October 1924.
122. Pim, 'General Hertzog's Smithfield Proposals', p. 6.
123. M. Legassick, 'The Rise of Modern South African Liberalism: Its
     Assumptions and its Social Base' (ICS seminar paper, London University, 1973), p. 21.
124. E. H. Brookes, *The Political Future of South Africa* (Pretoria, 1927),
     p. 48.
125. SAIRR papers, AD 843 B72. 1. 1, Brookes to D. Steyn (Hertzog's
     Private Secretary), 'confidential'. 20 October 1926.
126. E. H. Brookes, *A South African Pilgrimage* (Johannesburg, 1977),
     pp. 20–23.
127. *Ibid.*, p. 35.
128. Pim papers, A881 Fa 14/2, 'The Economic Position'; *Cape Times*,
     3 February 1927.
129. *The Star*, 24 April 1929.
130. *South African Native Affairs Commission 1903–5. Vol I*, (Cape Town,
     1905), pp. 895, 896.
131. SAIRR papers, AD 843 B72. 1. 1, Memo. on 1925 Native Conference
     by Rheinallt Jones, p. 1; Pim papers A881 Fa 14/2, 'The Land Question
     in South Africa', by J. D. Rheinallt Jones, pp. 10, 4.
132. F. J. Bagshawe Diaries, Mss. Afr. S. 288, Rhodes House, Oxford, vol.
     XI, 2 March 1929.
133. SAIRR papers, AD 843 B72. 2, Pim to Jones, 18 February 1929.
134. For a discussion of Macmillan's ideas, see chapter 2.
135. S. H. Frankel to C. T. Loram 18 December 1926, private possession
     of S. H. Frankel, Oxford.
136. 'Economic Aspects of the Native Problem'. Notes for lecture delivered
     in 2nd half of 1926 to Johannesburg Branch of the Economic Society
     of South Africa by S. H. Frankel. In Prof. Frankel's private possession.
137. S. H. Frankel, 'The Position of the Native as a Factor in the Economic
     Welfare of the European Population in South Africa', in *Journal of
     the Economic Society of South Africa*, II, 1, 1928, 24.
138. *Ibid.*, pp. 19, 17, 24–25 and *passim.*
139. S. H. Frankel and E. H. Brookes, 'Problems of Economic Inequality:
     The Poor White and the Native', in Brookes *et al., Coming of Age.
     Studies in South African Citizenship and Politics* (Cape Town, 1930).
140. *Ibid.*, pp. 158, 134. The internal quote is from Macmillan. Frankel and
     Brookes joined up again to give evidence to the Native Economic
     Commission.

2 Segregation and Cheap Labour

  1. Wolpe, 'Capitalism and Cheap Labour-Power'.
  2. M. Legassick, 'South Africa: Forced Labour, Industrialization and
     Racial Differentiation'. See also H. Wolpe and M. Legassick, 'The

Bantustans and Capital Accumulation in South Africa', in *Review of African Political Economy*, no. 7, 1976.

3. F. A. Johnstone, 'White Prosperity and White Supremacy in South Africa Today', in *African Affairs*, LXIX, p. 275, 1970.

4. F. A. Johnstone, 'Class and Race Relations in the South African Gold Mining Industry, 1910–26' (DPhil thesis, Oxford University, 1972).

5. Lacey, *Working for Boroko*, p. xi.

6. *Ibid.*, p. 4.

7. Wolpe, 'Capitalism and Cheap Labour', p. 437.

8. See, for example, Martin Legassick's research notes on permanent labour, housed at Warwick University. Also Sean Moroney's 'Mine Married Quarters: the Differential Stabilisation of the Witwatersrand Workforce, 1900–1920', in S. Marks and R. Rathbone (eds), *Industrialisation and Social Change*.

9. A. H. Jeeves, *Migrant Labour in South Africa's Mining Economy. The Struggle for the Gold Mines' Labour Supply 1890–1920* (Kingston and Johannesburg, 1985), p. 13.

10. W. Beinart, *The Political Economy of Pondoland*, p. 6.

11. P. Harries, 'Kinship, Ideology and the Nature of Pre-Colonial Labour Migration: Labour Migration from the Delagoa Bay Hinterland to South Africa, up to 1895', in Marks and Rathbone (eds), *Industrialisation and Social Change*. Similar arguments about migrant labour have been made by, among others, Judy Kimble and Peter Delius.

12. UG 22-'32, *Report of the NEC*. See pp. 117–25, paras 797–852 for sections on the mining industry.

13. D. Yudelman, *The Emergence of Modern South Africa* (Cape Town, 1984). Yudelman argues that state and capital formed a 'symbiotic' relationship as early as 1907, a relationship whose dominance 'has endured until the present, surviving important changes in the composition of both the state and capital', p. 7 and *passim*.

14. S. T. van der Horst, *Native Labour in South Africa* (London, 1942), p. 190; UG 14-'26, *Report of the Economic and Wage Commission (1925)*, p. 151, para. 273.

15. SAIRR papers, AD 843 B36.1.1, Memo. by Joint Councils of Europeans and Natives [1922], p. 10.

16. Evidence of Major H. S. Cooke, Director of Native Labour, to NEC, 4 May 1931, pp. 7226–7; 7229–30.

17. Evidence of H. M. Taberer, Advisor to the Transvaal Chamber of Mines to NEC, 5 May 1931, pp. 7310–15. Taberer said that the mines were employing 207–208 000 Africans, which was their full complement – though not all mines were equally well supplied. He qualified his claim by saying that in 1906–7 and 1909 there was a slight limitation on recruitment, and in 1924 there was a temporary restriction following the 1922 strike. See also evidence of F.G.A. Roberts, p. 9076.

18. NTS 2093 222/280, part II, General Circular no. 2 of 1932 from J. F. Herbst, 25 January 1932. Herbst claimed the gold mines were 'employing 147 000 Union Natives against a normal figure of 105 000 and already have within the compounds several thousand Natives who draw their daily food rations but for whom no work is available'.

19. F. A. Johnstone, *Class Race and Gold: A Study of Class Relations and Racial Discrimination in South Africa* (London and Boston, 1976).
20. R. H. Davies, *Capital, State and White Labour in South Africa, 1900–1960: An Historical Materialist Analysis of Class Formation and Class Relations* (Brighton, 1979).
21. Lacey, *Working for Boroko*, p. 207. See also R. H. Davies, *Capital, State and White Labour in South Africa*, p. 33.
22. M. Lipton, *Capitalism and Apartheid. South Africa, 1910–1986* (Aldershot, 1986), p. 184; Yudelman, *The Emergence*, p. 36.
23. D. Ticktin, 'The Origins of the South African Labour Party 1888–1910' (PhD thesis, UCT, 1973), pp. 422, 458.
24. W. M. Macmillan, *The Land, The Native and Unemployment* (Johannesburg, 1924), p. 2; Pim papers, A881 fa 9/7, 'Memo. re "Segregation" ' by Pim, 1914, p. 1.
25. Jeeves, *Migrant Labour*, p. 67.
26. *Joint Sitting of Both Houses of Parliament. Natives' Parliamentary Representation Bill, Coloured Persons' Rights Bill (1930)*, col. 9.
27. *Ibid.*, cols 9–13.
28. J. Lewis, *Industrialisation and Trade Union Organisation in South Africa, 1924–55* (Cambridge, 1984), p. 25.
29. Stubbs, *Tightening Coils. An Essay on Segregation* (Pretoria, 1925), pp. 8–9.
30. SC 19-'27, *Committee on Native Bills*, Evidence of C. T. Loram, 6 February 1928.
31. UG 22-'32, *NEC Report*, pp. 79–81, paras 541–61.
32. UG 14-'26, *Report of Economic and Wage Commission (1925)* pp. 152–8, paras 274–89 (Mills-Clay-Martin Report).
33. *Ibid.*, pp. 281–2 paras 44–5 (Andrews-Lucas-Rood Report).
34. For evidence and resolutions by the provincial farmers' organisations, see S. C. (Select Committee, henceforth SC) 10-'27, *Report of the Select Committee on the Union Native Council Bill, Coloured Persons Rights Bill, Representation of Natives in Parliament Bill, and Natives Land (Amendment) Bill*. The OFS Agricultural Union took the position (although it was not actively discussed at their April 1927 conference) that Free State whites were 'everywhere opposed to the representation of natives in Parliament', p. 218. It conceded that Africans should have 'everything they want in the way of representation in their own councils', p. 222.
35. Lacey, *Working for Boroko*, pp. 18–35, 44–5.
36. UG 17-'27, *Report of the Native Affairs Commission* (henceforth NAC) *for the Years 1925–26*, p. 4.
37. *Ibid.*, pp. 5–6.
38. SC 10-'27 *Committee on Native Bills*, pp. 87–8, 104–5. See also Elliot's speech at the 1926 Farmers' Conference in Pretoria, NTS 1697 42/276, p. 7677.
39. SC 19-'27, *Report of the Select Committee on the Union Native Council Bill, Coloured Persons Rights Bill, Representation of Natives in Parliament Bill, and Natives Land (Amendment) Bill*, p. 146.

40. *Ibid.*, Evidence of W. Stein, p. 165; Evidence of P. J. van Rooyen, p. 215.
41. *Ibid.*, P. 221.
42. NTS 1697 42/276, 1926 Farmers' Conference, Evidence of Mr Colenbrander, pp. 81–2; Evidence of Mnr. Spies, pp. 84–5.
43. *Ibid.*, Evidence of W. Elliot, p. 76.
44. *Ibid.*, Evidence of Sir Frederick Moore pp. 11–12, p. 34; W. Elliot p. 76; C. A. Wheelwright pp. 73–6; Mr Sinclair pp. 9, 18.
45. SC 19-'27, *Committee on Native Bills*, Evidence of Wheelwright p. 187. Wheelwright argued that his views would be 'equally applicable to the northern Transvaal', p. 196.
46. Bradford, 'The Industrial and Commercial Workers' Union of Africa', chap. 5.
47. SC 10-'27, *Committee on Native Bills*, Evidence of P. J. Marais, p. 234; SC 19-'27, *Committee on Native Bills*, Evidence of J. T. Brent, p. 67.
48. *Ibid.*, Evidence of T. W. C. Norton, pp. 65–6.
49. NTS 1697 42/276, 1926 Farmers' Conference, Evidence of Norton, pp. 69–70; Sinclair, pp. 33–4, 25, 9, 18.
50. NTS 8615 38/362, Border Farmers' League to Hon. PM 4 May 1927; NTS 1697 42/276, 1926 Farmers' Conference, Evidence of Mr Gilfillan, p. 18; Mnr. Spies p. 25.
51 NTS 1697 42/276, 1926 Farmers' Conference, Evidence of O. R. Nel, p. 32.
52. *Ibid.*, p. 19. See also SC 19-'27, *Committee on Native Bills*, Evidence of Lawrence Lever, Managing Director, Bellevue Cotton Estates, Transvaal, pp. 69–71. Lever requested that thirteen farms in the Waterberg district be included in the released area, as his experiments in cotton-growing had not proved commercially successful.
53. Lacey, *Working for Boroko*, p. 169.
54. See chapter 4.
55. For a definition of labour tenancy and squatting, see chapter 5.
56. See UG 22-'32, *Report of the NEC*, pp. 51–8 for a comprehensive survey of the conditions and variations in labour tenancy. See also M. L. Morris, 'The Development of Capitalism in South African Agriculture: class struggle in the countryside', in *Economy and Society*, V, 3, 1976. This important article analyses labour tenancy in terms of the 'phase of transition' of capitalist relations in the countryside.
57. SC 10-'27, *Committee on the Native Bills*, Evidence of G. A. Kolbe of OFS Agricultural Union, p. 218. See also evidence of G. Schoeman, p. 216.
58 *Ibid.*, Evidence of J. Venter & P. Marais of Cape Agriculture Union, pp. 237–8.
59. *Ibid.*, Evidence of J. C. Gilfillan, H. R. Abercrombie and Major Doyle of the Tvl. Agricultural Union, pp. 210–11.
60. NTS 1697 42/276, 1926 Farmers' Conference, Evidence of W. Elliot, p. 78; SC 19-'27, *Committee on Native Bills*, Evidence of F. J. Carless, p. 218.
61. NTS 1697 42/276, 1926 Farmers' Conference, Evidence of Mr Dicke, pp. 42–3.

62. *Ibid.*, Evidence of Ernest Stubbs, pp. 65–6.
63. *Ibid.*, General Hertzog, p. 67.
64. In 1985 a conference was held at the Institute of Commonwealth Studies, London University, to commemorate the 100th anniversary of Macmillan's birth. Attention is drawn to the papers presented, which are likely to be published shortly.
65. W. M. Macmillan, *Economic Conditions in a Non-Industrial South African Town* (Grahamstown, 1915); W. M. Macmillan, *The South African Agrarian Problem and its Historical Development*, (Johannesburg, 1919).
66. W. M. Macmillan, *The Land, The Native, and Unemployment*, (Johannesburg, 1924).
67. Macmillan, *The Land*, p. 11.
68. *Ibid.*, p. 3.
69. W. M. Macmillan, *Complex South Africa. An Economic Footnote to History* (London, 1930).
70. Macmillan, *The Land*, p. 4. It is possible that Macmillan framed this statement so as to attract the sympathetic attention of state officials.
71. SC 10-'27, *Committee on Native Bills*, Appendix A.
72. *The South African Outlook*, 1 July 1927; Pim papers, A881 Fa 14/2, Evidence submitted by Rev. James Henderson to 1927 European-Bantu Conference.
73. J. H. Pim, *A Transkei Enquiry* (Lovedale, 1934), pp. 37, 9–14.
74. UG 22-'32, *NEC Report*, p. 11 para. 73 (emphasis in original).
75. NTS 1772 64/276(6) part I, 'Destitute Natives: Feeding of or Finding Work for', 1 March 1932, pp. 3–4.
76. NTS 1772 64/276(6) part II, Thornton to SNA on the NEC Report, 27 June 1932.
77. Lord Hailey, *An African Survey* (London, 1938), p. 805.
78. Evans, *Black and White*, p. 150. See also pp. 83, 176–7.
79. Brookes, *History*, p. 402.
80. E. H. Brookes, 'Economic Aspects of the Native Problem', in *Journal of the Economic Society of Southern Africa* (henceforth *JESSA*), I, 2, 1927, pp. 45–6.
81. *Rand Daily Mail*, 22 May 1928.
82. E. H. Brookes, *The Colour Problems of South Africa*. See also *Cape Times*, 7 June 1933.
83. Nicholls papers, KCM 3348 file 5, Nicholls to F. H. Van Zutphen 28 May 1929, p. 7. See S. Marks's 'Natal, the Zulu Royal Family and the Ideology of Segregation', *JSAS*, IV, 2, 1978, in which she discusses how Nicholls's determination to revive tribalism in Natal led him to champion the reinstatement of Solomon kaDinuzulu as the Zulu paramount.
84. R. Phillips, *The Bantu are Coming. Phases of South Africa's Race Problem* (London, 1930), p. 32. See also foreword by C. T. Loram. And Tim Couzens's ' "Moralizing Leisure Time": the Transatlantic Connection and Black Johannesburg, 1918–36', in Marks and Rathbone (eds), *Industrialisation and Social Change*.

85. Foreword by J. Dexter Taylor to J. R. Sullivan, *The Native Policy of Sir Theophilus Shepstone* (Johannesburg, 1928).
86. J. C. Smuts, *South Africa and Some World Problems* (Oxford, 1930), p. 87.
87. NTS 1697 42/276, Hertzog to 1926 Farmers' Conference, p. 14.
88. *Ibid.*, pp. 97–8. These warnings probably refer to intelligence reports regarding the activities of the Communist Party, since Hertzog claimed that links had been traced to Moscow via London. The SA Communist Party adopted its 'Native Republic' policy in 1928.
89. Smuts Archive, A1 vol. 307 box N doc. 107. 'Note on Conversation with General Hertzog on Native Policy, 13/2/28', p. 1. Hertzog had in fact made public references to 'Bolshevism' before this date. See for example *House of Assembly Debates* vol. 9, 1927, col. 2913.
90. In 1928 Smuts stated his opposition to the creation of a General Native Council on the grounds that this would 'collect all the Kadalies and Communist agitators in South Africa into a body which might have a very unsettling effect on the Native mind'. Smuts Archive, A1 vol. 307 box N doc. 108, 'Note of a conversation with General Hertzog on 15/2/28'.
91. *Joint Sitting of Both Houses of Parliament (1930)*, cols 9–13 (Madeley); *House of Assembly Debates*, vol. 14, 1930, cols 230–1 (Stallard). In relation to the 1930 Urban Areas (amendment) Bill, Stallard said, 'the problem before South Africa at the present time is whether or not the black population is going to be the proletariat of South Africa. Are you willing, is the country willing to accept that position coolly and quietly?', col. 230.

3 Structure and Conflict in the NAD

1. Expenditure on 'native affairs' was approximately 1–2 *per cent* of total Union expenditure between 1912 and 1936. For figures see *Official Year Book of the Union of South Africa*, vol. 3 (1919), p. 798; vol. 7 (1924), p. 750; vol. 18 (1937), p. 584.
2. *Cape Times* 2 May 1934, address by Sir James Rose Innes.
3. Stubbs papers, A954 B4, draft of article dated February 1923, almost certainly by Stubbs, pp. 5–6.
4. The OFS was an exception, since its Native Affairs Department was abolished in 1908.
5. In 1921–2, T. W. C. Norton, then the Assistant Chief Magistrate of the Transkei, was appointed as the first Chief Native Commissioner of the Cape (Ciskei). His job was to coordinate the work of the NAD.
6. This schematic outline of the NAD is drawn from a variety of sources. For more detail, see Rogers, *Native Administration in the Union of South Africa* (Johannesburg, 1933), pp. 4–16, pp. 198–207; Brookes, *History*, chap. VII; *Official Year Book of the Union of South Africa* (annual).
7. UG 7-'19, *Report of the NAD for the Years 1913–1918*, p. 1. The NAD's district administration and its Native Labour branch were, for

practical purposes, distinct. This separation is replicated in the State Archives, Pretoria. Thus the SNA and NA series deal largely with district administration and matters pertaining to Head Office, whereas the Government Native Labour Bureau (GNLB) series is concerned with labour in the industrial areas. The scope of this work is limited to a study of the NAD's district administration and its Head Office. The best and most comprehensive account of the Native Labour Department is to be found in Jeeves's *Migrant Labour in South Africa's Mining Economy.*

8. JUS 750 1/683/22/1 part 4, Frank White to J. Raubenheimer, 23 April 1931.

9. *Umteteli Wa Bantu* (editorial), 29 September 1923; *SA Quarterly*, IV, 4, 1922, (editorial by Rheinallt Jones); *Cape Times*, 10 July 1922. E. G. Jansen became Minister of Native Affairs in 1929.

10. *Cape Times*, 1 June 1923. See also SNA Barrett's complaints of the NAD's 'cavalier treatment' by ministers since the time of Henry Burton and his criticisms of F. S. Malan in particular, in PM 1/2/61 18/1, E. Barrett to Hon. PM, 27 January 1923, 'Administration of Native Affairs'.

11. Stubbs papers, A954 B4, Harries to Stallard (confidential), 6 March 1922. Harries argued that 'a real live man' was needed as SNA and recommended Ernest Stubbs for the post. D. R. Hunt argued too that the NAD had been 'cussed with a succession of weak Secretaries' and provides further biographical comments on departmental officials. See D. R. Hunt to W. M. Macmillan, 23 October 1924, in W. M. Macmillan papers (possession of Mrs Mona Macmillan).

12. Only in 1936 was a CNC for the Northern Areas appointed. He had jurisdiction over the Transvaal (excepting the Witwatersrand), the OFS and parts of the Northern Cape.

13. This point is disputed by the writer William Plomer, who claims that the retrenchment of NAD officials in 1922 was part of an attempt to replace English with Afrikaners in the civil service. Plomer's father Charles had served as a NAD official in the Northern Transvaal and Johannesburg. Plomer's account of his father's career captures something of the ethos of 'native administration' in those days. See W. Plomer's *Double Lives. An Autobiography* (London, 1943), p. 136 and *passim*.

14. Both Edward Dower and J. B. Moffatt had been Chief Magistrates of the Transkei; E. Barrett had been Chief Clerk of the Cape NAD; Major Herbst had served for some time as a magistrate in the St Marks district of the Transkei. A possible exception of this rule was M. C. Vos. He, however, retired as SNA after only 6 months.

15. SDK 113 4/15/1 part IV, 'Confidential Impressions of Head Office Administration 1925', by S. Maynard Page.

16. Stubbs papers, A954 B4, 'Cliffy' (C. L. R. Harries) to 'My dear Ernest', 2 November 1922.

17. NA 273 585/20/f639, Garthorne to SNA, 4 June 1920.

18. UG 6-'21, *Fifth Report of the Public Service Commission of Enquiry (1920)*, p. 9.

19. E. Brookes, 'The Public Service' in Brookes *et. al.*, *Coming of Age. Studies in South African Citizenship and Politics* (Cape Town, 1930), pp. 335, 340. Brookes's 'Golden Age' refers to the period 1921–4, when the Commission was 'both strong and trusted'.
20. UG 18-'22, *Tenth Annual Report of the Public Service Commission (1921)*, p. 2.
21. SDK 112 4/15/1 unsigned memo. to Chairman PSC, 18 November 1922.
22. SDK 112 4/15/1 part I, V. G. M. Robinson Chairman PSC to Min. NA, 30 December 1922, pp. 1–2.
23. SDK 112 4/15/1, Robinson to Min. NA, received 2 February 1923.
24. SDK 112 4/15/1 part I, Robinson to Min. NA, 30 December 1922, p. 3.
25. SDK 112 4/15/1, Robinson to Min. NA, received 2 February 1923.
26. UG 14-'27, *Report of the NAD for the Years 1922–26*, p. 1.
27. SDK 112 4/15/1, unsigned memo. to the Chairman PSC on reorganis-ation of the NAD, 18 November 1922, p. 5.
28. *Ibid.*, p. 4.
29. SDK 112 4/15/1, 'Reorganisation Native Affairs Department', 13 March 1923, p. 2. At a meeting with the PSC the NAC advised that it would be unwise to change the system of administration in the Transkei since it 'had worked with such conspicuous success'. See UG 36-'23, *Report of the NAC for 1922*, p. 6.
30. SDK 117 4/15/31, 'Final Report on an Inspection of the Offices of the Public Service in the Transkeian Territories' by Edward Reading, 8 June 1922.
31. JUS 1607 1/53/44 part I, report by H. Britten on official conference of Transkeian magistrates, Umtata, May 1925, 11 May 1925.
32 NTS 1772 64/276(7), Herbst to Min. NA, 'Report of the NEC', 27 November 1933, p. 21.
33. PM 1/2/61 18/1, W. T. Welsh Chief Magistrate Transkei to SNA, 'Reorganization: Transkeian Territories', 23 December 1922.
34. PM 1/2/61 18/1, E. Barrett to Hon. PM, 27 January 1923, 'Adminis-tration of Native Affairs', p. 10.
35. *Ibid.*, p. 14.
36. SDK 4/15/1 part II, Smuts to Barrett, 13 February 1923.
37. *Cape Times*, 1 June 1923.
38. PM 1/2/61 18/1. See e.g. telegram from Lionel Phillips, Haenertsburg, 2 February 1923; E. J. Browning to Smuts, 4 March 1923; protests by the Bishops of Cape Town and Johannesburg, as well as the Vicar-General of Pretoria.
39. *Rand Daily Mail*, 27 February 1923 in PM 1/2/61 18/1.
40. *Rand Daily Mail*, 28 February 1923 in *ibid*.
41. *Rand Daily Mail*, 1 March 1923 in *ibid*.
42. *Rand Daily Mail*, 1 March 1923 (editorial), 'Wrecking the Native Affairs Department', in *ibid*.
43. *Cape Times*, 5 April 1923, letter from Wilfrid Parker.
44. *Cape Times*, 8 March 1923.
45. PM 1/2/61 18/1, Barrett to Hon. PM, 27 January 1923.

46. His Majesty's Stationery Office, London, Cd 4323. *Col. Reports-Miscellaneous no. 55, Cape Colony Report on the Rietfontein Area by J. F. Herbst*, Oct. 1908.
47. Herbst papers, BC 79 F2, Dower to Herbst, 25 February 1909. Dower recorded Merriman's thanks for the report on Kooper and his 'sense of the energy tact and discretion' displayed by Herbst. Merriman felt that Herbst had 'been the means of rendering very material service to the cause of peace in South Africa.'
48. A newspaper obituary to Herbst by Major K. R. Thomas (from which elements of this biography have been gleaned) incorrectly claims that Herbst was appointed by Hertzog to the post of SNA. I have not been able to establish the source or date of this clipping, which is in the Herbst papers.
49. Lacey, *Boroko*, pp. 94, 95. Margery Perham found Herbst rather enigmatic and was deeply suspicious of him at their meeting in 1930 – largely because she believed him to be 'Dutch'. She recorded in her diary, 'It is difficult to make him out. He has a cherubic smile. He smiles and smiles at everything but it is hard to say if he is a villain or not. His English accent is bad but it is not that that makes you know you are with a foreigner. He is cautious. I cannot draw him. All darts are turned by his smile'. From Perham, *African Apprenticeship*, p. 174. According to his son, Herbst was a severe, distant and private man of impeccable manners. He remained a SAP supporter all his life and was strongly pro-Empire. Interview with W. Herbst, Plumstead, Cape Town, 12 September 1984.
50. NTS 8456 1/360, Barrett to Roberts, 5/8/2; UG 34-'22, *Report of the NAD for the Years 1919–21*, p. 23.
51. NTS 8456 1/360, Barrett to Hon. Min. NA, 2/8/21. See also G. A. Godley to Chief Clerk, 19 July 1921. The NAC's report on the Bulhoek uprising was presented to Parliament in 1921 and is listed officially as A4-'21.
52. NTS 8456 1/360, A. W. Roberts to Hon. Min. NA, 1 September 1921.
53. Herbst papers, BC 79 D22, Barrett to Sec. Lands, 12 December 1921, p. 2. See also Sommerville to SNA, 6 May 1922.
54. Herbst papers, BC79 D22, memorandum (probably by E. R. Garthorne) on 'Native Occupation of Land', 24 October 1921, pp. 1–2.
55. Herbst papers, BC79 D25, memo. by Rogers, p. 5.
56. Herbst papers, BC 79 D22, SNA to Sec. Lands, 13 June 1922, p. 2.
57. Herbst papers, BC79 D25, memo by Rogers, p. 6. See also D22, memo by Garthorne.
58. Herbst papers, BC79 D22, notes of discussion at Prime Minister's Office on 5 December 1921.
59. Herbst papers, BC79 D22.1, J. Sommerville to SNA, 6 May 1922.
60. TES 2742 10/178. See e.g. Sec. Finance to Lands 30 September 1924; Acting Sec. Finance to Sec. Lands, 27 November 1923; Sec. Lands to Sec. Finance, 1 February 1924.
61. Smuts Archive, A1 vol. 125 doc. 14, D. L. Smit to Hon. Min., 21 August 1937. Smit pointed out that land purchases had been confined largely to Rustenburg (Minister P. G. W. Grobler's constituency)

and Pietersburg (Tom Naudé's constituency) and intimated that 'all sorts of unpleasant suggestions are being made', p. 4.

62. NTS 1695 35/276 part II, P. G. W. Grobler Min. Lands to Hertzog, 9 April 1927.
63. NTS 1695 35/276 part II, G. Denoon, Registrar Lands to Sec. Lands, 21 March 1927.
64. SDK 118 4/15/1 part I, Wheelwright to SNA, 4 October 1924.
65. Hunt papers, A1655 Ac.28, Hunt (unsigned) to Mr Niewenhuize, 23 March 1927.
66. NTS 8623 41/362, Norton to SNA 31/10/22, 'Native Administration in the Ciskei' (confidential), p. 2.
67. NTS 1698 45/276, Wheelwright to SNA, 7 January 1925.
68. Stubbs papers, A954 B4, article by Stubbs (for publication), Feb. 1923, pp. 4–5.
69. *House of Assembly Debates*, vol. 9, 1927, col. 5764. In 1929 Pirow (a Nazi-sympathiser during the war) himself led an armed police battalion in Durban to seek out African tax defaulters.
70. Naturally, the battle was most actively pursued by the NAD, for which more was at stake.
71. NTS 1700 45/276, Magistrate Herschel to CNC King Williamstown, 27 January 1925.
72. NTS 1700 45/276, D. R. Hunt to Native Commissioner Rustenburg (submitted by Ernest Stubbs, Magistrate and Native Commissioner Rustenburg, 29 December 1924).
73. NTS 1700 45/276, E. L. Matthews, Law Adviser, 'Report on Native Administration Bill', 11 December 1924. Submitted along with other papers from the Justice ministry to Hertzog, 17 December 1924.
74. Hertzog papers, A32 vol. 115, pp. 93–4, Matthews to Steyn, 18 January 1926.
75. NTS 1700 45/276, W. E. Bok to Minister, 17 December 1924.
76. JUS 750 1/683/22/1 part 2, Herbst to Sec. Finance, 9 October 1925; Sec. Finance to Sec. Justice, 27 November 1925.
77. JUS 750 1/683/22/1 part 2, Bok to Sec. Finance, 5 December 1925.
78. SDK 113 4/15/1 part IV, PSC Inspection Report on NAD Head Office 17 October 1928. These magistracies were probably Hlabisa, Ingwavuma, Melmoth, Mahlabatini, Nkhandla, Nongoma, Nqutu, Ubombo, Msinga, Ndwedwe, Mapumulo, Keiskamahoek, Middeldrift, Peddie and Victoria East. The remaining two might have been Barberton and Pilgrim's Rest in the E. Tvl.
79. See contents of JUS 750 1/683/22/1 part 3.
80. SDK 119 4/15/44 part I, Bok to Sec. PSC, 18 May 1928.
81. SDK 113 4/15/1 part IV, signed Inspection Report on the NAD Head Office 17 October 1928, pp. 5, 16.
82. In employing the term 'language of legitimation' as opposed to 'ideology' I am following Deborah Posel's useful distinction. 'An ideology includes, but is not exhausted by, a language of legitimation. The latter becomes an ideology once it is effectively persuasive, internalised into the experience and subjectivity of at least one audience.'

See her 'Language, Legitimation and Control: The South African State after 1978', *Social Dynamics*, X, 1, 1984, p. 13.

83. G. H. Searle, *The Quest for National Efficiency. A Study of British Politics and Political Thought, 1899–1914*, (Oxford, 1971), pp. 1 and 260.
84. L. Barnes, *Caliban in Africa. An Impression of Colour-Madness* (London, 1930), p. 212.
85. UG 15-'22, *Report of the NAD for the Year 1921*, p. 2.
86. NTS 1695 34/276 part I, SNA to Sec. PSC, 29? August 1925.
87. J. F. Herbst, 'The Administration of Native Affairs in South Africa', *Journal of the African Society*, XXIX, 117, 1930, p. 484. See also my paper ' "Understanding the Native Mind" '.
88. Rogers, *Native Administration*, p. 8.
89. See William Beinart, 'Soil Erosion, Conservationism and Ideas about Development: A Southern African Exploration, 1900–1960', *JSAS*, II, 1, 1984.
90. NTS 7313 75/327, 'The Agricultural Policy for Natives in the Union of South Africa', by R. W. Thornton, 1929; also NTS 1034 11/419, undated memo by Thornton to SNA on agricultural development of Native areas of the Union.
91. Attempts to arrive at a consensus over a uniform system of taxation based on a 'fair average' are evident in the debates of the annual Native Conferences of 1923 and 1924. Opposition was strongest in the Cape, which stood to lose most from a change in the taxation system. See UG 36-'23, *Report of the NAC for the Year 1922*, pp. 61–2; UG 40-'25, *Report of the NAC for the Year 1924*, pp. 31–8.
92. UG 36-'23, *Report of the NAC for the Year 1922*, pp. 34, 36. Likewise, Molema argued that 'Freedom in the Cape would be sacrificed for uniformity', p. 37.
93. J. F. Herbst, 'The Administration', p. 480.
94. Herbst papers, BC79 A1.1, 'Native Administration Bill, 1927', c. 1927.
95. NTS 1682 4/276 part I, 'Native Administration: Union of South Africa' by M. G. Apthorp, 1 October 1911 (draft of article for publication).
96. Senate SC 6-'13, *Report from the Select Committee on Native Customs and Marriage Laws*, p. 27.
97. UG 17-'27, *Report of the NAC for the Year 1925–26*, p. 21.
98. Herbst papers, BC79 A1.1, 'Native Administration Bill, 1927'.
99. *Ibid.*, p. 19.
100. *Ibid.*, p. 19.
101. Note that the clause (deriving from Natal) which proposed to make the Governor General 'Supreme Chief', was inserted only during the Bill's Committee stage.
102. *Ibid.*, p. 20. Act 29 of 1897 conferred powers of edictal legislation upon the Governor of the Cape Colony with respect to the Transkei.
103. *Ibid.*, p. 22.
104. NTS 8615 38/362, CNC Cape to SNA, 27/11/23; NTS 1696 36/276, Norton to SNA, 29 December 1924.
105. NTS 1695 35/276 part I, Norton to SNA, 22 December 1924.
106. For a more detailed consideration of the growing resistance from the

Cape to the Administration Bill, see my paper, ' "The Curious Native Administration Bill" of 1927 and the Native Affairs Department', (ICS seminar paper, London University, 1985).

107. A. G. Mcloughlin, 'The Transkeian System of Native Administration' (MA thesis, University of South Africa, 1936), p. 47.

4 The Ideology of Native Administration

1. SDK 112 4/15/1 part 1, E. Barrett to the Hon. PM, 28 November 1922. p. 2
2. J. H. Hofmeyr, *South Africa* (London, 1931), p. 315.
3. *Cape Times*, 8 March 1933.
4. NTS 1698 45/276, C. A. Wheelwright CNC Natal to SNA, 7 January 1925, pp. 1–2.
5. W. M. Macmillan, *Bantu, Boer and Briton* (London, 1929), p. 296. In the OUP edition of 1963 Macmillan was somewhat more ironical in referring to 'the almost vaunted success of this unique, tribally composite but roomy "Bantu Homeland" as a model of Native Administration . . .', p. 348.
6. Brookes in Schapera (ed.), *Western Civilisation*, p. 249.
7. F. Brownlee, 'The Administration of the Transkeian Territories', *Journal of the African Society*, XXXVI, 144, 1937, p. 337.
8. NTS 1772 64/276(6) part 1, 'Precis of CNCs' Opinions on NEC Report' by R. W. Thornton, 22 December 1932. See views of Welsh and Apthorp.
9. J. R. Sullivan, *The Native Policy of Sir Theophilus Shepstone* (Johannesburg, 1928), p. 82.
10. R. Martin, 'Political and Social Theories of Transkeian Administrators in the Late Nineteenth Century' (MA thesis, UCT, 1978), p. 51.
11. Schreuder, 'The Cultural Factor', p. 285.
12. Martin, 'Political and Social Theories', p. 84.
13. Mcloughlin, 'The Transkeian System', p. 193.
14. Biographical material drawn from Eric Rosenthal's *Southern African Dictionary of National Biography* (London, 1966); W. T. Brownlee, *Reminiscences of a Transkeian* (Pietermaritzburg, 1975).
15. Brownlee, 'The Administration', p. 339. See also F. H. Brownlee's evidence to the NEC, Kokstad, 4 November 1930, p. 2844.
16. JUS 750 1/683/22/1 part II, T. W. C. Norton CNC (Cape) to 'all magistrates in this area', circular no. 1/1923, 22 May 1923.
17. *Cape Times*, 24 September 1935.
18. Mcloughlin, 'The Transkeian System', pp. 68–9.
19. JUS 750 1/683/22/1 part II, Norton to all magistrates in this area, 22 May 1923.
20. SAIRR papers, AD 843.B30.1, Harding Barlow to Prof. Hoernlé, 'private', 29 July 1934.
21. See, for example, *Cape Times*, 24 September 1935, 'Native Administration in the Transkei'; Mcloughlin in 'The Transkeian System' says, 'The work is tedious and trying. It entails extensive knowledge of

native custom and habits, of human nature especially in its brown form . . .' p. 68.
22. Evidence of Frank Brownlee to NEC, Kokstad, 4 November 1930, p. 2842.
23. For details on the *Bunga* and council system, see Rogers, *Native Administration*, pp. 43–75; Brownlee, 'The Administration'.
24. Brookes in Schapera (ed.), *Western Civilisation*, p. 249.
25. One of Hertzog's original four segregation measures was the Natives Union Council Bill. The measure of success achieved by local councils in the Transkei and elsewhere was advanced as 'part of the reason for the Bill'. See J. B. M. Hertzog, *The Segregation .Problem. General Hertzog's Solution* (Cape Town, n.d. [1926]) p. 19.
26. NTS 7188 2/324, Welsh to 'Dear Barrett', 23 November 1920. See also JUS 1607 1/53/44 part I, report by H. Britten on the official conference of Transkeian magistrates, 11 May 1925.
27. Evidence of Rheinallt Jones to NEC, 11 June 1931, p. 8946.
28. *Cape Times*, 24 September 1935. Stanford condemned the transfer of criminal administration from the magistrate to the police in the Transkei.
29. Evidence of F. H. Brownlee to NEC, Kokstad, 4 November 1930 pp. 2841–5.
30. NTS 8623 41/362, Norton to SNA, 'Report on Native Administration in the Ciskei', 'confidential', 31 October 1922 p. 9 and *passim.*; SAIRR papers AD 843.B.30.1, Harding Barlow to Prof. Hoernlé, 29 July 1934, 'private', pp. 26–8.
31. NTS 1756 45/276 vol. 1, part I, report by R. Colson, Magistrate Harrismith, 8 October 1926. An annotated note by Howard Rogers of the NAD says that the report is 'excellent in parts' and may be regarded as 'typical of the OFS'.
32. SDK 118 4/15/35 part I, O. W. Staten to Sec. PSC, 'confidential', p. 3, received 31 January 1923.
33. NTS 1772 64/276(6) part I, Acting Native Commissioner Ixopo to CNC Pietermaritzburg, 5 September 1932, pp. 1–2; see also SDK 118 4/15/35 part 2, S. Maynard Page to Sec. PSC, 'Inspection Report of Office of the CNC Natal', 3 March 1928, p. 1.
34. In 1925 a number of Natal magistrates together with H. Britten, the Magistrate of King William's Town, attended the Transkeian magistrates' official conference in Umtata. See JUS 1607 1/53/44 part 1, Godley to Sec. Justice, 18 March 1925.
35. N. L. G. Cope, 'The Zulu Royal Family Under the South African Government, 1910–1933: Solomon KaDinuzulu, Inkatha and Zulu Nationalism' (PhD thesis, Natal University, 1985), p. 17.
36. *Ibid.* See also pp. 14–15, 18.
37. *Ibid.*, p. 143.
38. Brookes, *History*, pp. 149–53.
39. Mcloughlin, 'The Transkeian System', p. 193.
40. On this see Cope, 'The Zulu Royal Family', and Marks, *The Ambiguities of Dependence*, chapter 1.
41. See Paul Rich's interesting 'The Origins of Apartheid Ideology: The

Case of Ernest Stubbs and Transvaal Native Administration c.1902–1932', *African Affairs* CXXIX, p. 315, 1980.

42. PM 1/2/61 18/1, Stubbs to SNA, 'Minutes of a meeting of Native Chiefs and Indunas, Zoutpansberg District', 8/6/23; p. 5.
43. W. M. Macmillan, *My South African Years*, p. 180.
44. Evidence of Major D. R. Hunt to NEC, Lydenburg, 20/8/30, pp. 712–3.
45. PM 1/2/61 18/1, B. H. Dicke to General Smuts, 21/4/24. Amongst other letters in this file testifying to Stanford's indispensable role, are those from Lionel Phillips and Col. Mentz.
46. SDK 112 4/15/1 part I, W. I. S. Driver to SNA, 25/1/23, 'Bolshevism in the Bobibidi Tribe'.
47. PM 1/2/61 18/1, Archbishop Cape Town to PM, 10/3/23.
48. Evidence of H. M. Taberer to NEC, 5/5/31, p. 7336. See also evidence of Major H. S. Cooke, 4/5/31, pp. 7277–8.
49. Bradford, 'The Industrial and Commercial Workers' Union', p. 70.
50. SC 10a-'20, *Second Report of the Select Committee on Native Affairs*, p. 10.
51. Plans for the establishment of a permanent Native Affairs Commission were mooted in the NAD from at least as early as 1913. At about the same time (and perhaps coincidentally) Maurice Evans called for the creation of a permanent statutory council to 'study native affairs' and to advise the Governor General. The 1917 Native Administration Bill also proposed the creation of a Native Affairs Commission. See NA 269 210/14 f639, draft of 'A consolidated Bill dealing with Native Affairs Administration', 29/11/13; M. Evans, 'The Next Step in Native Government', *SA Quarterly*, I, 2, 1914.
52. See NA 273 585/20/f369 on the choice of the Commission's members. Amongst the many individuals who either applied or were nominated to sit on the body were M. Pelem, D. D. T. Jabavu, E. R. Garthorne and Fred Bell.
53. UG 15-'22, *Report of the Native Affairs Commission for the Year 1921*, p. 5.
54. *Cape Times*, (editorial), 29/10/24.
55. UG 40-'25, *Report of the Native Affairs Commission for the Year 1924*, p. 50.
56. *Ibid.*, pp. 28, 48.
57. NTS 8456 1/360, Roberts and Lemmer to PM, 1/6/21.
58. Brookes, *History*, p. 306.
59. UG 17-'27, *Report of the Native Affairs Commission for the Years 1925–26*, p. 9.
60. SC 19-'27, *Select Committee on Native Bills*, p. 25. See also individual evidence of Loram, Van Niekerk and Roberts. See SC 10-'27, *Select Committee on Native Bills*, pp. 6–8 for the NAC's 1927 memo on the Bills.
61. NTS 8624 41/362. See memo. by Roberts and Loram on the Natives Parliamentary Representation Bill (1929), as well as memo. by P. W. le R. van Niekerk. (Van Niekerk replaced Lemmer on the NAC in 1926.)

62. Pim papers, A881 BL 4/29, Roberts to Pim, 15 January 1924.
63. Pim papers, A881 BL 1, Roberts to Pim, 24 August 1921; 3/9/21.
64. M. M. S. Bell, 'The Politics of Administration', pp. 83–4.
65. In 1936 the NAC's members were G. Heaton Nicholls, W. R. Collins, J. Mould Young and E. A. Conroy. Aside from Mould Young, who was a member of the NAD, all were SAP parliamentarians.
66. NTS 7188 2/324, Welsh to Barrett, 23 November 1920.
67. UG 15-'22, *Report of the NAC for the Year 1921*, pp. 30–1.
68. SC 10-'27, *Select Committee on the Native Bills*, evidence of F. C. M. Thompson, p. 277.
69. Herbst, 'Native Administration' pp. 480–2; UG 36-'23, *Report of the NAC for the Year 1922*, p. 3.
70. NTS 8456 1/360, Norton to SNA, 7 February 1924; Wheelwright to SNA, 14 February 1924.
71. NTS 1694 30/276, 'Notes for the guidance of the conference by the acting PM', 5 November 1923, p. 2.
72. NTS 1772 64/276(7), Herbst to Min. NA, 'Report of the NEC', p. 7, 27 November 1923.
73. E. H. Brookes, *The Colour Problems of South Africa* (Lovedale, 1934), pp. 91–92.
74. For a list of the councils established between 1926 and 1933 with full powers under Act 23 of 1920, and with restricted powers under Act 27 of 1926, see Rogers, *Native Administration*, pp. 83–4.
75. This is a highly simplified account of a legislative maze. Useful contemporary summaries of the different legal systems are to be found in Brookes's *History*, esp. ch. IX, and Rogers's *Native Administration*, pp. 219–21.
76. Senate SC 6-'13, *Report from the Select Committee on Native Custom and Marriage Laws*, pp. iv-v.
77. SNA Edward Dower, for example, felt that customary law should be recognised where there was a call for it, but emphasised that it should not 'be enforced or crystallised into law so that advancing Natives cannot break away from it'. *Ibid.*, p. 27.
78. Brookes, *History*, pp. 246, 64. As in this example, what might be termed the 'missionary position' was frequently caricatured. But not all nineteenth-century missionaries were hostile to traditionalism. See, e.g. D. Welsh, *The Roots of Segregation. Native Policy in Natal 1854–1910* (Oxford and Cape Town, 1973), p. 261. In Jeff Guy's *The Heretic. A Study of the Life of John William Colenso 1814–1883* (Pietermaritzburg and Johannesburg, 1983), we learn that for Bishop Colenso 'the world was not divided between the enlightened, redeemed, Christian and the benighted, heathen, barbarian. While Christians had precious insights, special privileges, duties and responsibilities, all men were saved at birth through the love of God . . .', p. 44.
79. NTS 8623 41/362 part II, Memo. by 'E.R.G.' (Garthorne), 22 January 1920, pp. 3–4.
80. See NTS 1700 45/276, Official Conference on Native Marriage Bill, 14 November 1923; also NTS 1686 11/276, 'Native Marriage Bill', 19 November 1923. Among those present were C. T. Loram, C. A.

Wheelwright, W. T. Welsh, T. W. C. Norton, Dr Roberts, and Col. Pritchard.
81. NTS 1700 45/276, Official Conference on Native Marriage Bill, 14 November 1923, p. 8.
82. UG 22-'32 *Report of the Native Economic Commission 1930–32*, p. 102 para. 704.
83. *Ibid.*, p. 103, paras. 705–10.
84. NTS 1750 45/276(28), 'Annual Report on Native Affairs, Bergville District 1931', 26 January 1932.
85. UG 47-'23, *Report of the NAC for 1923*, pp. 20, 24.
86. See, e.g. NTS 1694 32/276, 'Notes of a meeting between the PM and deputation of Natives', 2 August 1920; NTS 1701 45/276, 'Minutes of Proceedings of Transkei Territories General Council', 2 May 1927; NTS 9313 9/378, 'Representation by chiefs and people of W. Pondoland to PM Hertzog on his tour of the Transkei', 29 August 1925.
87. NTS 1772 64/276(6) part 1, 'Precis of CNC's opinions on NEC Report' by R. W. Thornton, 22 December 1932. By 1932 the CNC's of the Cape (Apthorp), Transkei (Welsh) and Natal (Young) were all agreed that *lobolo* should not be interfered with for the present.
88. AD 1438, Native Economic Commission, Minutes of Evidence, (Church of the Province of South Africa Archives, University of the Witwatersrand – henceforth CPSA). Statement by H. Lugg, Magistrate Verulam, Natal to NEC, box 12, p. 1.
89. Statement by H. Britten, Magistrate JHB, to NEC, AD 1438 box 7 (CPSA), p. 2.
90. NTS 9454 2/392, Welsh to SNA, 6 August 1920.
91. NTS 1698 45/276, Norton to SNA, 22 December 1924.
92. NTS 1701 45/276, Report on the Proceedings of the Select Committee on the Administration Bill, 13 May 1927, p. 2.
93. NTS 9454 2/392, Welsh to SNA, 28 June 1927 and marginal note signed 'ERG' (Garthorne), 5 July 1927.
94. NTS 1772 64/276(6) part 1, 'Precis of CNC's opinions on NEC Report', by R. W. Thornton, 22 December 1932.
95. NTS 1704 45/276(3) (2), Herbst to Welsh, 12 August 1929.
96. NTS 1738 45/276(21) part 1, Welsh to Herbst, 15 November 1929. Jongintaba Dalindyebo was given jurisdiction over Tembuland and Victor Poto Ndamase jurisdiction over W. Pondoland. Welsh added that Regent Mswakeli, Paramount of E. Pondoland, had been omitted on the grounds of his being 'a drunken wastrel and wholly unfitted to be invested with judicial powers . . .'
97. NTS 1772 64/276(7), Herbst to Min. NA, 'Report of the NEC', 27/11/23, pp. 12–13, 16–17, 8.
98. *Ibid.*, pp. 10, 12–13.
99. F. S. Malan papers, Acc. 58/21, Herbst to Min. NA, 27 February 1931.
100. Welsh, *Roots*, p. 171. For a useful discussion of the Natal Code, see chap. IX.
101. NTS 1756 48/276 part 1, memo. from Burchell, Farrer and Lugg to CNC Pietermaritzburg, 28 February 1928, p. 1.
102. On the legalisation of customary law in the colonial context, see Martin

Chanock's *Law, Custom and Social Order. The Colonial Experience in Malawi and Zambia* (Cambridge, 1985).

103. For a selection of these protests see NTS 1758 48/276 vol. II, part 2. See also *The Round Table*, XXII, 87, 1932, p. 672.

104. Rheinallt Jones papers, AD 1715 5.3, 'Johannesburg Joint Council of Europeans and Natives. Criticisms of Draft Proclamation Amending the Natal Code of Native Law 1891'.

105. SAIRR papers, AD 843 box E, Rheinallt Jones to Sir Clarkson Tredgold, 5 March 1932.

106. SAIRR papers AD 843 box E, Clarkson Tredgold to Rheinallt Jones, 18 March 1932.

107. See for e.g. NTS 1756 48/276 vol. I part 1, Norton CNC Natal to SNA, 19 March 1931.

108. NTS 1756 48/276 vol. I, part 1, Wheelwright to SNA, 2 May 1928.

109. NTS 1756 48/276 vol. I part I, Norton to SNA, 7 January 1931. See also note from J. S. Allison to SNA, 9 March [1931]; NTS 1758 48/276 part II, 'Draft Revised Code of Native Law' n.d. The amended Natal Code was published in the *Government Gazette* of 6 November 1931.

110. NTS 1698 11/276, 'Native Marriage Bill', 19 November 1923.

111. NTS 1701 45/276, Report of the Select Committee on the Native Administration Bill, 13 May 1927; NTS 1695 35/276 part 1, Wheelwright to SNA, 26/6/26. Wheelwright associated himself with a leader in the *Natal Witness* of 26 June 1926 and argued that Africans should have access to the Supreme Court rather than being subject to the Natal Native Court.

112. Rheinallt Jones papers, A394 C9a/17, J. M. Young, CNC Natal, to Rheinallt Jones, 3 May 1932.

113. NTS 2009 9/280 part I, O. Pirow to Min. NA, 2 March 1925.

114. PM 1/2/32 7/15, Williams, for Sec. Agriculture, to Sec. PM, 6 January 1926.

115. For copies of these petitions see NTS 2009 9/280 part I. See also NTS 2093 22/280 vol. II.

116. NTS 2009 9/280 part I, Herbst to Pirow, 11 March 1925.

117. NTS 2093 222/280 vol. I, Welsh to SNA, 23 May 1928.

118. NTS 2093 222/280 vol. I, H. S. Cooke, Director of Native Labour to SNA 12 May 1928, p. 2; Cooke to SNA, 3 August 1928.

119. NTS 2093 222/280, vol. I. See article by Herbst in *The S. A. Farmer*, 22 June 1928, entitled 'Native Farm Labour'. For farmers' response see *The S. A. Farmer*, 6 July 1928. See also typescript of article dated 25 January 1920 by H. G. Falwasser for *The Sunday Times*. Falwasser argues that the role of the NAD was to serve as the arbiter between 'employer and employee' and that it should not engage in 'actual recruiting of natives' on behalf of farmers.

120. PM 1/2/32 7/15, 'ERG' (Garthorne), to Sec. Agriculture 18 January 1926. 'This Department would assist such a Bureau in every way possible short of identifying itself with the actual recruiting of natives.' p. 4.

121. Without free access to the national archives it is difficult to assess how long the NAD was able to resist being drawn directly into farm labour

recruitment. It is possible that by the 1930s the Department was more amenable in this respect. See e.g. NTS 2093 222/280 part II, General Circular 10 of 1934, 'Native Farm Labour', 10 September 1934. Baruch Hirson, however, is of the view that SNA Douglas Smit refused to involve the NAD in direct farm labour recruitment during the mid-1930s for reasons similar to those outlined in the argument above.

122. Act 24/1932.
123. For a description of the Act's intentions see JUS 1/10/11(53), Report by law adviser A. A. Schoch; Rogers, *Native Administration*, pp. 159–65.
124. *Cape Times* (editorial), 10 May 1932. See also *House of Assembly Debates*, vol. 19, 1932, col. 4278.
125. See, e.g. UG 26-'32, *Report of the NAC for the Years 1927–31*, pp. 21–23; *Imvo*, 16 February 1932; *Round Table*, 87, 1932, pp. 671–2.
126. NTS 8632 61/362. See, e.g. J. S. Marwick to Sec. Justice, 4 November, 1932; *Sunday Times*, 31 July 1932; Report of meeting between O. Pirow and representatives of Tvl. Landowners Association, 13 July 1932 and memo.
127. *Cape Times* (editorial), 10 September 1930.
128. See, e.g. NTS 1779 77/276 part I, 'Proceedings of Native Commissioners' Conference, Durban 15–17/11/33'; NTS 8633 61/362, Herbst to Sec. Justice, 1 July 1933; NTS 8631 61/362 part II, A. L. Barrett, Director of Native Labour, to SNA, 15 June 1933.
129. NTS 8633 61/362, H. C. Lugg CNC Natal to SNA, 18 September 1933. Lugg made a conservative estimate that some 150 000 African squatters and rent-paying tenants (40 000 families) with 'huge herds of cattle' faced eviction in Natal should the Contract Act's provisions be enforced. There was little room for them in the existing reserves which were already congested.
130. NTS 8633 61/362, Note to Minister from D. L. Smit; Herbst to Sec. Justice, 27 January 1933.
131. NTS 8633 61/362, Note to Minister from D. L. Smit, 15 September 1933; Herbst to Sec. Justice, 18 July 1933. At some point the responsibility for the Act must have devolved upon the NAD, though it is unlikely that it was ever effectively administered. See D. C. Hindson, 'The Pass System and the Formation of an Urban African Proletariat in South Africa' (PhD thesis, Sussex University, 1983), p. 94.
132. NTS 1741 45/276/26 part I, Maynard Page to SNA, 4 December 1928.
133. Hunt Papers AD 1655 Ac 28, D. R. Hunt (unsigned) to Mr Niewenhuize, 23 March 1927.
134. NTS 1741 45/276/26 vol. 2, A. L. Barrett to SNA, 17 September 1934, p. 2.
135. See, e.g. evidence of Dr Seme to NEC, 6 May 1931, p. 7421. In the *Cape Times* of 25 September 1935, W. Elliot Stanford argued that criminal jurisdiction should remain in the hands of the magistrate. The police were 'a foreign body thrust into the administrative system and social structure of the native and incapable of assimilation'.
136. NTS 1695 35/276 part I, Norton to SNA, 22 December 1924.

137. NTS 1741 45/276(26) part II, SNA D. L. Smit to CNC Pietermaritz-burg, 4 January 1935, pp. 1–2
138. UG 15-'22, *Report of the NAC for the Year 1922*, pp. 25–8, pp. 34–6; UG 34-'22, *Report of the NAD for the Years 1919–21*, pp. 13–15.
139. UG 41-'22, *Report of the Inter-Departmental Committee on the Native Pass Laws 1920*, pp. 9, 11. Section 12 of the 1923 Urban Areas Act embodied elements of the Native Registration and Protection Bill. At the 1923 native conference in Pretoria, G. A. Godley described the Registration and Protection Bill as 'an earnest and honest attempt to secure the minimum of control and the maximum measure of protection to the natives'. See UG 47-'23, *Report of the NAC for the Year 1923*.
140. See R. Davenport, 'African Townsmen? South African Natives (Urban Areas) Legislation through the Years', *African Affairs*, LXVIII, 271, 1969. For an analysis of the differences between the Godley and Stal-lard Commissions in terms of a 'differentiated labour system', see also D. Hindson, *Pass Controls and the Urban African Proletariat in South Africa* (Johannesburg, 1987), pp. 35–9.
141. UG 56-'37, *Notes on Conference Between Municipalities and Native Affairs Department . . . to Discuss the Provisions of the Native Laws Amendment Act (no. 46 of 1937)*, p. 2. Cancellation of the 1931 census renders figures somewhat speculative. For detailed estimates of African urbanization 1904–36, see Shannon, 'Urbanization', *SAJE*, V. 2, 1937. Also UG 22-'32, *Report of the NEC*.
142. AD 843 SAIRR-Rheinallt Jones papers, A1.11 Unsorted Head Office Memoranda 'Natives (Urban Areas) Further Amendment Bill', n.d., [1935] p. 2.
143. NTS 4147 11/313 part III, 'Natives (Urban Areas) Act Amendment Bill, 1927'.
144. In 1937 General Smuts admitted to being mystified that only eleven towns had availed themselves of the 1930 Amendment permitting municipalities to restrict Africans' entry to urban areas. See UG 56-'37, *Notes on Conference Between Municipalities and the NAD*, p. 3.
145. NTS 4153 11/313, Memorandum on (Urban Areas) Act Further Amendment Bill, 12 December 1932, p. 1.
146. Nicholls referred to the 1937 Act as 'the last of a trilogy of Bills which were designed to translate into law the principle of trusteeship established by the Natives Representation Act and the Native Trust and Land Act . . .' See UG 54-'39, *Report of the NAC for the Year 1937–38*, p. 8.
147. The Committee was appointed by the SNA on 2 July 1935 and reported in January 1936. It comprised J. Mould Young (member of the NAC and formerly CNC Natal and Chief Magistrate Transkei) and A. L. Barrett (CNC Cape, former Director of Native Labour and CNC Witwatersrand). The Secretary was F. Rodseth (Inspector of Urban Locations). The report was laid before the Joint Select Committee, but was suppressed because of opposition from the Minister of Native Affairs, P. G. W. Grobler.
148. Smuts Archive, A1 vol. 123 doc. 3, 'Minute and Report of Depart-

mental Committee on Proposed Amendments to the Native's (Urban Areas) Act of 1923', 15 January 1936, paras 49–50.

149. See M.M.S. Bell, 'The Politics of Administration: A Study of the Career of Dr D.L. Smit with Special Reference to his Work in the Department of Native Affairs, 1934–45', MA thesis (Rhodes University, 1978) p. 22, also pp. 19–23. Bell claims that Smit, like J. H. Hofmeyr, saw the 1937 legislation as an opportunity for increasing departmental control in the urban areas in order to ensure that local authorities 'would treat "their responsibilities" in a more serious light'. The 1942 Smit Report recommended the abolition of the pass laws.

150. J. Van der Poel, *Selections From the Smuts Papers vol. VI*, letter no. 414, Smuts to M. C. Gillett, 15 May 1937.

151. Rogers, *Native Administration*, p. 18.

5   The Passage of Hertzog's Native Bills, Part One

1. Trapido, ' "The Friends of the Natives" ', in Marks and Atmore (eds), *Economy and Society*.

2. Acts 12 of 1936 and 18 of 1936, respectively. The 1937 Native Laws Amendment Act may be said to have completed the segregationist trio.

3. Representation of Natives Act, 1936, no. 12 of 1936, *Union Gazette Extraordinary* 23 April 1936.

4. Native Trust and Land Act, 1936, no. 18 of 1936, *Union Gazette Extraordinary*, 19 June 1936.

5. For a description of the 1936 Representation Act, see M. Ballinger, *From Union to Apartheid. A Trek to Isolation* (Folkestone, 1969), chap. 1.

6. Section 49 of Act 18 of 1936 defined 'labour tenant' as any native male adult not in continuous employment, who (together with any dependents) rendered service to a farmer in excess of 180 days per calendar year. The term 'squatter' referred to adult native males resident on a farm but who were neither servants in continuous employment nor labour tenants, e.g. sharecroppers, rent-paying tenants.

7. The decision not to enforce Chapter IV immediately was announced by the Minister of Native Affairs to Parliament on 30 April 1936. See *House of Assembly Debates* vol. 26, 1936, col. 2750.

8. Hertzog papers, A32 vol. 112, Hertzog to Brookes, 23 March 1924; O. Pirow, *James Barry Munnik Hertzog* (Cape Town, n.d., [1957]), pp. 197–8; P. Lewsen, *John X. Merriman. Paradoxical South African Statesman* (New Haven and London), 1982, p. 353.

9. Text of Smithfield speech in J. B. M. Hertzog, *The Segregation Problem* (Cape Town, n.d.).

10. *Ibid.*, p. 2.

11. *Ibid.*, pp. 4–6.

12. *Ibid.*, pp. 3–4.

13. UG 17-'27, *Report of the NAC for 1925–6*, p. 20.

14. Hertzog, *The Segregation Problem*, pp. 13, 15.

15. *Ibid.*, pp. 14–15.
16. J. C. Smuts, *Memorandum on Government Natives and Coloured Bills* (Pretoria, 1926).
17. *Ibid.*, p. 5.
18. *Ibid.*, p. 7.
19. *Ibid.*, p. 19.
20. *Ibid.*, p. 8.
21. *Ibid.*, pp. 11–12.
22. GG 934 19/945. See e.g. *Cape Times*, 28 September 1926; *Rand Daily Mail*, 29 September 1926; *Natal Mercury*, 29 September 1926; *The Star*, 29 September 1926.
23. Smuts, *Memorandum*, p. 19.
24. Hertzog papers, A32 vol. 115, p. 69, Hertzog to Smuts, 16 January 1926.
25. *Ibid.*, pp. 75–6, Smuts to Hertzog, 21 January 1926.
26. *Ibid.*, p. 77, 80, Hertzog to Smuts, 23 January 1926; Smuts to Hertzog, 26 January 1926.
27. Duncan papers, BC 294 D15.9.4, Patrick Duncan to Smuts, 29 December 1927.
28. Smuts archive, A1 vol. 307 Box N doc. 107, 'Note of Conversation with General Hertzog on Native Policy', 13 February 1928, p. 1.
29. *Ibid.*, pp. 1–2.
30. *Ibid.*, pp. 2–3. In addition to the common qualification Smuts proposed the introduction of an 'education and civilisation test' applicable only to 'non-Europeans'.
31. Smuts archive, A1 vol. 307 box N. doc. 108, 'Note of Conversation with General Hertzog on 15/2/28'.
32. Smuts archive, A1 box N vol. 307 doc. 109, 'Note of a Conversation with General Hertzog on Native Bills 27/2/28'.
33. Pim papers, A881 cc36, Pim (unsigned) to Arthur Gillett, 19 July 1929; J. Krikler, 'The South African Party and the Cape African Franchise, 1926–36' (BA(Hons) thesis, University of Cape Town, 1978), pp. 66–7; Pirow, *Hertzog*, p. 192.
34. Pim papers, A881 BL1, Pim to Brookes (confidential), 23 July 1929. See also Margery Perham, *African Apprenticeship*, p. 140, who recorded in her 1929 diary that the SAP 'is divided between the old stalwarts of the Cape and those, especially from Natal, who would vote with the Dutch on the native question'.
35. A. Paton, *Hofmeyr* (London and Cape Town, 1964), p. 222.
36. J. T. Cameron, 'An Analysis of Smuts' Attitude Towards Hertzog's "Native Bills" From 1926 to 1936' (MA thesis, UNISA, 1982), p. 12.
37. Millin Papers, A539/C1, Hofmeyr to Millin, 16 June 1935.
38. B. Friedman, *Smuts: A Reappraisal* (London, 1975), p. 87.
39. *Cape Times*, 29 January 1929.
40. *Ibid.*
41. Indeed, during the 1929 Joint Sitting of Parliament, Smuts stated emphatically that neither he nor his party were 'bound finally or irrevocably to the Cape basis' and he indicated his willingness to 'collaborate'

with Hertzog. *Joint Sitting of Both Houses of Parliament 1929*, col. 68, 18 February 1929.
42. *Ibid.*
43. *Cape Times* (editorial) 25 February 1930. The original 1930 Joint Committee comprised J. B. M. Hertzog, N. C. Havenga, H. W. Sampson, E. G. Jansen; Senators C. J. Langenhoven, F. S. Malan, Rev. C. J. Smit, A. T. Spies, F. C. Thompson, P. W. le Roux van Niekerk and P. J. Wessels; and MPs Col-Cdt. Collins, P. C. De Villiers, Patrick Duncan, J. H. Hofmeyr, C. J. Krige, S. P. le Roux, J. S. Marwick, Tom Naudé, G. H. Nicholls, A. O. B. Payn, General J. C. Smuts, Col. C. F. Stallard, Dr A. J. Stals, Strydom, G. B. van Zyl, and J. B. Wessels.
44. For official details of the Joint Select Committee's sittings see Supplement to Joint Committee No. 1–1935, *Reports and Proceedings of the Joint Committees on Natives and Coloured Persons During the Period 1930–34* (1935) (henceforth *JSC Proceedings 1930–4*). And Joint Committee No. 1–1935, *Reports and Proceedings of the Joint Committee on the Representation of Natives and Coloured Persons in Parliament and Provincial Councils and the Acquisition of Land by Natives* (April, 1935) (henceforth, Joint Committee No. 1–1935, *Reports and Proceedings*).
45. Nicholls, *South Africa in My Time*, pp. 284–5. p. 285.
46. Hancock, *Smuts vol II*, p. 262.
47. Smuts Archive, A1 Box N vol. 307 docs 116–128; doc. 111 pp. 1–6. See also NTS 38/362, 'Comparative Schedule of Proposals Submitted Regarding the Representation of Natives in Parliament', for summaries of the individual proposals of Nicholls, Stallard, Malan, Payn and G. B. van Zyl.
48. *JSC Proceedings 1930–34*, p. 19.
49. *Ibid.*, p. 20. Those voting against Hertzog's motion were F. S. Malan, Collins, Duncan, Hofmeyr, Krige, Payn, Smuts, G. B. van Zyl. van Zyl's proposals fell away on 14 May 1930.
50. Nicholls, *South Africa in My Time*, p. 288.
51. *JSC Proceedings 1930–4*, p. 21.
52. *Ibid.*, pp. 13–15, 17–18. Note that the JSC accepted Stallard's scheme for a Senatorial Grand Council on 14 May 1930, subject to the substitution of 'European' for 'Native' senators. For Stallard's view that 'Natives should be represented in the Senate by men of their own race', see NTS 8618 38/362, 'Comparative Schedule of Proposals Submitted Regarding the Representation of Natives in Parliament'.
53. Nicholls papers, KCM 3309 file 2, text of speech made by Nicholls in introducing his proposals to the Committee, 2 May 1930, p. 1. It is possible that Nicholls did not actually deliver the full text.
54. *Ibid.*, p. 1.
55. *Ibid.*, p. 2.
56. *Ibid.*, p. 2.
57. *Ibid.*, p. 3.
58. *Ibid.*, p. 3.
59. *Ibid.*, p. 4.

60. *Ibid.*, p. 4, pp. 5–6.
61. *Ibid.*, p. 7.
62. *JSC Proceedings 1930–4*, p. 12.
63. *Ibid., pp. 71, 129.*
64. *Natal Advertiser*, 15 May 1935. See also G. Heaton Nicholls, *The Native Bills* (Durban, 1935).
65. Nicholls, *The Problem of the Native in South Africa* (Pretoria, 1937), p. 5.
66. *Natal Advertiser*, 15 May 1935.
67. Nicholls papers, KCM 3359 file 5, Nicholls to editor *Cape Argus*, 4 March 1936.
68. Nicholls papers, KCM 3416(4) file 12, Nicholls to 'my dearest one' [Ruby], Sunday [1931?].
69. Nicholls papers, KCM 3416(5) file 12, Nicholls to 'my darling' [Ruby], Wednesday [1931?].
70. Van der Poel, *Selections Vol V* docs 314, 321.
71. Joint Committee No. 1–1935, *Reports and Proceeedings*, p. 80. Note that Smuts and other members of the SAP refused to participate in the Joint Select Committee during November 1932 and were therefore not signatories to the 1932 Representation Bill. Smuts excluded himself from the Committee probably because he believed that a general election was near and that the SAP would find itself deeply divided should the Native Bills come before Parliament in 1933. See Duncan papers, BC 294 D1.35.31, Smuts to Duncan, 24 October 1932.
72. On coalition and fusion see D. O'Meara, *Volkskapitalisme. Class, Capital and Ideology in the Development of Afrikaner Nationalism 1934–48* (Cambridge and Johannesburg, 1983), pp. 39–48; D. W. Kruger, *The Making of a Nation. A History of the Union of South Africa 1910–1961* (Johannesburg, 1969), pp. 154–74.
73. Macmillan papers, Olivier to Macmillan, 17 April 1928.
74. *Round Table*, March 1930, p. 149.
75. Lacey, *Working for Boroko*, pp. 292–5, 61–2.
76. *Ibid.*, pp. 62, 295.
77. The above analysis is drawn from Friedman, *Smuts*, pp. 101–3. On fusion, see Hancock, *Smuts Vol. II*, chap. 13; Pirow, *Hertzog*, chaps 13–15; N. M. Stultz, *Afrikaner Politics in South Africa 1934–48* (California, 1974), chap. 2.

6   The Passage of Hertzog's Native Bills, Part Two

1. UG 17-'27, *Report of the NAC for the Years 1925–26*, p. 12.
2. *Ibid.*, p. 13.
3. *Ibid.*, p. 11.
4. SC 10-'27, *Report of the Select Committee on the Subject of the Union Native Council Bill, Coloured Persons Rights Bill, Representation of Natives in Parliament Bill, and Natives Land (Amendment) Bill* (1927). Henceforth SC 10-'27, *Select Committee on Native Bills*.

5. *Ibid.*, p. 45. See also NTS 8624 41/362 for a copy of the *Bunga*'s resolutions on the Native Bills.
6. SC 10-'27, *Select Committee on Native Bills*, p. 46.
7. *Ibid.*, p. 47.
8. *Ibid.*, p. 48.
9. See, e.g. NTS 8624 41/362, J. A. Sishuba, President Cape Native Rights Protection Association to Select Committee on Native Bills, 21 May 1927, p. iv: 'Nothing has happened since Union which would justify the abrogation of the native franchise solemnly granted and preserved by the Act of Union which was a sacred contract entered into by the parties concerned'.
10. SC 10-'27, *Select Committee on Native Bills*, p. 241. For an amplification of Jabavu's views, see his pamphlet *The Segregation Fallacy and Other Papers* (Lovedale, 1928).
11. SC 10-'27, *Select Committee on Native Bills*, pp. 245–8.
12. *Ibid.*, p. 252.
13. For Selope Thema's views, see *Ibid.*, evidence on behalf of Johannesburg Joint Council; also his 'In Defence of the Cape Franchise', in *The South African Outlook*, 1 September 1928. For Plaatje, see B. Willan, *Sol Plaatje. A Biography* (Johannesburg, 1984).
14. See, e.g. D. D. T. Jabavu's *'Native Disabilities' in South Africa* (Lovedale, [1932]); *Native Taxation* (Lovedale, [1932]).
15. SC 10-'27, *Select Committee on Native Bills*, pp. 252, 263.
16. W. Beinart and C. Bundy, *Hidden Struggles in Rural South Africa. Politics and Popular Movements in the Transkei and Eastern Cape 1890–1930* (Johannesburg, 1987), p. 34.
17. *Ibid.*, pp. 36–7.
18. Hertzog papers, A32 vol. 209, p. 7. Telegram from Chief Maitse Moloi to General Hertzog, 3 April 1935. Consider also the case of Botomane Umtini (?) who advised Hertzog, 'I have much pleasure to urge your honour to push forward the segregation policy in spite of all opposition . . . Rely upon me, Sir, in future to do my uttermost to help you to build up the South Africa tribes, the Bantu race, my dear people, on Constitutional lines . . .' NTS 1696 38/276, Botomane Umtini (?) Deputy President of the Tvl. ANC to Hertzog, 28 May 1926; also Umtini to SNA, 28 July 1926. For evidence of further support for Hertzog, see Hertzog papers, A32 vol. 112, Isaac Makappa and B. B. Kondlo ('Native Nationalists of the Cape') to Hertzog, 25 June 1924, p. 46; E. E. Victor Tetyana to Hertzog 25 June 1924, p. 46; Jas D. Nzojo to Hertzog, 27 August 1924, p. 65. See also NTS 9313 9/378, 'Address by the Gaikas and Gcalekas of Kentani District to Hertzog on his Visit to the Transkei', [1925].
19. NTS 8624 41/362, 'Memo. of the League of Economic Independence, 1933' signed S. M. Bennet Ncwana (General Secretary) and Rev. James A. S. Rune (President).
20. SC 10-'27, *Select Committee on the Native Bills*, pp. 254, 286–7. Note that Dr W. Rubusana disputed Pelem's views in the select committee and denied that they were shared by the Bantu Union as a whole.

21. Peter Walshe, *The Rise of African Nationalism in South Africa. The African National Congress 1912–1952* (London, 1970), p. 54.
22. *The Star*, 4 January 1926. The newspaper described the meeting as the 'biggest and most representative gathering of the Bantu races that has ever met in South Africa' and referred to its being held under the auspices of the 'African National Convention'.
23. SC 10-'27, *Select Committee on Native Bills*, p. 298, 303.
24. *Ibid.*, pp. 301–2, 294, 296, 306–7.
25. *Ibid.*, p. 296. Mahabane presented a paper to the 1923 DRC European Bantu Conference in which he said 'no right-thinking black man would take exception' to segregation based on a 50–50 division of land. See *European and Bantu* (Johannesburg, 1923), p. 39.
26. Evidence of P. Seme to NEC, 6 May 1931, p. 7404.
27. C. Bundy, 'Land and Liberation: Popular Rural Protest and the National Liberation Movements in South Africa, 1920–1960', in Marks and Trapido, *The Politics of Race, Class and Nationalism*, p. 264.
28. NTS 8615 38/362, Clements Kadalie to Hertzog, 16 February 1927, with enclosed ICU resolutions on Native Bills.
29. *Ibid.*, p. 1.
30. *Ibid.*, p. 1.
31. *Ibid.*, p. 2.
32. P. L. Wickins, *The Industrial and Commercial Workers' Union of Africa* (Oxford, 1978), p. 66.
33. Cited in Ibid., p. 79. Wickins adds that Kadalie's statement was at variance with his 'fundamental belief in a racially integrated society'. In return for Kadalie's help in influencing the ANC to urge the black electorate to vote for a change of government in 1924, Hertzog printed 10 000 copies of the ICU newspaper, *The Workers' Herald*.
34. R. Elphick, 'Mission Christianity and Interwar Liberalism', in J. Butler *et. al.*, *Democractic Liberalism in South Africa. Its History and Prospect* (Connecticut and Cape Town, 1987).
35. For a sympathetic account of the Joint Council movement, see J. W. Horton, 'South Africa's Joint Councils: Black-White Cooperation between the two World Wars', in the *South African Historical Journal*, no. 4, November 1972. A critical account of the Joint Councils' role in damping down African radicalism is to be found in Baruch Hirson's 'Tuskegee, The Joint Councils and the All African Convention' (ICS Collected Seminar Papers, London University, X, 1981).
36. Joint Council of Europeans and Natives, *General Hertzog's Solution of the Native Question. Memorandum no. 1* (Johannesburg [1927]) (on the Natives' Land Act 1913, Amendment Bill, 1927); *General Hertzog's Solution of the Native Question. Memorandum no. 2* (Johannesburg [1927]) (on the Union Native Council Bill, 1927 and Representation of Natives in Parliament Bill, 1927).
37. SC 10-'27, *Select Committee on the Native Bills*, p. 136 (emphasis in original).
38. *Ibid.*, pp. 137–8.
39. *Ibid.*, p. 164.
40. *Ibid.*, pp. 138–9.

41. *Ibid.*, p. 140.
42. *Ibid.*, p. 188.
43. *Ibid.*, p. 174. See also SAIRR papers, AD 1438 B72.1.1, Memo. on PM's Bills by Pretoria Joint Council, December 1926.
44. *Ibid.*, p. 176. In 1928 the Johannesburg Joint Council took a more definite stand in support of the Cape franchise with the publication of its pamphlet, *In Defence of the Cape Franchise. Memorandum no. 4* (Johannesburg, n.d., [1928]).
45. Pim papers, A881 Fa 13/1, Resolutions of Conference on Native Affairs convened by Federal Council of the Dutch Reformed Churches, 1923, p. 3.
46. SC 10-'27, *Select Committee on Native Bills*, p. 344.
47. The resolutions of the 1927 DRC European-Bantu Conference are presented and discussed in *Ibid.*, pp. 339–64.
48. *The Friend*, 8 February 1927; *Cape Times*, 4 February 1927 (editorial); *Cape Times*, 3 February 1927.
49. On the formation of the NRFA, see SAIRR papers, AD 843 B72.2, Burton to Pim, 6 April 1929; Burton to Rheinallt Jones, 13 March 1929; Rose Innes to Pim, 29 April 1929; Burton to Rheinallt Jones, 10 May 1929, and other letters. Rose Innes had been Attorney General under Rhodes and Chief Justice of South Africa, 1914–27; Henry Burton held cabinet posts (including that of Native Affairs) under Botha and Smuts, 1910–24; J. W. Jagger was a member of the Cape delegation to the 1909 Union Convention; Clarkson Tredgold was Senior Judge of S. Rhodesia.
50. Sir James Rose Innes, *The Native Franchise Question* (Cape Town, 1929). This speech was read to the opening meeting of the NRFA. See *Cape Times*, 23 May 1929.
51. *Cape Times*, 23 May 1929.
52. J. W. Jagger and Sir Clarkson Tredgold, *The Native Franchise Question* (Cape Town, 1930), p. 4. See also H. Burton, *The Native Franchise Question* (Cape Town, 1930).
53. SAIRR papers, AD 843 B72.2, Frames to Pim, 22 March 1929 (telegram).
54. SAIRR papers, AD 843 B72.2, Burton to Pim, 3 July 1929; Pim papers, A881 cc35, Pim to Brookes, 16 July 1929.
55. Cape Times, 3 June 1929.
56. SAIRR papers, AD 843 B72.2, Burton to Pim (confidential), 10 May 1929.
57. Van Der Poel, *Selections Vol. V*, Smuts to M. C. Gillett, vol. 43 no. 115, 11 June 1929, p. 409.
58. W. K. Hancock, *Survey of British Commonwealth Affairs Vol. II Part 2* (London, 1942), p. 8.
59. J. D. Rheinallt Jones, 'Cape Franchise and Bantu Status', in *The South African Outlook*, 1 September 1928, pp. 166–7.
60. Johannesburg Joint Council, *In Defence of the Cape Franchise. Memorandum no. 4* (Johannesburg, n.d., [1928]).
61. SAIRR papers, AD 843 B99.2, Confidential Memorandum by Rheinallt Jones, January 1930.

62. SAIRR-RJ papers, AD 843 Franchise Box 'F', J. Rose Innes to Rheinallt Jones, 10 December 1929.
63. Pim papers, A881 BL1, Brookes to Pim, 4 July 1929.
64. E. H. Brookes, 'General Hertzog's Native Franchise Proposals', in *Cape Times*, 12–15 February 1930. Henry Burton criticised Brookes's proposal as 'unworkable' in his *Native Franchise Question*, p. 13.
65. *The South African Outlook*, 1 June 1928.
66. See *The South African Outlook*, 2 June 1928, 1 September 1928.
67. *The South African Outlook*, 2 June 1928, p. 140.
68. Pim papers, A881 BL4 136, Rheinallt Jones to Pim, 15 December 1930.
69. SAIRR papers, AD 843 B72.2, Rheinallt Jones (unsigned) to Jabavu (strictly private and confidential), 28 March 1931.
70. SAIRR papers, AD 843 B72.2, Jabavu to Hofmeyr, 8 April 1931.
71. Nicholls papers, KCM 3350b, Nicholls to Dube, 11 February 1931 (confidential) pp. 1–2. An analysis of Dube's alliance with Nicholls was first presented by Shula Marks in 'The Ambiguities of Dependence: John L. Dube of Natal', in *JSAS*, I, 2, 1975.
72. Nicholls papers, KCM 3350d, Dube to Nicholls, 13 May 1931, pp. 2–3.
73. Nicholls papers, KCM 3350a, undated document.
74. SAIRR-RJ papers, AD 843 Box 'F' 'franchise' file, Rheinallt Jones (unsigned) to Jabavu, 20 April 1931.
75. *Ibid.*, Jabavu to Rheinallt Jones, 13 May 1931.
76. Joint Committee No. 1–1935, *Report and Proceedings*.
77. Walshe, *The Rise*, p. 117 says that the 1935 AAC meeting represented a 'genuine African consensus'.
78. *Cape Times*, 18 December 1935.
79. *Ibid.*
80. *Ibid.*
81. *Ibid.*, 19 December 1935.
82. *Ibid.*
83. *Ibid.*
84. SAIRR papers, AD 843 B100.1, Rheinallt Jones (unsigned) to Richard Stuttaford, 12 July 1935.
85. *Ibid.*, Chairman SAIRR (Hoernlé) to Smuts, 13 July 1935.
86. *Cape Times* (editorial), 27 September 1935.
87. *Cape Times*, 5 September 1935. In October a further conference of 'Zulu chiefs' met to reconsider the Bills and took a stronger stand on the Cape franchise. For details see SAIRR papers, AD 843, B100.1, Brookes to Rheinallt Jones, 22 October 1935; Z. K. Matthews to Brookes, 22 October 1935; Brookes to Rheinallt Jones, 29 October 1935.
88. 'Description of the Native Trust and Land Bill' and 'Description of Representation of Natives Bill', *Race Relations*, August 1935.
89. SAIRR-RJ papers AD 843 box 'E', 'Legislation'. See, e.g. Rheinallt Jones to F. S. Malan, 24 June 1935.
90. *Cape Times*, 29–30 January 1936. The resolution proposed to extend the franchise throughout the Union, subject in the case of Africans, to an acceptable 'civilisation test'.

91. For an account of the Institute's activities in connection with the Native Bills, see SAIRR papers AD 843 B99.1. 'The Native Bills', 1 April 1936 (confidential).

92. Xuma papers ABX 360203b, S. Msimang (General Secretary AAC) to Xuma, 3 February 1936.

93. Rheinallt Jones papers AD 1715 1.3, Rheinallt Jones to Hoernlé, 6 February 1936.

94. *Rand Daily Mail*, 11 February 1936; *Cape Times*, 11 February 1936.

95. Xuma papers ABX 360211, Telegram from Hoernlé, Ramsbottom and Schreiner to Rheinallt Jones 11 February 1936; ABX 360213, Telegram from Hoernlé to Xuma, 13 February 1936; ABX 360215, Telegram from Ballinger to Xuma, 15 February 1936.

96. *Cape Times*, 17 February 1936. See also *Cape Times*, 11–15 February 1936 for more details and speculation about the compromise.

97. *Joint Sitting of Both Houses of Parliament 1936*, cols 22–3, cols 301–2.

98. SAIRR papers AD 843 B100.1, Payn to Makiwane, 20 February 1936, p. 2.

99. *Joint Sitting of Both Houses of Parliament 1936*, cols 1151–3; cols 473–5.

100. SAIRR papers AD 843 B99.1, 'Representation of Natives Bill' (statement by D. D. T. Jabavu), [1936].

101. *Ibid.*

102. See Walshe, *The Rise*, p. 130 for a similar account of the compromise.

103. SAIRR papers AD 843 B100.1, Brookes to Rheinallt Jones, 24 February 1936; Hoernlé to Rheinallt Jones, 8 February 1936, pp. 1–2.

104. *Ibid.*, Hoernlé to Rheinallt Jones, 27 February 1936 and 8 February 1936, pp. 1–2.

105. *Cape Times*, 18 February 1936.

106. *Joint Sitting of Both Houses of Parliament 1936*, 19 February 1936, col. 47.

107. Duncan papers, BC 294/D5.28.4, Duncan to Lady Selbourne, 20 February 1936.

108. *Cape Times* (editorial), 1 May 1935.

109. Nicholls, *South Africa*, p. 291.

110. *Joint Sitting of Both Houses of Parliament 1936*, col. 391; col. 1194.

111. *Ibid.*, cols. 309–10.

112. The Representation Bill was passed in April 1936 by 169 votes to 11.

113. *Joint Sitting of Both Houses of Parliament 1936*, cols 1083–4.

114. *Ibid.*, cols 1085–6.

115. *Ibid.*, col. 1089.

116. Paton, *Hofmeyr*, pp. 231, 233–4.

117. P. Lewsen, 'Liberals in Politics and Administration, 1936–1948', in J. Butler *et. al.*, *Democratic Liberalism*, p. 99.

118. SAIRR papers AD 843 B72.2, Hofmeyr to Stohr, 14 October 1929 (emphasis in original). Hofmeyr was strongly attacked by Rheinallt Jones and P. R. Frames for this statement, though he tried to explain that he was not actually abandoning the Cape franchise, so much as indicating a willingness to bargain. See *Ibid.*, Rheinallt Jones (unsigned) to Hofmeyr, [19 October 1929]; Hofmeyr to Rheinallt

Jones, 24 October 1929 and Pim papers A881 BL1, P. R. Frames to Pim, 8 December 1929.

119. *JSC Proceedings 1930–34*, p. 15. See also *Cape Times* (editorial) of 7 April 1936, which took Hofmeyr to task for his speech during the Third Reading, reminding him of his 1930 proposal and questioned the moral basis on which he had arrived at the figure of 10 per cent.

120. On 'constructive segregation', see Hofmeyr's 'The Approach to the Native Problem', *Journal of the Royal African Society*, XXXVI, 144, 1937.

121. F. S. Malan papers Acc. 583/21, editorial in *Imvo* 14 May 1936; Eric Walker to 'My dear Senator', 17 February 1935; Hoernlé to Malan, 12 May 1935.

122. See, e.g. *Cape Times*, 18 February 1929 'Facts and Figures' (editorial); *Cape Times*, 20 February 1928 'Cape Native Voters' (editorial); *Cape Times*, 25 February 1929; J. H. Pim, 'The Native Bills', in *The South African Outlook*, 2 April 1928.

123. Figures derived from SAIRR-RJ papers, AD 843 A1.11 'Head Office Memoranda', 'Description of Representation of Natives Bill' 1935, pp. 1–3. According to Noel Garson's figures, the combined African and coloured vote peaked in 1927, when it reached a total of 45 572. The purely African vote increased by 148 per cent from 1909 (6 637) to a peak in 1927 (16 481), when it represented some 7.6 per cent of the Cape electorate. N. Garson, 'The Cape Franchise In Action: The Queenstown By-Election of December 1921', Witwatersrand University History Workshop 1984, pp. 3–5.

124. Duncan papers, BC 294 D5.27.28, Duncan to Lady Selbourne, 23 October 1935. See also D5.28.3, Duncan to Lady Selbourne, 13 February 1936.

125. *Joint Sitting of Both Houses of Parliament 1936*, col. 388, 2 March 1936.

126. *Ibid.*, col. 21, 14 February 1936.

127. T. Karis and G. M. Carter, *From Protest to Challenge Vol. 1*, (Stanford, 1972), p. 49.

128. R. J. Haines, 'The Opposition to General Hertzog's Segregation Bills, 1929–36: A Study in Extra-Parliamentary Protest' (MA thesis, University of Natal, 1978), pp. 290, 288.

129. J. T. Gumede, Acting President ANC, reported in *Rand Daily Mail* 26 October 1926.

130. Marks, *The Ambiguities of Dependence*, p. 2.

131. ICU Records, A924 file 3, Margaret Hodgson to Dr Leys, 12 July 1933.

132. M. L. Legassick, 'Race, Industrialization and Social Change in South Africa: The Case of R. F. A. Hoernlé', *African Affairs*, LXXV, 299, 1976, 237–8. See also Hirson, 'Tuskegee, The Joint Councils and the All African Convention'.

133. SAIRR papers, AD 843 B100.1, Brookes to Rheinallt Jones, stamped 16 May 1935.

134. *Ibid.*, Rose Innes to Rheinallt Jones, 15 July 1935. See also the more

ography.

radical criticisms of the Institute mounted by George Findlay and the response by Mrs E. Rheinallt Jones in ibid.
135. SAIRR papers, AD 843 B72.1.1. See unmarked newspaper clipping of the Manifesto of the Native Franchise Vigilance Committee – I have been unable to locate its source or date.

Conclusion

1. See J. W. Lazar, 'The Role of the South African Bureau of Racial Affairs (SABRA) in the Formulation of Apartheid Ideology, 1948–1961' (ICS seminar paper, London University, 1986).
2. This is not to say that apartheid ideology was incapable of modification, nor that it was unable to speak to different constituencies with different voices. See D. Posel, 'The Meaning of Apartheid before 1948: Conflicting Interests and Forces within the Afrikaner Nationalist Alliance', in *JSAS*, 14, 1, 1987.
3. Cell, *White Supremacy*, p. 18.

Bibliography

I MANUSCRIPT SOURCES

(i) Official
(ii) Unofficial

II PRINTED PRIMARY SOURCES

(i) Official Records
(ii) Newspapers and Periodicals

III SECONDARY SOURCES

(i) Select Books and Pamphlets
(ii) Select Journal, Book, and Unpublished Articles
(iii) Theses and Dissertations

I MANUSCRIPT SOURCES

(i) Official: State Archives Pretoria, Intermediate and Central Archives Depot

GG : Archives of the Governor General
JUS: Archives of the Justice Department
K26: Archives of the Commission of Enquiry into Social and Economic Conditions of Natives in South Africa, 1930–32 (Native Economic Commission)
NA : Archives of the Transvaal Native Affairs Department (prior to Union)
NTS: Archives of the Native Affairs Department (post-Union)
PM : Archives of the Prime Minister's Office
SDK: Archives of the Public Service Commission
TES: Archives of the Treasury

(ii) Unofficial

(a) *University of Cape Town, Jagger Library, Manuscripts Division*
BC 79 : J. F. Herbst Papers
BC 255: G. P. Lestrade Papers
BC 294: P. Duncan Papers
BC 618: E. Walker Papers

(b) *University of the Witwatersrand, William Cullen Library, Church
of the Province of South Africa Archives*
A 146 : Fortnightly Club Papers
A 394 : J. D. Rheinallt Jones Papers
A 419 : W. A. Norton Papers
A 539 : S. G. Millin Papers
A 881 : J. H. Pim Papers
A 924 : Industrial and Commercial Workers Union Records
A 954 : E. Stubbs Papers
A 1007 : C. T. Loram Papers
A 1655 : D. R. Hunt Papers
ABX : A. B. Xuma Papers
AD 843 : South African Institute of Race Relations Records
AD 843 : South African Institute of Race Relations/Rheinallt Jones
Papers
AD 1438: Native Economic Commission, Minutes of Evidence
AD 1623: R. F. A. Hoernlé Papers
AD 1715: J. D. Rheinallt Jones Papers (additional)

(c) *State Archives, Pretoria*
A 32: J. B. M. Hertzog papers
A 1 : J. C. Smuts Papers

(d) *Killie Campbell Library, University of Natal*
G. Heaton Nicholls Papers
M. Webb Papers

(e) *Cape Archives*
A 583 : F. S. Malan Papers

(f) *Rhodes House, Oxford*
Mss. Afr. S. 288 : F. J. Bagshawe Diaries

(g) *Privately held papers*
W. M. Macmillan Papers (in possession of Mrs Macmillan, Long Wittenham, Oxfordshire)
M. Legassick Papers (housed at Warwick University)

II PRINTED PRIMARY SOURCES

(i) Official Records

(a) Government and Departmental Reports
UG 33-'13, *Report of the Native Affairs Department for the Year 1912*
UG 19-'16, *Report of the Natives Land Commission. Volume I* (Beaumont)
UG 22-'16, *Report of the Natives Land Commission. Volume II* (Beaumont)
UG 8-'18, *Report of the Local Natives Land Committee, Cape Province* (Scully)
UG 23-'18, *Report of the Natives Land Committee, Western Transvaal* (Lemmer)
UG 31-'18, *Majority Report of the Eastern Transvaal Natives Land Committee* (Stubbs)
UG 34-'18, *Report of the Local Natives' Land Committee (Natal Province)* (Mackenzie)
UG 7-'19, *Report of the Native Affairs Department for the Years 1913–1918*
UG 24-'20, *Eighth Annual Report of the Public Service Commission (1919)*
UG 34-'20, *Report of the Low Grade Mines Commission*
UG 6-'21, *Fifth Report of the Public Service Commission of Enquiry*
UG 15-'22, *Report of the Native Affairs Commission for the Year 1921*
UG 42-'22, *Report on Native Location Surveys*
UG 17-'22, *Eleventh Annual Report of the Public Service Commission (1922)*
UG 18-'22, *Tenth Annual Report of the Public Service Commission (1921)*
UG 41-'22, *Report of the Inter-Departmental Committee on the Native Pass Laws 1920*

UG 34-'22, *Report of the Native Affairs Department for the Years 1919–21*

UG 16-'23, *Report of the Commission Appointed to Enquire into the Rebellion of the Bondelzwarts*

UG 36-'23, *Report of the Native Affairs Commission for the Year 1922*

UG 47-'23, *Report of the Native Affairs Commission for the Year 1923*

UG 49-'23, *Final Report of the Drought Investigation Commission. October 1923*

UG 40-'25, *Report of the Native Affairs Commission for the Year 1924*

UG 14-'26, *Report of the Economic and Wage Commission (1925)*

UG 14-'27, *Report of the Native Affairs Department for the Years 1922–26*

UG 17-'27, *Report of the Native Affairs Commission for the Years 1925–6*

UG 35-'28, *Report of the Committee Appointed to Inquire Into the Training of Natives in Medicine and Public Health*

UG 16-'32, *Report of the Low Grade Ore Commission*

UG 22-'32, *Report of the Native Economic Commission 1930–1932*

UG 26-'32, *Report of the Native Affairs Commission for the Years 1927–31*

UG 30-'32, *Report of the Unemployment Investigation Committee*

UG 3-'34, *Report of the Native Affairs Commission for the Years 1932–3*

UG 29-'36, *Report of the Interdepartmental Committee on Native Education 1935–36*

UG 48-'37, *Report of the Native Affairs Commission for the Year 1936*

UG 56-'37, *Notes on Conference Between Municipalities and Native Affairs Department Held at Pretoria on 28th and 29th September, 1937, to Discuss the Provision of the Native laws Amendment Act (no. 46 of 1937)*

UG 54-'39, *Report of the Native Affairs Commission for the Years 1937–38*

(b) *Select Committee Reports*

Senate SC 6-'13, *Report from the Select Committee on Native Custom and Marriage Laws*

SC 10a-'20, *Second Report of the Select Committee on Native Affairs*

SC 3-'23, *First Report of the Select Committee on Native Affairs*
SC 12-'25, *Report of the Select Committee on Subject Matter of Masters and Servants Law (Transvaal) Amendment Bill*
SC 14-'25, *Report of the Select Committee on the Wage Bill*
SC 15-'25, *Report of the Select Committee on the Mines and Works Act, 1911, Amendment Bill*
SC 11-'27, *Report of the Select Committee on the Native Administration Bill*
SC 10-'27, *Report of the Select Committee on the Subject of the Union Native Council Bill, Coloured Persons Rights Bill, Representation of Natives in Parliament Bill, and Natives Land (Amendment) Bill*
SC 19-'27, *Report of the Select Committee on the Subject of the Union Native Council Bill, Coloured Persons Rights Bill, Representation of Natives in Parliament Bill, and Natives Land (Amendment) Bill*
SC 6a-'29, *Second Report of the Select Committee on Native Affairs*
SC 7-'31 *Report of the Select Committee on the Subject of the Native Service Contract Bill 1931*
Joint Select Committee No. 1–1935, *Report and Proceedings of the Joint Committee on the Representation of Natives and Coloured Persons in Parliament and Provincial Councils and the Acquisition of Land by Natives* (April, 1935)
Report of the South African Native Affairs Commission 1903–5, Vol. I (Cape Town, 1905)
Supplement to the Joint Committee No. 1–1935, *Reports and Proceedings of the Joint Committees on Natives and Coloured Persons During the Period 1930-'34* (1935)

(c) *Parliamentary Debates*
House of Assembly Debates, vol. 5, 1925; vol. 6, 1926; vol. 9, 1927; vol. 12, 1929; vol. 14, 1930; vol. 26, 1936
Joint Sitting of Both Houses of Parliament. Natives' Parliamentary Representation Bill, Coloured Persons' Rights Bill (1929)
Joint Sitting of Both Houses of Parliament, Natives' Parliamentary Representation Bill, Coloured Persons' Rights Bill (1930)
Joint Sitting of Both Houses of Parliament, Natives' Parliamentary Representation Bill, Coloured Persons' Rights Bill (1936) (JS 1–36 & JS 2–36)

(d) *Government Gazettes*
Union Gazette Extraordinary, 23 April 1936, 19 June 1936
Union Government Gazette, 6 November 1931

(e) *British Government (Command Papers)*

Cd. 4119, *Colonial Reports – Miscellaneous No. 52. Report on Native Education in South Africa; Part III – Education in the Protectorates; by E. B. Sargant* (1908)

Cd. 4323, *Colonial Reports – Miscellaneous No. 55. Cape Colony Report on the Rietfontein Area by Mr J. F. Herbst* (1908)

Cd. 7707, *Dominions Royal Commission. Minutes of Evidence Taken in the Union of South Africa in 1914 Part II*

(ii) Newspapers and Periodicals

Africa (1928–36)
Bantu Studies (1921–36)
Cape Times (1920–36)
Journal of the African Society (1919–37)
Journal of the Economic Society of South Africa / South African Journal of Economics (1928–36)
Race Relations (1933–36)
The Round Table (1921–35)
The South African Journal of Science (1920–36)
The South African Outlook (1922–37)
The South African Quarterly (1914–26)

III   SECONDARY SOURCES

(i) Select Books and Pamphlets

Adler, T. (ed.), *Perspectives on South Africa. A Collection of Working Papers* (Johannesburg, 1977)

Armstrong H. C., *Grey Steel (J. C. Smuts). A Study in Arrogance* (London, 1937)

Ballinger, M., *From Union to Apartheid. A Trek to Isolation* (Folkestone, 1969)

Ballinger, W. G., *Race and Economics in South Africa* (London, 1934)

Banton, M., *The Idea of Race* (London, 1977)

Baptist, R. Hernekin (Ethelreda Lewis), *Wild Deer* (London, 1933)

Barnes, L., *Caliban in Africa: An Impression of Colour Madness* (London, 1930)

Barnouw, A. J., *Language and Race Problems in South Africa* (The Hague, 1934)

Beinart. W., *The Political Economy of Pondoland, 1860–1930* (Cambridge, 1982)

Beinart, W. and Bundy, C., *Hidden Struggles in Rural South Africa. Politics and Popular Movements in the Transkei and Eastern Cape 1890–1930* (Johannesburg, 1987)

Bell, F. W., *Open Letter to Members of the Legislature of the Union of South Africa in Connection with the Native Franchise* (Johannesburg, 1936)

Bonner, P. (ed.), *Working Papers in Southern African Studies. Vol. 2* (Johannesburg 1981)

Bozzoli, B., *The Political Nature of a Ruling Class. Capital and Ideology in South Africa, 1890–1933* (London, 1981)

Bozzoli, B., *Town and Countryside in the Transvaal* (Johannesburg, 1983)

Brookes, E. H., *The History of Native Policy in South Africa From 1830 to the Present Day*, first edition (Cape Town, 1924)

Brookes, E. H., *The Political Future of South Africa* (Pretoria, 1927)

Brookes, E. H. *et. al., Coming of Age. Studies in South African Citizenship and Politics* (Cape Town, 1930)

Brookes, E. H., *The Colour Problems of South Africa* (Lovedale, 1934)

Brookes, E. H., *A South African Pilgrimage* (Johannesburg, 1977)

Brownlee, W. T., *The Progress of the Bantu* (Lovedale, 1928)

Brownlee, W. T., *Reminiscences of a Transkeian* (Pietermaritzburg, 1975)

Buell, R. L., *The Native Problem in Africa*, 2 vols (New York, 1928)

Bundy, C., *The Rise and Fall of the South African Peasantry* (London, 1979)

Burton, H., *The Native Franchise Question* (Cape Town, 1930)

Butler, J. *et. al.*, (eds) *Democratic Liberalism in South Africa. Its History and Prospect* (Cape Town and Connecticut, 1987)

Carnegie Commission, *The Poor White Problem in South Africa*, 5 vols (Stellenbosch, 1932)

Cell, J. W., *The Highest Stage of White Supremacy: The Origins of Segregation in South Africa and the American South* (Cambridge, 1982)

Chanock, M., *Law, Custom and Social Order. The Colonial Experience in Malawi and Zambia* (Cambridge, 1985)

Continuation Committee of National Conference on the Native Bills,

Native Vote v. Native Land. 'Shadow' v. 'Substance' (Cape Town, 1936)

Continuation Committee of National Conference on the Native Bills, *The Native Trust and Land Bill* (Cape Town, 1936)

Cotton, W. A., *Racial Segregation in South Africa* (London, 1931)

Crocker, H. J., *The South African Race Problem. The Solution of Segregation* (Johannesburg, 1908)

Davenport, T. R. H. and Hunt, K. S. (eds), *The Right to the Land* (Cape Town, 1974)

Davenport, T. R. H., *South Africa: A Modern History*, second edition (Johannesburg, 1980)

Davies, R. H., *Capital, State and White Labour in South Africa 1900–1960. An Historical Materialist Analysis of Class Formation and Class Relations* (Brighton, 1979)

Dubow, N. E., *Irma Stern* (Cape Town, 1974)

Dutch Reform Church Federal Council, *European and Bantu. Papers and Addresses Read at Conference on Native Affairs Johannesburg 1923* (Johannesburg, n. d., [1924])

Du Toit, D., *Capital and Labour in South Africa: Class Struggle in the 1970's* (London, 1981)

Elster, J., *Making Sense of Marx* (Cambridge, 1985)

Eiselen, W., *Die Naturelle-Vraagstuk* (Cape Town, 1929)

Evans, I., *Native Policy in South Africa* (Cambridge, 1934)

Evans, M. S., *The Native Problem in Natal* (Durban, 1906)

Evans, M. S., *Black and White in South East Africa. A Study in Sociology*, first edition (London, 1911)

Evans, M. S., *Black and White in the Southern States. A Study of the Race Problem in the United States From a South African Point of View* (London, 1915)

Findlay, G., *Miscegenation* (Pretoria, 1936)

FitzPatrick, Sir P., *The Situation in South Africa* (London, 1919)

Franklin, J. S., *South Africa – A Glimpse into the Future* (Cape Town, 1923)

Fredrickson, G. M., *White Supremacy. A Comparative Study in American and South African History* (Oxford and New York, 1981)

Friedman, B., *Smuts: A Reappraisal* (London, 1975)

Galton, Sir F., *The Narrative of an Explorer in Tropical South Africa*, fourth edition (London, 1891)

Godley, R. S., *Khaki and Blue: Thirty Five Years Service in South Africa* (London, 1935)

Greenberg, S. B., *Race and State in Capitalist Development: Comparative Perspectives* (New Haven, 1980)

Guy, J., *The Heretic. A Study in the Life of John William Colenso 1814–1883* (Pietermaritzburg and Johannesburg, 1983)

Hailey, Lord, *An African Survey. A Study of Problems Arising in Africa South of the Sahara*, first edition (London, 1938)

Hancock, W. K., *Survey of British Commonwealth Affairs, I: Problems of Nationality, 1918–1936; II. 1 and 2: Problems of Economic Policy, 1918–1939, Parts I and II* (London 1937–42)

Hancock, W. K., *Smuts* Vol. II., *The Fields of Force, 1919–1950* (Cambridge, 1968)

Harris, M., *The Rise of Anthropological Theory* (London, 1968)

Herskovits, M. J., *The Cattle Complex in East Africa* (Wisconsin, 1926)

Hertzog, J. B. M., *The Segregation Problem, General Hertzog's Solution* (Cape Town, n. d., [1926])

Hindson, D. C., *Working Papers in Southern African Studies Vol. III* (Johannesburg, 1983)

Hindson, D. C., *Pass Controls and the Urban African Proletariat in South Africa* (Johannesburg, 1987)

Hobsbawm, E. J., *Industry and Empire* (London, 1968)

Hoernlé, R. F. A., *South African Native Policy and the Liberal Spirit* (Cape Town, 1939)

Hofmeyr, J. H., *South Africa* (London, 1931)

Hogben, L., *Dangerous Thoughts* (London, 1939)

Hunter, M., *Reaction to Conquest. Effects of Contact with Europeans on the Pondo of South Africa* (Oxford, 1936)

Hyam, R., *Elgin and Churchill at the Colonial Office 1905–8* (London, 1968)

Jabavu, D. D. T., *The Black Problem* (Lovedale, 1920)

Jabavu, D. D. T., *The Segregation Fallacy and Other Papers* (Lovedale, 1928)

Jabavu, D. D. T., *Native Taxation* (Lovedale, 1932)

Jabavu, D. D. T., *Native Views on the Native Bills* (Lovedale, 1935)

Jagger, J. W. and Tredgold, C., *The Native Franchise Question* (Cape Town, 1930)

Jeeves, A. H., *Migrant Labour in South Africa's Mining Economy. The Struggle for the Gold Mine's Labour Supply, 1890–1920* (Johannesburg, Kingston and Montreal, 1985)

Johannesburg Joint Council, *General Hertzog's Solution of the Native Question. Memorandum No. 1* (Johannesburg, n. d., [1927])

Johannesburg Joint Council, *General Hertzog's Solution of the Native Question. Memorandum No. 2* (Johannesburg, n. d., [1927])

Johannesburg Joint Council, *The Native in Industry. Memorandum No. 3* (Johannesburg, n. d.)

Johannesburg Joint Council, *In Defence of the Cape Franchise. Memorandum No. 4* (Johannesburg, n. d., [1928])

Johannesburg Joint Council, *Forced Labour in Africa. Memorandum No. 6* (Johannesburg, n. d., [1930])

Johannesburg Joint Council, *Summary of Native Disabilities. Memorandum No. 7* (Johannesburg, n. d., [1930])

Johnstone, F. A., *Class, Race and Gold. A Study of Class Relations and Racial Discrimination in South Africa* (London, 1976)

Jones, G., *Social Darwinism and English Thought* (Sussex and New Jersey, 1980)

Kallaway, P. (ed), *Apartheid and Education. The Education of Black South Africans* (Johannesburg, 1984)

Karis, T. and Carter, G. (eds), *From Protest to Challenge. A Documentary History of African Politics in South Africa (1882–1964)*, 4 vols (Stanford, 1972–7)

Kentridge, M., *Unemployment in South Africa. A Simple Outline* (Johannesburg, n. d.)

Kirk, J., *The Economic Aspects of Native Segregation in South Africa* (London, 1929)

Kruger, D. W., *South African Parties and Policies 1910–1960* (London, 1960)

Kruger, D. W., *The Making of a Nation. A History of the Union of South Africa, 1910–1961* (Johannesburg, 1969)

Kuper, A., *Anthropologists and Anthropology. The British School, 1922–72* (London, 1972)

Lacey, M., *Working for Boroko. The Origins of a Coercive Labour System in South Africa* (Johannesburg, 1981)

Leach, G., *South Africa. No Easy Path to Peace*, 2nd edition (London, 1987)

Lehfeldt, R. A., *The National Resources of South Africa* (Johannesburg, 1922)

Lestrade, G. P., *Die Naturellevraagstuk en die Studie van die Naturel* (Johannesburg, n. d., [1932])

Levy, N., *The Foundations of the South African Cheap Labour System* (London, 1982)

Lewis, J., *Industrialisation and Trade Union Organisation in South Africa, 1924–55* (Cambridge, 1984)

Lewsen, P., *John X Merriman. Paradoxical South African Statesman* (New Haven and London, 1982)

Long, B. K., *In Smuts's Camp* (London, 1945)

Loram, C. T., *The Education of the South African Native* (London, 1917)

Lorimar, D. A., *Colour, Class and the Victorians* (Leicester, 1978)

Lugard, F. J. D.,(Lord), *The Dual Mandate* (Edinburgh, 1922)

Lugg, H. C., *A Natal Family Looks Back* (Durban, 1970)

MacCrone, I. D., *Race Attitudes in South Africa. Historical, Experimental and Psychological Studies* (Johannesburg and London, 1937)

Macmillan, W. M., *Economic Conditions in a Non-Industrial South African Town* (Grahamstown, 1915)

Macmillan, W. M., *The South African Agrarian Problem and its Historical Development* (Johannesburg, 1919)

Macmillan, W. M., *The Land, the Native and Unemployment* (Johannesburg, 1924)

Macmillan, W. M., *Bantu, Boer and Briton: The Making of the South African Native Problem* (London, 1929)

Macmillan, W. M., *Complex South Africa. An Economic Footnote to History* (London, 1930)

Macmillan, W. M., *My South African Years. An Autobiography* (Cape Town, 1975)

Madden, F. and Fieldhouse, D. K. (eds), *Oxford and the Idea of Commonwealth* (London, 1982)

Mair, L., *Native Policies in Africa* (London, 1936)

Marks, S. and Atmore, A. (eds), *Economy and Society in Pre-Industrial South Africa* (London, 1980)

Marks, S. and Rathbone, R. (eds), *Industrialisation and Social Change in South Africa. African Class Formation, Culture and Consciousness, 1870–1930* (London, 1982)

Marks, S., *The Ambiguities of Dependence in South Africa. Class, Nationalism and the State in Twentieth-Century Natal* (Baltimore and Johannesburg, 1986)

Marks, S. and Trapido, S. (eds), *The Politics of Race, Class and Nationalism in Twentieth-Century South Africa* (London, 1987)

Millin, S. G., *God's Step-Children* (London, 1924)

Millin, S. G., *The South Africans* (London, 1926)

Millin, S. G., *General Smuts*, 2 vols (London, 1936)

Molema, S., *The Bantu Past and Present. An Ethnographical and*

Historical Study of the Native Races of South Africa (Edinburgh, 1920)

Molteno, D. B., *The Betrayal of 'Natives Representation'* (Johannesburg, 1959)

Moodie, T. D., *The Rise of Afrikanerdom. Power, Apartheid and the Afrikaner Civil Religion* (Berkeley, 1975)

Mosse, G. L., *Toward the Final Solution. A History of European Racism* (London, 1978)

Msimang, H. S., *The Crisis* (Johannesburg, 1936)

Murray, B. K., *Wits: The Early Years* (Johannesburg, 1982)

Nathan, M., *The South African Commonwealth* (Johannesburg, 1919)

Nathan, M., *South Africa from Within* (London, 1926)

Neame, L. E., *General Hertzog* (London, 1930)

Newby, I. A., *Jim Crow's Defense. Anti-Negro Thought in America, 1900–1930* (Louisiana, 1965)

Nicholls, G. H., *Bayete!* (London, 1923)

Nicholls, G. H., *The Problem of the Native in South Africa* (Pretoria, 1937)

Nicholls, G. H., *South Africa in My Time* (London, 1961)

Nielsen, P., *The Black Man's Place in Africa* (Cape Town, 1922)

Olivier, S. H., *The Anatomy of African Misery* (London, 1927)

O'Meara, D., *Volkskapitalisme. Class, Capital and Ideology in the Development of Afrikaner Nationalism, 1934–1948* (Cambridge and Johannesburg, 1983)

Paton, A., *Hofmeyr* (London and Cape Town, 1964)

Pelzer, A. N., *Die Afrikaner-Broederbond: Eerste 50 Jaar* (Cape Town, 1979)

Perham, M., *African Apprenticeship. An Autobiogaphical Journey in Southern Africa 1929* (London, 1974)

Phillips, R. E., *The Bantu are Coming. Phases of South Africa's Race Problem* (London, 1930)

Pim, J. H., *Introduction to Bantu Economics* (Lovedale, 1930)

Pim, J. H., *A Transkei Enquiry* (Lovedale, 1934)

Pirow, O., *James Barry Munnik Hertzog* (Cape Town, n. d., [1957])

Plomer, W., *Turbott Wolfe* (London, 1926)

Plomer, W., *Double Lives. An Autobiography* (London, 1943)

Porter, B., *The Lion's Share. A Short History of British Imperialism 1850–1983* (London and New York, 1975)

Poulantzas, N., *State, Power, Socialism* (London, 1978)

Report of the National European-Bantu Conference (1929) (Lovedale, 1929)

Rich, P. B., *White Power and the Liberal Conscience. Racial Segregation in South Africa and South African Liberalism 1921–60* (Johannesburg and Manchester, 1984)

Rich, P. B., *Race and Empire in British Politics* (Cambridge 1986)

Rodseth, F., *NDABAZABANTU. The Life of a Native Affairs Administrator* (Johannesburg, 1984)

Rogers, *Native Administration in the Union of South Africa*, first edition (Johannesburg, 1933); see also second edition revised by P. A. Linington, Pretoria, 1949

Rose Innes, J., *The Native Franchise Question* (Cape Town, 1929)

Rose Innes, J., *Autobiography* (Oxford, 1949)

Rosenthal, E., *Southern African Dictionary of National Biography* (London, 1966)

Roux, E., *Time Longer Than Rope. The Black Man's Struggle for Freedom in South Africa* (London, 1948)

Schapera, I. (ed.), *Western Civilization and the Natives of South Africa. Studies in Culture Contact* (London, 1934)

Scully, W. C., *The Ridge of White-Waters* (London, 1912)

Searle, G. R., *The Quest for National Efficiency. A Study of British Politics and Political Thought, 1899–1914* (Oxford, 1971)

Searle, G. R., *Eugenics and Politics in Britain, 1900–1914* (Leyden, 1976)

Semmel, B., *Imperialism and Social Reform. English Social-Imperialist Thought, 1895–1914* (London, 1960)

Simons, H. J., *African Women. Their Legal Status in South Africa* (London, 1968)

Simons, H. J. and R. E., *Class and Colour in South Africa, 1850–1950* (Harmondsworth, 1969)

Smuts, J. C., *Memorandum on Government Natives and Coloured Bills* (Pretoria, 1926)

Smuts, J. C., *Africa and Some World Problems* (Oxford, 1930)

Smuts, J. C., *Jan Christian Smuts* (London, 1952)

South African Institute of Race Relations, *Report of the Fifth National European-Bantu Conference (1933)* (Johannesburg, n. d., [1933])

South African Institute of Race Relations, *Some Aspects of the Native Question. Selected Addresses Delivered at the Fifth National European-Bantu Conference Bloemfontein 1933* (Johannesburg, n. d., [1933])

Stauffer, M. (ed.), *Thinking with Africa* (London, 1928)

Stepan, N., *The Idea of Race in Science: Great Britain 1800–1960* (London, 1982)

Stocking, G. W., *Race, Culture and Evolution. Essays in the History of Anthropology* (New York, 1968)

Stubbs, E., *Tightening Coils. An Essay on Segregation* (Pretoria, 1925)

Stultz, N. M., *Afrikaner Politics in South Africa 1934–48* (California, 1974)

Sullivan, J. R., *The Native Policy of Sir Theophilus Shepstone* (Johannesburg, 1928)

Tatz, C. M., *'Shadow and Substance in South Africa'. A Study in Land and Franchise Policies Affecting Africans, 1910–1960* (Pietermaritzburg, 1962)

Van Bruggen, J., *Booia* (Pretoria, 1931)

Van der Horst, S. T., *Native Labour in South Africa* (Oxford, 1942)

Van den Heever, C. M., *General J. B. M. Hertzog* (Johannesburg, 1946)

Van Jaarsveld, F. A., *The Afrikaners' Interpretation of South African History* (Cape Town, 1963)

Walker, E. A., *A History of South Africa* (London, 1928)

Walker, E. A., *The Frontier Tradition in South Africa* (Oxford, 1930)

Walker, E. A., *The Cape Native Franchise* (Cape Town, 1936)

Webster, E. (ed.), *Essays in Southern African Labour History* (Johannesburg, 1978)

Walshe, P., *The Rise of African Nationalism in South Africa. The African National Congress 1912–1952* (London, 1970)

Welsh, D., *The Roots of Segregation. Native Policy in Natal (1854–1910)* (Cape Town, 1973)

Werskey, G., *The Visible College* (London, 1978)

Wickins, P. L., *The Industrial and Commercial Workers' Union of Africa* (Oxford, 1978)

Willan, B., *Sol Plaatje. A Biography* (Johannesburg, 1984)

Williams, R., *Keywords. A Vocabulary of Culture and Society* (London, 1976)

Willoughby, W. C., *The Soul of the Bantu. A Sympathetic Study of the Magico-Religious Practices and Beliefs of the Bantu Tribes of Africa* (London, 1928)

Wilson, M. and Thompson, L. (eds), *The Oxford History of South Africa*, 2 vols (Oxford, 1969, 1971)

Xuma, A. B., *Bridging the Gap Between White and Black in South Africa* (Lovedale, 1930)

Yudelman, D., *The Emergence of Modern South Africa. State, Capital and the Incorporation of Organized Labour on the South African Goldfields, 1902–1939* (Connecticut, 1983)

(ii) Select Journal, Book and Unpublished Articles

Archer, S., 'The Industrialization Debate and the Tariff in the Inter-War Years', seminar paper, Institute of Commonwealth Studies, London University, 1981

Beinart, W., 'Conflict in Qumbu: Rural Consciousness, Ethnicity, and Violence in the Colonial Transkei, 1880–1913', *JSAS*, VIII, 1, 1981

Beinart, W., 'Soil Erosion, Conservationism and Ideas about Development: A Southern African Exploration, 1900–1960' *JSAS*, XI, 1, 1984

Bennie, W. G., 'A National System of Native Education: Observations on Dr Loram's Paper', *SAJS*, XXVI, 1929

Bonner, P., 'The Transvaal Native Congress 1917–1920: The Radicalisation of the Black Petty-Bourgeoisie on the Rand', in S. Marks and R. Rathbone, *Industrialisation and Social Change*

Brookes, E. H., 'Economic Aspects of the Native Problem', *Journal of the Economic Society of Southern Africa*, I, 2, 1927

Brownlee, F., 'The Administration of the Transkeian Territories', *Journal of the Royal African Society*, XXXVI, 144, 1937

Bundy, C., 'Land and Liberation: Popular Rural Protest and the National Liberation Movements in South Africa, 1920–1960', in Marks and Trapido, *The Politics of Class, Race and Nationalism*

Coetzee, J. M., 'Blood, Flaw, Taint, Degeneration: The Case of Sarah Gertrude Millin', *English Studies in Africa*, XXIII, 1, 1980

Couzens, T., ' "Moralizing Leisure Time": The Transatlantic Connection and Black Johannesburg 1918–36', in S. Marks and R. Rathbone, *Industrialisation and Social Change*

Davenport, R., 'African Townsmen? South African Natives (Urban Areas) Legislation Through the Years', *African Affairs*, LXVIII, 271, 1969

Davis, R. Hunt, 'Charles T. Loram and the American Model for African Education in South Africa', in P. Kallaway (ed.), *Apartheid and Education*

Dubow, S. H., ' "Understanding the Native Mind": Anthropology, Cultural Adaptation and the Elaboration of a Segregationist Discourse in South Africa, c. 1920–36', seminar paper, Centre for African Studies, University of Cape Town, 1984

Dubow, S. H., ' "The Curious Native Administration Bill" of 1927 and the Native Affairs Department', seminar paper, Institute of Commonwealth Studies, London University, 1985

Dubow, S. H., 'Holding "a Just Balance Between White and Black" ', The Native Affairs Department in South Africa c. 1920–33', *JSAS*, XII, 2, 1986

Duerden, J. E., 'Social Anthropology in South Africa: Problems of Race and Nationality', *South African Journal of Science*, XVIII, 1–2, 1921

Duerden, J. E., 'Genetics and Eugenics in South Africa: Heredity and Environment', *SAJS*, XXII, 1925

Evans, M. S., 'The Next Step in Native Government', *The South African Quarterly*, I, 2, 1914

Fick, M. L., 'Intelligence Test Results of Poor White, Native (Zulu), Coloured and Indian School Children and the Educational and Social Implications', *SAJS*, XXVI, 1929

Frankel, S. H., 'The Position of the Native as a Factor in the Economic Welfare of the European Population in South Africa', *Journal of the Economic Society of South Africa*, II, 1, 1928

Garson, N., 'The Cape Franchise in Action: The Queenstown By-Election of December 1921', seminar paper, History Workshop 1984, Witwatersrand University

Gluckman, M., 'Anthropology and Apartheid: The Works of South African Anthropologists', in M. Fortes and S. Patterson (eds), *Studies in African Social Anthropology* (London and New York, 1975)

Green, A. D., 'On the Political Economy of Black Labour and the Racial Structuring of the Working Class in England', (mimeo.), Centre for Contemporary Cultural Studies, Birmingham, 1979

Gluckman, M. 'Anthropology and Apartheid: The Work of South African Anthropologists', in M. Fortes and S. Patterson (eds), *Studies in African Social Anthropology* (London and New York, 1975)

Hammond-Tooke, W., 'The Natives and Agriculture', *SAJS*, XVIII, 1922

Harries, P., 'Kinship, Ideology and the Nature of Pre-Colonial Labour Migration: Labour Migration from the Delagoa Bay

Hinterland to South Africa, up to 1895', in Marks and Rathbone, *Industrialisation and Social Change*

Hellman, E., 'Native Life in a Johannesburg Slum Yard', *Africa*, VIII, 1, 1935

Herbst, J. F., 'Administration of Native Affairs in South Africa', *Journal of the African Society*, XXIX, 117, 1930

Hill, R. A. and Pirio, G. A., ' "Africa for the Africans": The Garveyite Movement in South Africa, 1920–1940', in S. Marks and S. Trapido, *The Politics of Race, Class and Nationalism*

Hirson, B., 'Tuskegee, the Joint Councils, and the All African Convention', seminar paper, Institute of Commonwealth Studies, 1981

Hofmeyr, J. H., 'The Approach to the Native Problem', *Journal of the Royal African Society*, XXXVI, 144, 1937

Hoernlé, A. W., 'New Aims and Methods in Social Anthropology', *SAJS*, XXX, 1933

Holloway, J. E., 'The American Negro and the South African Abantu - A Study in Assimilation', *South African Journal of Economics*, I, 4, 1933

Horton, J. W., 'South Africa's Joint Councils: Black-White Co-operation between the Two World Wars', *South African Historical Journal*, no. 4, 1972

Hunter, M., 'The Effects of Contact with Europeans on the Status of Pondo Women', *Africa*, VI, 3, 1933

Hunter, M., 'Methods of Study of Culture Contact', *Africa*, VII, 3, 1934

Huss, B., 'The Evolution of the Native Mind', *Africa*, IV, 4, 1931

Innes, D. and Plaut, M., 'Class Struggle and Economic Development in South Africa: The Inter-War Years', seminar paper, Institute of Commonweath Studies, London University, 1977–8

Johnstone, F. A., 'White Prosperity and White Supremacy in South Africa Today', *African Affairs*, LXIX, 275, 1970

Kallaway, P., 'F. S. Malan, the Cape Liberal Tradition, and South African Politics, 1908–1924, *Journal of African History*, XV, 1, 1974

Kaplan, D., 'Capitalist Development in South Africa: Class Conflict and the State', in T. Adler (ed.), *Perspectives on South Africa* (Johannesburg, 1977)

Krige, E. J., 'Changing Conditions in Marital Relations and Parental Duties among Urbanized Natives', *Africa*, IX, 1, 1936

Lazar, J. W., 'The Role of the South African Bureau of Racial

Affairs (SABRA) in the Formulation of Apartheid Ideology, 1948–1961', seminar paper, Institute of Commonwealth Studies, London University, 1986

Legassick, M., 'The Rise of Modern South African Liberalism: Its Assumptions and its Social Base', seminar paper, Institute of Commonwealth Studies, London University, 1973

Legassick, M., 'The Making of South African "Native Policy", 1903–1923: The Origins of "Segregation" ', seminar paper, Institute of Commonwealth Studies, London University, 1973

Legassick, M., 'British Hegemony and the Origins of Segregation in South Africa, 1901–14', seminar paper, Institute of Commonwealth Studies, London University, 1974

Legassick, M., 'Ideology and Legislation of the Post–1948 South African Government', seminar paper, Institute of Commonwealth Studies, London University, 1974

Legassick, M., 'Legislation, Ideology and Economy in Post–1948 South Africa', *JSAS*, I, 1, 1974

Legassick, M., 'South Africa: Forced Labour, Industrialization and Racial Differentiation', in R. Harris (ed.), *The Political Economy of Africa* (Massachusetts, 1975)

Legassick, M. and Wolpe, H., 'The Bantustans and Capital Accumulation in South Africa', *Review of African Political Economy*, 7, 1976

Legassick, M., 'Race, Industrialization and Social Change in South Africa: The Case of R. F. A. Hoernlé, *African Affairs*, LXXV, 299, 1976

Legassick, M. and Innes D., 'Capital Restructuring and Apartheid: A Critique of Constructive Engagement', *African Affairs*, LXXVI, 305, 1977

Lonsdale, J., 'States and Social Processes in Africa: A Historiographical Survey', *African Studies Review*, XXIV, 2–3, 1981

Loram, C. T., 'The Claims of the Native Question Upon Scientists', *South African Journal of Science*, XVIII, 1921

Loram, C. T., 'A National System of Native Education in South Africa', *SAJS*, XXVI, 1929

Loram, C. T., 'Native Labour in Southern Africa', in American Geographical Society, *Pioneer Settlement. Co-operative Studies* (New York, 1932)

MacCrone, I. D., 'Psychological Factors Affecting the Attitude of White to Black in South Africa', *SAJS*, XXVII, 1930

Mair, L., 'The Study of Culture Contact as a Practical Problem', *Africa*, VII, 4, 1934

Malinowski, B., 'Practical Anthropology', *Africa*, II, 1, 1929

Marks, S., 'The Ambiguities of Dependence: John L. Dube of Natal', *JSAS*, I, 2, 1975

Marks, S., 'Natal, the Zulu Royal Family and the Ideology of Segregation', *JSAS*, IV, 2, 1978

Marks, S. and Trapido, S., 'Lord Milner and the South African State', in P. Bonner (ed.), *Working Papers in Southern African Studies. Vol. 2* (Johannesburg, 1981)

Moroney, S., 'Mine Married Quarters: The Differential Stabilisation of the Witwatersrand Workforce 1900–1920', in S. Marks and R. Rathbone (eds), *Industrialisation and Social Change*

Morris, M. L., 'The Development of Capitalism in South African Agriculture: Class Struggle in the Countryside', *Economy and Society*, V, 3, 1976

Moschke, H. 'Is Segregation Necessary?', *Journal of the Economic Society of South Africa*, I, 1, 1927

Parry, R., ' "In a Sense Citizens, But Not Altogether Citizens . . ." Rhodes, Race, and the Ideology of Segregation at the Cape in the Late Nineteenth Century', *Canadian Journal of African Studies*, XVII, 3, 1983

Perham, M., 'A Restatement of Indirect Rule', *Africa*, VII, 3, 1934

Posel, D., 'Language, Legitimation and Control: The South African State after 1978', *Social Dynamics*, X, 1, 1984

Posel, D., 'The Meaning of Apartheid before 1948: Conflicting Interests and Forces within the Afrikaner Nationalist Alliance', *JSAS*, XIV, 1, 1987

Pim, J. H., 'General Hertzog's Smithfield Proposals', *The South African Quarterly*, VII, 3–4, 1925–6

Radcliffe-Brown, A. R., 'Some Problems of Bantu Sociology', *Bantu Studies*, I, 3, 1922

Radcliffe-Brown, A. R., 'The Methods of Ethnology and Social Anthropology', *SAJS*, XX, 1923

Rheinallt Jones, J. D., 'The Need for a Scientific Basis for South African Native Policy', *SAJS*, XXIII, 1926

Rheinallt Jones, J. D., 'Cape Franchise and Bantu Status', *The South African Outlook*, LVIII, 688, 1928

Rich, P., 'The Agrarian Counter-Revolution in the Transvaal and the Origins of Segregation, 1902–1913', seminar paper, African Studies Institute, Witwatersrand University, 1975

Rich, P., 'Ministering to the White Man's Needs: The Development of Urban Segregation in South Africa, 1913–23', *African Studies*, XXXVII, 2, 1978

Rich, P., 'Liberalism and Ethnicity in South African Politics, 1921–48', *African Studies*, XXXV, 3–4, 1976

Rich, P., 'The Origins of Apartheid Ideology: The Case of Ernest Stubbs and Transvaal Native Administration, c. 1902–1932', *African Affairs*, LXXIX, 315, 1980

Rich, P., 'Segregation and the Cape Liberal Tradition', seminar paper, Institute of Commonwealth Studies, London University, 1981

Robertson, H. M., '150 Years of Economic Contact Between Black and White. A Preliminary Survey', *South African Journal of Economics*, II, 4, 1934 (Part I); III, 1, 1935 (Part II)

Schapera, I., 'Economic Changes in South African Native Life', *Africa*, I, 2, 1928

Schapera, I., 'Changing Life in the Native Reserves', *Race Relations* I, 1, 1933

Schapera, I., 'Field Methods in the Study of Modern Culture Contacts', *Africa*, VIII, 3, 1935

Schreuder, D. M., 'The Cultural Factor in Victorian Imperialism: A Case-Study of the British "Civilising Mission" ', *Journal of Imperial and Commonwealth History*, IV, 3, 1976

Shannon, H. A., 'Urbanization, 1904–1936', *South African Journal of Economics*, V, 2, 1937

Simkins, C., 'Agricultural Production in the African Reserves of South Africa, 1918–1969', *JSAS*, VII, 2, 1981

Smith, E. W., 'The Story of the Institute. A Survey of Seven Years', *Africa*, VII, 1, 1934

Smuts, J. C., 'Native Policy in Africa', *Journal of the African Society*, XXIX, 115, 1930

Swanson, M. W., ' "The Durban System": Roots of Urban Apartheid in Colonial Natal', *African Studies*, XXXV, 3–4, 1976

Swanson, M., 'The Sanitation Syndrome: Bubonic Plague and Urban Native Policy in the Cape Colony 1900–09', *JAH*, XVIII, 3, 1977

Thema, R. V. S., 'In Defence of the Cape Franchise', *The South African Outlook*, LVIII, 688, 1928

Trapido, S., ' "The Friends of the Natives": Merchants, Peasants and the Political and Ideological Structure of Liberalism in the Cape, 1854–1910', in Marks and Atmore, *Economy and Society*

Van der Horst, S. T., 'Some Effects of Industrial Legislation on the

Market for Native Labour in South Africa', *South African Journal of Economics*, III, 4, 1935

Van der Post, A. P., 'Social and Economic Aspects of the Poor White and Native Problem', *Journal of the Economic Society of South Africa*, II, 1, 1928

Welsh, D., 'The State President's Power Under the Bantu Administration Act', *Acta Juridica*, 1968

Wheelwright, C. A., 'Native Administration in Zululand', *Journal of the African Society*, XXIV, 94, 1925

Wolpe, H., 'Capitalism and Cheap Labour-Power in South Africa: From Segregation to Apartheid', *Economy and Society*, I, 4, 1972

(iii) Theses and Dissertations

Ashford, A, 'On the "Native Question": A Reading of the Grand Tradition of Commissions of Inquiry into the "Native Question" in Twentieth-Century South Africa', DPhil thesis, University of Oxford, 1987

Bell, M. M. S., 'The Politics of Administration: A Study of the Career of Dr D. L. Smit with Special Reference to his Work in the Department of Native Affairs, 1934–45', MA thesis, Rhodes University, 1978

Bradford, H., 'The Industrial and Commercial Workers' Union of Africa in the South African Countryside, 1924–1930', PhD thesis, University of the Witwatersrand, 1985

Bridgman, F. B., 'The Native Franchise in the Union of South Africa'. PhD thesis, Yale University, 1939

Cameron, J. T., 'An Analysis of Smuts' Attitude Towards Hertzog's "Native Bills" From 1926 to 1936', MA thesis, University of South Africa, 1982

Cobley, A. G., ' "On the Shoulders of Giants": The Black Petty Bourgeoisie in Politics and Society in South Africa, 1924–1950', PhD thesis, London University, 1986

Cope, N. L. G., 'The Zulu Royal Family under the South African Government, 1910–1933: Solomon kaDinuzulu, Inkatha and Zulu Nationalism', PhD thesis, University of Natal, 1985

Dubow, S. H., 'Segregation and "Native Administration" in South Africa, 1920–36', DPhil thesis, Oxford University, 1986

Haines, R. J., 'The Opposition to General J. B. M. Hertzog's Segregation Bills, 1925–36: A Study in Extra-Parliamentary Protest', MA thesis, University of Natal, Durban, 1978

Hexham, I., 'Totalitarian Calvinism – The Reformed (Dopper) Community in South Africa, 1902–1919', PhD thesis, University of Bristol, 1975

Hindson, D. C., 'The Pass System and the Formation of an Urban African Proletariat in South Africa', PhD thesis, University of Sussex, 1983.

Johnstone, F. A., 'Class and Race Relations in the South African Gold Mining Industry, 1910–26', PhD thesis, Oxford University, 1972

Kaplan, D. E., 'Class Conflict, Capital Accumulation and the State: An Historical Analysis of the State in Twentieth Century South Africa', PhD thesis, University of Sussex, 1977

Kavina, S. B. D., 'The Political Thought and Career of Hon. Dr. Edgar H. Brookes of South Africa', PhD thesis, Bombay University, 1972

Klein, V., 'African Responses in the Eastern Cape to Hertzog's Representation of Natives in Parliament Bill, 1926–36', BA(Hons) thesis, University of Cape Town, 1978

Krikler, J. M., 'The South African Party and the Cape African Franchise, 1926–36', BA(Hons) thesis, University of Cape Town, 1980

Martin, S. J. R., 'The Political and Social Theories of Transkeian Administrators in the Late Nineteenth Century', MA thesis, University of Cape Town, 1978

Mcloughlin, A. G., 'The Transkeian System of Native Administration', MA thesis, University of South Africa, 1936

Nuttall, T. A., 'Principle and Pragmatism: Dr E. H. Brookes and the Natives Representative Council Crisis, 1946–49', BA(Hons) thesis, University of Natal, Pietermaritzburg, 1981

Smurthwaite, A. G., 'The Policy of the Smuts Government Towards Africans, 1919–1924', MA thesis, University of South Africa, 1975

Steele, M. C., 'The Foundations of a "Native" Policy: Southern Rhodesia, 1923–33', Simon Fraser University, 1972

Taylor, J. S., 'The Emergence and Development of the Native Department in Southern Rhodesia, 1894–1914', PhD thesis, London University, 1974

D. Ticktin, 'The Origins of the South African Labour Party 1888–1910', PhD thesis, University of Cape Town, 1973

Index

African National Congress
(ANC) 18, 41, 42, 153–5,
173
Africanism 18, 40, 152, 173, 180
Afrikaner Broederbond 22, 183
n. 7
Aggrey, James K. 155
agriculture 60–6, 95, 119–20
decline of in reserves 68–9
see also reserves
Alexander, M. 84
All-African Convention
(AAC) 18, 164–5, 166–8
Allison, J. S. 80
anthropology 5, 8, 27, 34–5, 37,
38, 72, 113, 159
see also cultural relativism
apartheid vii, 1, 11, 18, 177–8,
179–80
and Afrikaner nationalism 22,
27, 177
Apthorp, M. G. 96
Ashforth, A. 5–6

Ballinger (Hodgson) M. 174
Ballinger, W. 15, 16, 167
Bantu Union 153
Barlow, H. 102, 103
Barnes, L. 5, 94
Barrett, A. L. 122, 124, 125
Barrett, Edward 40, 41, 79, 82,
83–6, 88, 89, 99, 107
Basutoland 21, 24, 183 n. 2
Beinart, W. viii, 12, 54, 152, 174
biology 33, 35
as societal metaphor 29, 36–7
see also eugenics, social
Darwinism
Boas, F. 35
Bok, W. E. 92, 93
Bondelswarts 84
Bonner, P. 41
Bradford, H. 10, 41, 42, 107, 174
Brent, J. T. 63

Bridgman, F. 72
Britten, H. 115
Brookes, E. 6, 49, 81, 102, 105,
113
and segregation 8, 17, 21, 28–9,
46–7, 48, 50, 158
fear of proletarian
consciousness 70–1
on Native Affairs
Department 84–5
opposition to industrial colour
bar 44
preparedness to
compromise 162, 164, 168,
175
rejection of classic liberalism 34
Brownlee, C. P. 101
Brownlee, Frank 101, 103
Brownlee, Reverend J. 101
Brownlee, W. T. 101
Bulhoek 41, 84, 88
Bundy, C. 152, 154, 174
Bunga see Transkeian Territories
General Council
Bunting, S. 107
Burchell, F. B. 118
Burton, H. 17, 159, 160

Cameron, J. T. 141
Cape 4, 63, 65, 107, 112, 116, 121
franchise 14, 132, 136
liberalism in 7, 22, 80, 159, 173
see also Ciskei, franchise, Native
Affairs Department
Cape Native Franchise Vigilance
Committee 159, 175
Cape Native Rights Protection
Association 150
Cape Native Voters'
Convention 150
Carless, F. J. 62
Carnegie Corporation 156
Carter, G. 172

242